"Stress at work has become a major public health problem ... While industries in developed countries have addressed chemical and physical sources of risks, they are now faced with a new, more insidious, difficulty: the threat to the quality of life of their employees. Research has demonstrated that stress has consequences on mental health, but also on physical health, be it directly (such as high blood pressure, back pain, susceptibility to infections...), or indirectly, through accident-prone behavior, smoking, alcohol consumption, and unfortunately, even suicide ... life expectancy has been long demonstrated to be correlated to stressful life events. Absence at work has been shown to be one of the most sensitive predictors of health outcomes. No wonder that WHO defines health as a state of complete physical and mental well-being. Dr Simon Dolan's new book, as all the previous ones and the extensive research work he has conducted over the years on stress – including stress-related health outcomes – is an extremely important contribution in this regard. I believe every modern manager should read it!" — **Lucien Abenhaim**, MD, PhD, medical doctor and a professor of public health at the University of Paris 5. Former General Director of Health of France and former member of the WHO Executive Board.

"Simon Dolan addresses an increasing challenge facing organizations in the 21st century: How can they meet individual needs for growth, respect and meaning and organizational needs for peak performance? Managers all too often see this in either–or terms, neglecting employee needs, resulting in the stress epidemic we see all around us. He identifies important antecedents of workplace stress and provides realistic suggestions for keeping stress levels manageable. His use of self-esteem – both individual and organizational – as a central organizing concept is both unique and interesting. This book is a must-read for both managers and stress researchers interested in leaning more about high performing individuals and organizations." — **Ron Burke**, PhD, Professor at York University, and one of Canada's most prolific researchers. He specializes on the relationship between the work environment and the individual's overall well-being.

"Living with work-related stress is an escapable reality of modern life, but not all employees suffer equally. Dolan explores the complex sources of work-related stress and offers practical suggestions for how to minimize the negative effects of stress while building healthy and productive organizations. This thought-provoking book will be useful to everyone who wants to ensure that their work place is a source of energy and positive self-esteem." — **Susan Jackson**, PhD, Professor of Human Resource Management in the School of Management and Labor Relations at Rutgers University. Former President of the Academy of Management's Division of Organizational Behavior, and former editor of the *Academy of Management Review*. Earlier in her career, she co-developed with Cristina Maslach the MBI (the most widely used burnout measure).

"Professor Dolan's new work is centered around four concepts of fundamental importance for our present lives which interact in a systemic way, usually outside of our awareness. As he aptly mentions, each of them needs to be kept in a 'middle way', to prevent or correct deviations on individual and organizational levels. Those corporate leaders who still maintain the attitude of 'I am OK, You are OK, the firm is OK and the world is OK' might benefit from reading this book in reassessing their leadership style; their effort to increase productivity should be viewed within the context of their own stress and the stress they generate in their respective organizations. There is no doubt that this book will serve as an eye opener to these corporate leaders." — **Roberto Kertez**, MD, a psychiatrist and Rector of the University of Flores in Buenos Aires, Argentina. A past President of the Latin American Association of Transactional Analysis, he introduced multimodal therapy and stress management in Argentina and several other Latin American countries.

"This book provides an engagingly novel vista of the occupational stress field. It is a novel vista in several respects. First, it blends updated scientific findings in this area with vignettes reflecting case-studies of executive stress and with the author's personal experiences, including those of working with the harbinger of modern stress research, the late Hans Selye of the University of Montreal. This is an effective mix, bound to expand readers' understanding of the phenomenon of executive stress and its organizational and individual manifestations. Second, it incorporates individual predispositions in the employee–organization interactions leading to work-related stress. The role of stable individual predispositions, like self-esteem, in the stress process has only recently been explored. Third, the book develops the important notion of an organizational-level equivalent of individual-level self-esteem, referred to as collective self-esteem. It also outlines how an organization may have an impact on individual self-esteem by promoting in its culture and normative supervisory behaviors procedures that incorporate employee recognition, fair treatment, and positive feedback. Finally, all these novel elements are integrated in one unifying framework, allowing readers to comprehend the complexity of interacting employee predispositions, job features, and perceived stress in organizations. I would like to salute the author, Professor Simon Dolan, for being able skilfully to combine these novel elements in one highly readable new book!" — **Arie Shirom**, PhD, Professor of Organizational Behavior at the Leon Recanati Graduate School of Business Administration, Tel Aviv University, Israel. He is a leading scholar in the fields of stress, strain and performance, burnout at work, and healthcare systems management.

Stress, Self-Esteem, Health and Work

Simon L. Dolan

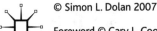
First published 2007 by
PALGRAVE MACMILLAN
Houndmills, Basingstoke, Hampshire RG21 6XS and
175 Fifth Avenue, New York, N.Y. 10010
Companies and representatives throughout the world

PALGRAVE MACMILLAN is the global academic imprint of the Palgrave Macmillan division of St. Martin's Press, LLC and of Palgrave Macmillan Ltd. Macmillan® is a registered trademark in the United States, United Kingdom and other countries. Palgrave is a registered trademark in the European Union and other countries.

ISBN-13: 978-0-230-00642-3
ISBN-10: 0-230-00642-6

This book is printed on paper suitable for recycling and made from fully managed and sustained forest sources.

A catalogue record for this book is available from the British Library.

Library of Congress Cataloging-in-Publication Data
Dolan, Simon L.
   Stress, self-esteem, health, and work / Simon L. Dolan.
      p. cm.
   Includes bibliographical references and index.
   ISBN 0-230-00642-6
      1. Job stress. 2. Job stress—Prevention. 3. Work—Psychological aspects.
I. Title.
   HF5548.85.D65 2006
   158.7'2—dc22   2006048295

10   9   8   7   6   5   4   3   2   1
16   15   14   13   12   11   10   09   08   07

Printed and bound in Great Britain by
Creative Print & Design (Wales), Ebbw Vale

Note: The Dali drawing appearing on the jacket of this book was handed to the author during the 2nd International Symposium on the Management of Stress which was held in Monte Carlo, Monaco, 18–22 November 1979. Reproduced with the explicit permission of © DASA Edicions N.V. 2005.

This book is dedicated to my family, friends and acquaintances to whom I have inadvertently caused stress in their lives, and to Adela Maldonado (my stress reliever) who really pushed me to complete this book

Contents

List of Tables and Figures

Tables

Figures

Foreword

The enterprise culture of the 1980s and 1990s helped to transform economies in Western Europe and North America, and led to sustained growth in many countries. This period saw an expansion of the short-term contract culture, major restructurings, outsourcing, more monitoring of individual performance and less autonomy, and a long working hours culture throughout the developed world, which has been carried forward to the first decade of the 21st century. Although this has meant enhanced growth rates, there has been a substantial personal cost for many employees. This cost was captured by a single word – **stress**. Indeed, stress has found as firm a place in our modern vocabulary as faxing, fast food and the internet. We use the term casually to describe a wide range of aches and pains resulting from our hectic pack of work and domestic life. "I feel really stressed", someone says to describe a vague, yet often acute sense of disquiet. "She's under a lot of stress", we say trying to understand a colleague's irritability or forgetfulness. But, to those whose ability to cope with day to day matters is at crisis point, the concept of stress is no longer a casual one; for them, stress can be a four letter word – pain.

This book explores this 21st century plague as we live more frenetic lives, overloaded by work, pushed by new technology, and involved in intrinsically insecure work environments. It highlights the importance of self-esteem, both individually and in the culture of the organization ... this is a class-act book which will help you to better understand yourself and the organization you work for – buy it, read it, live it.

CARY L. COOPER, CBE
Professor of Organizational Psychology and Health at Lancaster University Management School and Pro Vice Chancellor (External Relations), Lancaster University

Introduction and Acknowledgements

I believe that this book appears at a very fitting time, because the corporate world is being subject to productivity demands that we still do not know how to take on board with a suitable degree of sanity. While many senior managers believe that pushing employees to their limit will increase their productivity, both qualitatively as well as quantitatively, they very often fail to see the hidden costs of stressed employees. They either do not see or neglect to diagnose the impact on their own lives and health resulting from operating in these types of environments. It is obvious that in the 21st century corporate world, we cannot operate in a stress free environment; this is a utopia. We also understand that while factors generating stress seem to be on the rise, there are also work environments where stimulus is very low, and although this is not a factor in generating stress, it does create boredom, giving rise to a "do-nothing" attitude and bureaucracy.

The common wisdom is that a high level of stress generates a drop in productivity. Hyperactivity may result in more effort being required to get through a task, but it does not necessarily lead to the successful accomplishment of the latter in the long run. As the famous cliché suggests: "You can be a superman (or superwomen) for a day, a week or a month, but not throughout your working life". Attempting to become a super-person on a chronic basis, causes significant wear and tear to the body and the soul, and the end result is poor health and poor performance. Being under excessive stress at work also interferes in life outside the workplace, resulting in a reduction of creative ideas and making the attempt at balancing work and private life virtually impossible. Therefore, managing workloads and other stress generating demands is of vital importance.

Among the individual differences that can explain capacities and risk factors in terms of suffering from stress is the individual's self-esteem. Self-esteem varies from person to person, and some authors connect the lack of self-esteem to occupational stress. In my personal experience, which is based on interviews with hundreds of managers and professionals working in various organizations world wide, a lack of self-esteem produces more stress because the insecurity that goes along with it is an unnecessary drain on people's energy. In addition, business environments themselves can often produce 'attacks' on people's self-esteem or lead to emotion-generated conflicts, which in turn may lead to stress. People with healthy self-esteem cope better in these circumstances.

An important innovation in this book deals with the novel concept of "corporate self-esteem". I propose that self-esteem can also be analysed on a collective and business level, and this produces a sensation of pride in belonging to a company. An organization that generates such a feeling of pride and commitment among its employees benefits from greater productivity derived from higher levels of motivation and creativity among its employee. Similarly, a lack of pride associated with belonging to a company can produce quite the opposite effect.

But neither can we ignore the fact that there are also organizations that have an excess of self-esteem and pride, which leads to commercial arrogance and a lack of humility, limiting their growth given that many potential clients may be put off by just such an attitude. Something similar can be observed in people whose self-esteem is too low, although at first sight this would appear to be just the opposite.

The above comments provide the framework for this book. It is intended to offer conceptual and practical models to respond to one of the greatest challenges of our time: how to go about generating "wealth and health", creating jobs in hypercompetitive global environments without producing excessive stress levels and at the same time attempting to address the issue of our self-esteem as human beings.

The book takes the reader through an interesting voyage that ends up demystifying the concept of stress and providing no-nonsense understanding and tools from a menu of options about how to manage stress individually and organizationally.

As is usually the case with books of this particular genre, innumerable quotes from respected presidents of multinationals, large corporations and business leaders, as well as academic and scientific scholars have been included.

At present, due to companies relocating in the east, closures, mergers, crisis, etc., many CEOs often repeat the saying, "our people are our best asset". Reality, however, demonstrates more and more that this sounds hollow, rhetorical and barely credible, as the same CEOs do not really put their resources into treating people well or showing respect by not pushing them to the edge. Stress levels at many of the Fortune 500 companies appear to be at records that have never been seen before.

It seems reasonable to imagine the large number of combinations that can be made out of the four words in the title of the book. In fact, if we look at the hypothesis that each of these words could be given a positive or negative meaning, based on their level of intensity, and on the way in which they affect the individual, we would reach the conclusion that an excess or a lack of self-esteem, stress and workload, could result in a variety of disorders and complications for the individual, as well as productivity losses for the organization. This could lead us to think that the key may lie in striking a balance between these four forces that act simultaneously on the human being. An illustration of these possible combinations is given by the CEO of Philips Iberoamérica who was quoted as saying the following in a book I published in Spanish: "Think about a tire with three independent chambers. If one of the chambers has either too little or too much air, the wheel would probably be off balance" (Felipe Pérez Gimenéz, in Dolan et al., 2005 p. xxii).[1]

It has been said that the problem being debated is the consequence of the ferocious struggle being waged for competitiveness in the 21st century. This cannot be denied, but what is certain is that extreme pressures of all type have been exerted upon workers for centuries. These pressures have come in various forms, based on the different economic, political and social circumstances of each case. Almost all of us can call these to mind, in one guise or another, to one extent or another and the spectre of this controversial trinomial has always gravitated around the worker.

Any worker knows that work and organizational demands are an important source of stress in their daily life. The typical expression nowadays in most organizations around the world is, "we need the project done by yesterday". From Monday to Friday, deadlines, emergencies, daily relationships with colleagues, subordinates and supervisors govern the lives of employees on all hierarchical levels, professional categories and levels of responsibility in commercial organizations. At one time, in a society considered as "underdeveloped", people competed with each other and even used physical violence in order to survive. Nowadays, in a society in which physical violence is no longer accepted, controlled by laws and social codes, we are witnessing a new form of psychological violence – subtler and more indirect – but whose results are just the same; in the end people suffer, become ill and even die from it. This is stress.

Paradoxically, in spite of all our advances in technology, nutrition, medicine, and an increase in scientific, social, legal and behavioral knowledge, those who run organizations are unable to realise that the means that they use every day in what seems to be a fight for economic survival, cause catastrophic suffering, deception, sadness, bitterness, pain and agony among the very people who have built up the organizations. Neither do they appreciate that they themselves can become victims of the stress generated

---

[1] Cited in S.L. Dolan, S. Garcia and M. Diez-Piñol (2005) *Autoestima, estrés y trabajo*. Madrid: McGraw-Hill.

amid the corporate culture that they themselves have created. Making the matter more complex, we need to understand that stress in the workplace is a phenomenon that has neither odor nor color, but its negative effects on the health and well-being, both of individuals as well as organizations, is devastating.

In the first decade of the 21st century, a syndrome of epidemic proportions is starting to appear all over the planet: several billion inhabitants in the most economically and technologically developed regions are suffering from a serious ethical and emotional development disorder that prevents them from fully developing their self-esteem and aspiring to being happy individuals.

One of the main ethiopathogenic hypotheses of this atrophic syndrome is based on Aristotelian wisdom: their excess of work is preventing them from appreciating truth and beauty. In all likelihood, this excess of work is based on a compulsive need to display their worth to others, due to an increasing fear of poverty and of being excluded from the system. In addition, it comes mainly out of a lack of deep-rooted self-esteem, derived cyclically from a lack of ethical and emotional development throughout their lives.

Those affected by this occupational stress syndrome associated to a lack of self-esteem find it increasingly difficult to develop essential aspects of their life such as playing, taking a walk, reading a book, enjoying cultural events or simply chatting with their partner, children or friends. Their understanding of self-esteem is based on working chronically and incessantly, with a sensation of being "trapped with no way out", never being able to enjoy or get satisfaction out of the results of their efforts.

However, there is also another kind of problem connected with self-esteem: excessive self-esteem. Too much self-esteem can make people arrogant, and if those who run organizations show an excess of self-esteem, although they are not stressed as such, this may lead to generating a lot of stress in those who share their surroundings. Such people are usually authoritarian, they fail to listen and expect those who work with them to fulfil impossible tasks. An excess of collective self-esteem explains corporative arrogance and the repercussions on the members of such an organization can be severe. In this book, we share the idea that a lack or an excess of self-esteem provoke stress and that, ideally, we need an optimal level of self-esteem to feel good about ourselves and not create stress in our fellow workers.

In other words, at the threshold of the 21st century, we may have learned how to work but we do not know how to relax, how to love ourselves, how to live or share our lives as fully developed human beings. This book sets out to contribute some individual and organizational ways of confronting this new psychopathological mass phenomenon.

This book is not intended to be an example of how to get rid of pressure in the workplace. In fact there is no simple remedy albeit the quest for simple formulae. On the contrary, we will present all the complex elements of this phenomenon, as simply and synthetically as possible, so that you can understand what stress is, how it relates to your own self-esteem, and the options available for reducing your level of stress. We will focus our attention on diagnosis and on remedies. We will also put forward and demonstrate some examples of organizational policies and strategies. In this book, we pay particular attention to those executives and professionals who display high levels of stress at work. More specifically, the book is organized into seven chapters:

- **Chapter 1** puts forward the bases for reflection between the need for high productivity, quality of life in the workplace, stress and health.
- **Chapter 2** helps understand the phenomenon of stress in general and occupational stress in particular, analysing its determining and regulating factors, their symptoms and their results.
- **Chapter 3** develops the concept of self-esteem within the broad context of stress and health. In addition, related aspects such as narcissism and arrogance are introduced. It also reflects on self-esteem and other individual differences such as youth or gender. Finally, it analyses the relationships between self-esteem and occupational stress.
- **Chapter 4** closely examines the antecedent factors of occupational stress, as well as their costs and consequences in terms of the mental and physical health of employees.
- **Chapter 5** provides practical keys for individual strategies in dealing with stress, including instructions for its prevention through developing healthy personal self-esteem. A variety of techniques and school of thoughts are introduced.
- **Chapter 6** refers to organizational strategies for managing occupational stress, analysing the obstacles to be overcome and possible levels of intervention.
- **Chapter 7** proposes an innovative concept of organizational self-esteem. It describes a new philosophy for managing organizations and prescribes a menu for future leaders for redesigning culture based on common core values of organizations. The utility and possible gains from empowering employees and freeing them from the tyranny of excessive stress is described and the blueprint is proposed for a new organization that is healthy emotionally, economically and ethically.

Stress, Self-Esteem, Health and Work has been prepared with four objectives in mind: to deliver material that is easy to read and understand, to cover the main subject matter, to adapt the contents to the current situation in organizations and to provide stimulating material for readers. I hope that the result is a book that provokes thought, discussion and reflection in the field of managing occupational stress. The book is equally intended for entrepreneurs and company directors, as well as professionals working in the field of occupational health.

As a result, the following are some of the main characteristics included in this book:

- *Use of simple language and terminology.* In writing this book, I have attempted to use language that would be easily understood by professionals, avoiding the use of abstract and non-specific examples. The intention has been to write a straightforward text that is quick and easy to read.
- *Use of up-to-date examples.* The contents are rounded off with company cases and comments by respected specialists on the subject.
- *Use of stimulating material.* Each chapter includes material that can be used in debates to discuss the aspects being analysed. Self-evaluation tools are suggested aimed at assessing how well the material has been understood and mini cases are described which provide an analysis of real situations.

The idea behind this work is to create awareness amongst leaders and organizations that understand the heavy toll of working under stress. We must bear in mind that our working environment depends on us, and that together, we can create work environments that are healthy, emotive and productive. If there is no solidarity in the future, there will be no future for mankind.

A personal concluding note. The reflections and key points of action mentioned in this book are largely the result of my personal and professional experience. My interest in the field of occupational stress began after an experience I had at the Mayo Clinic in Minnesota. While still studying for my doctorate at the University of Minnesota (back in the 1970s), I was involved in research that studied the perceptions of patients who had survived their first heart attack. All of the patients had no previous history of heart disease, and were actively working; essentially these were patients who had considered themselves healthy all of their lives. Out of the 210 patients, it came as a surprise to corroborate that more than 90 percent of them attributed their heart attack to their work. Obviously, this was only the perception of the patients, and as it was not a scientific test, important conclusions could not be extracted from such findings. Nevertheless, the revelation was sufficiently important for me to spend more than 30 years of my life involved in research in this field. The impetus for this research can be summarized as following: in spite of the fact that work can be positive and increase people's well-being (economically, socially and psycho-emotionally[2]), though when things are going badly at work the impact on health can be devastating. I arrived at the conclusion that in the 20th and of course the 21st centuries, we are dealing with a new form of toxicity; it is colourless and odourless, but its accumulated effect on the individual health and organisational well-being can be devastating. This gave rise to a new interest in an occupational field that was labelled: "psychotoxicology of work". After attaining my doctoral degree in Minnesota, I joined the international team headed by Hans Selye in Montreal. At that time, Hans was considered to be the greatest "guru" in the field of stress and many called him "the father" of stress. This book is based largely on the work I did with Hans Selye early in my career and has been influenced by the work of other distinguished scholars whom I have had the pleasure of collaborating with.

I therefore wish to dedicate this book to these colleagues whom I owe deeply for helping me evolve and develop. First I wish to express my gratitude to my two spiritual mentors in Minnesota: Professor Dick Hall, my doctoral thesis supervisor (currently at SUNY – Albany), and Professor John Campbell (active member of my doctoral committee). I also wish to express my deepest and most sincere appreciation to the late Dr Hans Selye, for his belief in me, and for the support and opportunities provided to me during my initial years at the University of Montreal. I also wish to thank Doctor André Arsenault from Montreal (a physician and nuclear medicine specialist, a great humanist and brilliant statistician), for his wisdom and collaboration throughout almost 15 years of joint work and joint directorship of the Centre for Occupational Health and Stress at the University of Montreal. In fact, an earlier version of this book was written with André Arsenault in French in 1980 (prefaced by Hans Selye) and turned out to be my record best-selling book in Canada.[3] We jointly created the Centre for Occupational Health and Stress, which was very active and produced a large number of scholarly published works in the forms of monographs and scientific articles until the mid-1990s. Another collaborator with us during this period at the University of Montreal was Doctor Lucien Abenhaim (physician and epidemiologist), who later on rose become the Surgeon General of France. Professor Arie Shirom (of Tel Aviv University – Israel) discovered my scholarly interest and potential,

[2] This is the principal message expressed in another book which I had co-authored and published with the same publisher: S.L. Dolan, S. Garcia and B. Richley (2006) *Managing by Values: A Corporate Guide to Living, Being Alive and Making a Living in the 21st Century.* London: Palgrave Macmillan.

[3] S.L. Dolan and A. Arsenault (1980) (foreword by Hans Selye) *Stress, santé et rendement au travail.* Montreal: ERI-Presse de la Université de Montréal.

and was instrumental in convincing me to abandon the corporate world and reorient my career towards academia. I learned from Professor Shirom the importance of conducting research on stress from a multidisciplinary perspective, and I have the utmost admiration for him as a scholar and a humble personality. Professor Shirom is still one of the leading scholars in stress research. Professors Susan Jackson and Randall Schuler (formerly from Stern School of Business in New York and presently at Rutgers University in the U.S.) have been my friends and co-authors for the past 20 years or so. Both were involved in stress research earlier in their careers. More specifically, Susan was a co-developer of the MBI (the most widely used measure of burnout). I would like to thank them for their confidence in me and their investment in maintaining our friendship in spite of the large geographical distance that separates us. Lastly, I wish to thank my current collaborators and colleagues with whom I conduct stress-related research at ESADE, namely Mrs Miriam Diez-Piñol, Dr Salvador Garcia Sanchez (my collaborators on the Spanish version of a stress-related book), Dr Angel Guavara (a physician working for the Catalan Public Health Service) as well as Ms Bonnie Richley and Dr Anthony Lingham. Finally, I wish to thank Chad Albrecht, a doctoral student at ESADE, for his instrumental copyediting assistance. May the passion for satisfying intellectual curiosity live forever and the benefits to humanity triumph.

SIMON L. DOLAN
Barcelona, March 2006

Every effort has been made to trace all copyright-holders, but if any have been inadvertently missed the publishers will be pleased to make the necessary arrangement at the first opportunity.

Prof. Simon L. Dolan – Short biography

Simon L. Dolan is currently a Ramón Llul Professor of HRM in ESADE, one of the world's leading academic institutions in Business (see: www.esade.edu). Formerly, he has been a full tenured Professor of Human Resource Management and Organizational Behavior at the School of Industrial Relations, The University of Montreal. He begun his research and academic career there in 1977. Dr Dolan obtained his Ph.D. from the Carlson Graduate School of Management, the University of Minnesota. After initial work with Hans Selye (during 1977–81), he became director of a multidiciplinary research centre for Occupational Stress and Health. Professor Dolan taught as visiting professor/scholar in many universities across the globe on MBA, Ph.D. and Executive Education programs, including: Boston University, Northeastern University, The University of Minnesota, The University of Colorado, in the U.S.; Tel Aviv University and Haifa University in Israel; McGill University, Concordia University, and St. Mary's University in Canada; Remini University of Beijing (China), Vienna University, ESSEC-Paris, Toulouse University, and Alba Business School in Europe; Federal University of Rio (Brazil), ITESM (Mexico), Cadiz University, Pablo de Olavide University (Seville), Instituto de Empresa (Madrid) and Pompeu Fabra Universities in Spain.

Professor Dolan has written extensively in the fields of human resource management, organizational psychology and on occupational stress. He has published about 100 papers in refereed journals, refereed proceedings and chapters in published books. He speaks several languages (English, French, Spanish and Hebrew, and understands German and Polish) and has given over 400 speeches around the globe on issues pertaining to management and I/O psychology themes. He has written (and co-authored) 26 books and monographs, some of which are on the "best-selling" lists in management series.

As the scientific director of IEL (Institute for Labor Studies) in ESADE, Prof. Dolan provides leadership to the various research projects undertaken by the Institute. At present there are numerous ongoing projects; more information on these can be found at: www.esade.es/pfw files/cma/institution/institutos/IEL/iel2006.pdf.

An updated detailed c.v. of Prof. Dolan can be found at: www.mbvsuite.com/dolancv

1 Work, Stress and Health: An Overview

Can the goal of high productivity be reconciled with the goal of quality work life?

The importance of improving productivity and quality of work life is evident to anybody who has ever worked in a company. For many years, workers and organizations believed that they were protected from global competition; therefore, few incentives were devised to increase productivity. However, this panorama has rapidly changed due to the following factors:

- Longer-lasting cycles of economic recession;
- Globalization of markets and increasing international competition.

As companies realize that their survival is at stake, pressures to increase productivity are mounting. A great number of companies face the definitive test of survival that, on the one hand is related to the economy, and on the other hand is due to their low productivity levels. A drop in productivity has an effect on people's standard of living as well as the community in general, resulting in companies becoming less competitive. The need to improve productivity coincides with a period in which the workforce is better trained and calls for greater participation in and control over their work. Employees prefer not to be dealt with as just another cog in the wheel, calling for innovative approaches to simultaneously improve the quality of their work life and productivity.

This chapter focuses on the changes in certain aspects of the organization, which can lead to increasing quality of work life without lowering productivity and affecting the well-being of an organization's employees.

In the past, attempts to increase productivity were centred on technological change, which, over time, gave rise to one by-product in particular: the deterioration in the quality of work life for a greater number of employees. In general, people were asked to work faster, to produce more, to spend less time thinking (that was the task of the machines) and to program their work activity according to the available technology. Although this approach seemed to be effective in the short-term, we now know that this is no longer the case. This has given rise to employees currently trying to exert greater control, having more choices and participating in all of the aspects related to work that concern them.

Consequently, over the last forty years efforts have been made to create a more global approach in terms of increasing productivity without having to forfeit the physical and psychological well-being of the workforce. This approach is centred on the concept of quality of work life. In spite of being a commendable and humanist approach in relation to how work is organized, quality of work life is not the final goal of

> Quality of work life is a work organization concept and philosophy, aimed at improving the lives of employees within organizations.

organizations. The strategic objective of companies is their survival, growth and profits, and, therefore, productivity. Interest in quality of work life is based on the supposition that its improvement will result in healthier, happier and more satisfied workers, who are, as a result, likely to be more productive.

It is difficult to define and measure quality of work life. This chapter refers to a process by which all of the members of the organization participate in the decisions that affect their jobs in particular and their work surroundings in general. This is done through open and appropriate communication channels, resulting in workers having greater involvement in their work as well as greater job satisfaction, in addition to lower levels of stress and fatigue. In essence, quality of work life represents an organizational culture, or innovative management style, in which employees have the sensation of belonging, a say in what goes on, responsibility and dignity. Generally, the organization that is characterised as having a high quality of work life promotes industrial democracy: suggestions, questions and criticisms are seen as possibly leading to improvements in one sense or another. In an environment such as this, constructive dis-agreement is considered a manifestation of concern for the organization instead of being viewed as a destructive complaint. The promotion of this type of participation by management often leads to ideas and actions that increase the efficiency and effectiveness of how the organization is run, improving both working conditions and atmosphere.

Quality of work life (QWL) is a process by which all members of the organization, through appropriate and open channels of communication set up for this purpose, have some say in decisions that affect their jobs in particular and their work environment in general, resulting in greater job involvement and satisfaction, and less stress and fatigue. QWL represents a management style in which employees experience feelings of ownership, self-control, responsibility and self-respect. In an organization with a high QWL, industrial democracy is encouraged; suggestions, questions and criticism that might lead to improvements of any kind are welcomed. Creative discontent is viewed as a manifestation of constructive caring about the organization rather than destructive griping. Management's encouragement of such feelings of involvement often leads to ideas and actions for upgrading efficiency.

Interesting to know

The organization of work has great implications for the quality of working life, and this is clearly demonstrated by the ongoing debates on changes in work organization in the direction of greater flexibility and their potential and actual effects on workers. While it is widely assumed that flexible forms of work organization can have desirable influences on both the enterprise and its workers, these outcomes are often not real-ized in practice. Even when a new form of work organization results in positive out-comes overall, the gain is not always shared by all the participants involved: in many cases, some workers benefit from the change, but others do not. Thus, changes in work organization should be approached from the perspective of workers as well as employers, in order to allow their social implications to be fully explored

Howard Gospel, *Quality of Working Life: A review on changes in work organization, conditions of employment and work-life arrangements.* ILO Report, Geneva 2003

Thus, quality of work life is a concept and philosophy, aimed at improving the lives of employees within organizations. In order to bring this about, its advocates follow several methods, ranging from the strictest and simplest scientific reorganization of work tasks, as defended by Taylor and his colleagues, to the more complex process of continuous change, introduced by the socio-technical group and the defenders of the more recent system and contingency theories. The quality of work life concept can be translated into operational terms and be applied to the specific context of the organization through programs. Some of these programs are specific and limited in scope, whereas others are intended to produce multiple changes in a wide variety of areas. To better understand the role of quality of work life programs, we will present a brief description of its relationship with other management areas and several theories on work organization.

From the historical point of view, the term "QUALITY OF WORK LIFE" (QWL) originated from a series of conferences sponsored by the US Labor Department and the Ford Foundation in the late 1960s and early 1970s. These conferences were stimulated by the then widely popular phenomenon of "*workers' alienation*".

Many of these factors, and the worker discontent that accompanied them, were on display at General Motors' infamous Lordstown, Ohio, plant. A modern automated plant, Lordstown was designed by automotive engineers in the late 1960s for the efficient production of a small and inexpensive car. General Motors wanted something to compete with the small foreign automobiles that began to eat their way into the American automobile market. The Lordstown plant soon manufactured a possible competitor, the Chevrolet Vega. Lordstown's line speed greatly exceeded that of older plants, and eventually Lordstown came to symbolize the worker discontent and worker alienation of the auto-industrial age – the "Blue Collar Blues." It also epitomized the heady and rebellious youthful working-class militancy of the late 1960s and early 1970s.

A Youngstown State University oral history project captured the recollections of some of the Lordstown autoworkers. Jim Graham, a Greek-born union activist, expressed the familiar refrain that autoworkers no longer needed brains for their work. When questioned about the early 1970s wildcat strikes, Graham replied that management "came in and said look, when you come in the plant leave your brain at the door, just bring your body in here, because we don't need any other part. Leave your brain at the door, we'll tell you what to do, how to do it, when to eat, when to drink coffee."

So, the series of conferences led to a conclusion that a job is more than a mere pay and repeating routine tasks and following orders. Those who attended these conferences considered that the term referred to more than job satisfaction and that it included other concepts. These concepts included participation in at least some of the decision-making processes, an increase in autonomy for daily work schedules, and redesigning jobs, systems and structures within the organization, with the aim of stimulating learning and promoting a satisfactory form of employee-backed interest and participation in work issues.[1]

The term Quality of Work Life remained ambiguous for a long time, until in the 1970s a handful of companies expressed interest in putting it into practice, such as Procter & Gamble and General Motors in the United States, and Volvo in Scandinavia. Successful results were achieved with the implementation of programs geared toward improving the quality of work life in their new plants. From the positive results obtained by these companies, in the late 1970s other companies, among them Ford, applied similar projects and also obtained good results. At the beginning of the 80s, there was a deep recession in the U.S. Asian competition, offering cheap and high-quality products, seriously concerned American corporate executives, leading many of them – along with many public sector organizations – to opt for quality and begin to apply quality of work life programs.

Although quality of work life can be defined in many ways, an interesting definition would be the combination of four requirements and perceptions expressed by workers towards their company:

Interesting to know

The Sodexho Alliance Observatory for Quality of Daily Life has carried out a study on "The Quality of Work Life". In order to carry out the project, 2.6 million questionnaires were sent out to 138 different sources in 11 countries around the world. Data were-gathered, classified and studied from all of the companies to which Sodexho Alliance offered its services.

According to the main results:

- In relation to the number of hours given over to workdays, in the year 2000 employees in the United States worked an annual average of 1,976 hours, whereas in Spain each employee worked an average of 1,634 hours, representing 342 hours less.
- As far as quality of work life is concerned, employees' perception of their jobs has varied remarkably over the last 40 years. In 1960, 91.6% of workers thought that their professional life was more important than their personal life, whereas at present 53.7% of the adult working population give greater importance to their personal life. In the Spanish case, workers gave 52.6% importance to their professional life and 47.4% to their private life in 2000.

Source: http://www.mujeractual.com/trabajo/empleo/calidad.html

---

1   **The perception of feeling supported and looked after by the company**. Some companies provide employees with a series of services related to their private lives, which form part of an increase in

employee benefits. For example, in Belgium it is a common practice to provide free legal services to employees who are in divorce proceedings.

2   **The need for companies to make employees lives easier**. In Sweden, companies have reached a series of agreements with certain suppliers, in such a way that employees can make purchases via the Intranet with the added advantage of considerable discounts and free delivery of goods to the employee's home or place of work.

3   **The need to fulfil personal wishes**. Employees increasingly call for their private life to be taken into consideration at work. The company, therefore, provides a series of activities that help to reduce stress and increase employee productivity. For example, the possibility of employees working from home, or even making a 24-hour, human resources hot-line available.

4   **The need to maintain good personal relationships**. Company recognition for each and every employee helps to maintain a good working relationship, not only with the management, but also among colleagues themselves.

Quality of work life and stress at work

Quality of work life has significant repercussions on the quality of emotional life and in the socio-emotional and affective balance that may or may not be obtained by individuals. Work is, for many, one of the fundamental activities of human existence. It is the activity that allows people to produce the goods and services that are necessary and indispensable for modern-day life, and enables them to become integrated into the system of relationships that makes up the very fabric of society.

By means of efficient and productive jobs, societies improve the quality of organizational and social life, and through this, workers find the satisfaction they need in terms of their personal, family and social life.

> Quality of work life has significant repercussions on the quality of emotional life and in the socio-emotional and affective balance that may affect stress and lead to a variety of illnesses.

Given the time that people spend at work, we must be aware of the implications and consequences that this has on their lives. The latter is valid for any type of work relationship: a group of professionals, a company of consultants, a micro-company as well as large companies. Certainly, dynamics and the relationships between people will be different in each case since there is an intimate link between the organizational structure and the inherent psychosocial processes.

In terms of personal relationships, obtaining a positive relationship in the workplace has always been an aspiration. Many workers who are proficient in the art of work and friendship – camaraderie – have been and are still daily examples that enable us to renew and reshape our faith and hope in that it is possible to create positive and rewarding human environments in the workplace.

We should bear in mind that the crux of the problem lies in the fact of a perceived hazard or disturbance considered threatening, such as natural catastrophes and emotional loss (the death of a spouse or child, the break up of a marriage, job-loss, retirement, etc.). Today, however, work-related stress also takes on special significance. Each person may consider stimuli or disturbances in their place of work differently: what some see as a challenge that stimulates them toward self-improvement and development, others may see as posing a terrible threat. This plays an important role in the appraisal of self-esteem, tolerance of frustration, optimism, creativity and the sensation of security – internally as well as externally – through affective, social and economic support networks, amongst other aspects.

Transposing this to work and its relationship with quality of life, there is no doubt that the presence of non-motivating work demands may drastically affect performance and the workplace environment, disrupting personal as well as family and career development. The balance between work-family quality of life, the existence of a good working atmosphere, a satisfactory level of organizational mental health, the existence of good risk-prevention programs, and minimum accident and professional illness levels, make it possible to minimize the existence of pathological stress.

Today, we speak of new, emerging causes of work-related stress, increasing job uncertainty for instance, which implies a permanent risk and an exaggerated sense of the short-term (an end to long-term career paths such as those in the Civil Service, and the introduction of possible job changes – between 5 and 10 – in the course of an adult's working life). On the one hand, this clashes with family life projects in the long-term, and, on the other hand, makes it difficult to develop loyalty and commitment (weak bonds), socialization, solidarity and, especially, trust. We would have to add the need for permanent change, the extreme submission to the computer (the screen replacing person to person contact), and the difficulty in finding a quiet moment amid the accelerated pace of today's technical, economic and cultural events.

Today, there is special significance between the fragmentation of the personal, family and work world and the disappearance of the spiritual and cultural world in work environments, which brings with it an increasing sense of loss of meaning regarding work. On all levels, life in the last few decades has become accelerated and has exposed people to increasing pressures. In the work environment, employees are expected to produce better quality and more work in less time and using less resources.

The effects of stress upon health are becoming more and more relevant. According to a survey carried out by the European Foundation for the Improvement of Living and Working Conditions (Paoli, 1997), there has been an important transformation in terms of how work is organized in Europe. At the same time, the workforce has also been transformed. According to this study, in 1996, 45 percent of the 147 million workers in the EU considered that they carried out monotonous tasks; 44 percent did not rotate tasks; 50 percent carried out simple and repetitive tasks; 35 percent stated that they did not have any say in what they did or how they did their work, whereas 54 percent mentioned that they worked too fast. These data indicate that, if we try to approach the health problems of today's workers, a thorough revision of the concept of occupational health is required.[2]

Diverse opinions exist with regards to whether or not organizations should be concerned about their employees' emotions. By way of a brief summarized version, we can put forward four reasons why executives and management should be concerned about the emotions of their employees, emotions that might then translate into stress or tension:

1   From the perspective of the quality of their work, workers feel more satisfied when their working environments are safe and comfortable.
2   Executives should make an effort in terms of reducing occupational stress because this is a factor that leads to negative results. Specialists in mental health consider that 10 percent of the workforce suffers from depression or high stress levels that will end up affecting their performance.
3   From the enormous economic costs derived from stress, experts consider that the illnesses related to stress represent many millions of euros (pounds or dollars) a year.
4   The last reason has to do with the recent cases of employees who have taken their companies to court over unpaid compensation for problems derived from stress.

Work, stress and health

According to the definition given by the World Health Organization (hereafter WHO), the promotion of health includes all the measures that allow people, groups and organizations to have greater control over

> Stress is one of the direct causes of the commonest and most lethal psychological and physiological illness that affects mankind.

the factors that affect their health. The objective of these measures is to improve the health of people, groups, organizations and communities.

For this reason, it can be said that promoting health is a process that allows people to reach a higher level of self-esteem as far as their health is concerned. In this sense, health represents a resource for daily life that allows people or groups to fulfil expectations and desires to take action, and, at the same time, take on society at large and change the world.

Promoting health in the workplace is a combined effort involving companies, workers and society at large to improve the health and well-being of individuals in the workplace. This promotion is obtained through a combination of measures:

- Improving the organization of work tasks and the working environment.
- Encouraging active participation in the process.
- Promoting personal development.

An active workforce that is healthy motivated and well-qualified constitutes a fundamental element of companies in the 21st century. Growing evidence demonstrates that health improvements in working environments can represent a key ingredient in a company's efficiency and competitiveness. In innovative companies, the quality of work life and the quality of products or services are part and parcel of the same strategy.

Promoting health in the workplace makes it possible to reduce occupational stress. Its objective is to influence those factors that promote employee health. Its success is due to improving working conditions, encouraging employee participation and bolstering personal competencies. Among the main elements involved in health promotion in a company are the methodological approaches and procedures used. With the purpose of analysing the point of reference, the workloads as well as the subjective effects on well-being have been identified by means of different instruments, including questionnaires, tools for identifying health risk factors, and "health circles". Like "quality circles" on which they are based, health circles offer workers the opportunity to participate and to take part, as experts in their own affairs, in the stress reduction process within their capacity.

CHRONIC WORK STRESS AND HEALTH

Short or infrequent episodes of stress pose little risk. But when stressful situations go unresolved, the body is in a constant state of activity which increases the pace at which the biological systems are worn down.

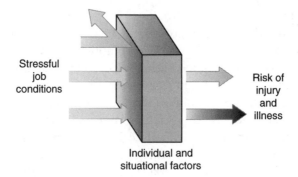

Figure 1.1 **NIOSH model of job stress**
Source: http://www.cdc.gov/niosh/stresswk.html

Ultimately, this leads to fatigue and/or injury, and the body's capacity to defend itself can be seriously weakened. As a result, this increases the risk of disease or accident (Figure 1.1).

In the last 20 years, many studies have looked into the relationship between work-related stress and a variety of diseases. Mood swings and alterations of sleeping patterns, gastrointestinal and stomach problems, headaches and changing attitudes towards family and friends, are examples of problems related to stress that develop quickly and which are commonly seen in these studies. These early symptoms of work-related stress are usually easy to recognize. But the effects of occupational stress in chronic diseases are more difficult to diagnose given that these take a long time to develop and can be influenced by many other factors in addition to stress. However, there is increasing evidence to suggest that stress has an important role in different chronic health problems – particularly cardiovascular disease, muscular-skeletal conditions, and psychological alterations.

Interesting to know

Work-related stress and health: an American perspective

Cardiovascular disease

Many studies suggest that jobs that are psychologically demanding and which give employees little control over the work results in increased risk of cardiovascular disease.

Muscular-skeletal conditions

On the basis of research done by the National Institute for Occupational Safety and Health (NIOSH) and other organizations, it is believed that work-related stress increases the risk of developing muscular-skeletal conditions affecting the back and lower extremities.

Psychological conditions

Several studies suggest that the differences between the instances of mental health problems (such as depression and exhaustion) for several occupations are partly due to the differences between the levels of work-related stress (the economic and lifestyle differences between occupations can also contribute toward some of these problems).

Accidents in the workplace

Although more in-depth studies are needed, it is believed that stressful working conditions impede work from being carried out safely and that they cultivate conditions for industrial accidents.

Suicide, cancer, ulcers and affected immune disorders

Some studies suggest a relationship between stressful working conditions and these health problems. Nevertheless, more research is needed before firm conclusions can be drawn.

(Encyclopedia of Occupational Health and Safety)

Interesting to know

Work-related stress and health: a European perspective

Work-related stress, its causes and its consequences are frequent in the 15 member states of the European Union. More than half of the 160 million European workers state that they work very fast (56%) and have tight schedules (60%). More than a third of those interviewed have no say in how their work tasks are organized; 40% point out that they perform monotonous tasks.

It is probable that these work-related stress generators have contributed to the present manifestations of disease and illness: 15% of workers complain of headaches, 23% complain of neck and shoulder pains, 23% of fatigue, 28% of "stress" and 33% of backache. They also contribute toward many other diseases, including life-threatening diseases (European Foundation, 2001).

Stress related to prolonged work is a significant determining factor in depressive disorders. These disorders represent the fourth main cause in terms of volume of disease for the entire world. It is anticipated that by the year 2020 this will become the second cause, behind ischemic cardiopathy, but ahead of all the other diseases (World Health Organization, 2001).

In the 15 member EU countries, the average cost of these mental health problems and other associated problems totals between 3% and 4% of the GDP (ILO, 2000) which totals around €256,000 million per year (1998).

It is quite probable that work-related stress is a significant determining factor of the metabolic syndrome (Folkow, 2001; Björntorp, 2001).This syndrome contributes toward heightening ischemic cardiopathic morbility and type-2 diabetes.

In the EU guideline, examples of ischemic cardiopathy, strokes, cancer, muscular-skeletal and gastrointestinal diseases, anxiety and depressive disorders, accidents and suicides are commented on in detail.

Source: European Agency for Occupational Health and Safety, 2004
http://agency.osha.eu.int/publications/magazine/5/es/index_5.htm

The great paradox of the 21st century: better physical conditions in the workplace, but worse psychological conditions and more work-related stress

In spite of the enormous tensions and psychological pressures that are experienced every day at work, in most countries we continue to associate occupational health with safety and hygiene. The present fluctuating context of organizations, the uncertainty of the job market and the randomness with which competitive companies have to be run in order to guarantee their existence, nevertheless directly affect the psychological well-being of their workers. The effects of stress on health, for example, are increasingly visible and important. And so, in trying to approach the present-day health problems of workers, there would need to be a thorough revision of the occupational health concept in order to extend it beyond physical well-being to also include psychological well-being.

Various opinions exist with regards to whether or not organizations should be concerned about the emotions of their employees. By way of a brief summarized version of these, we can put forward four reasons why executives and management should be concerned with the emotions of their employees which might then translate into stress or tension:

1   Workers feel more satisfied when their work surroundings are safe and comfortable, increasing the quality of their work.
2   Occupational stress produces negative results that affect performance and productivity.

Interesting to know

What people say...

- I lead a very hectic lifestyle. I work with my husband who is a lawyer and I am also a housewife. I don't know how to cope with everyday stress, and, in addition, I suffer from kidney problems. I need help.
- I'm a sales director and manage a team of 11 sales executives. In our jobs, we have to deal with a lot of pressure as part of meeting our daily targets. I'd like to discover some sort of simple methodology to apply to my work team.
- I'm in charge of the Quality Control Department in a Clinic and, in some areas, mistakes get made resulting from a lack of concentration, for instance in dispensing medicines, surgical-medical material, etc.
- I'm the manager of a Customs Agency, and last week I had a problem with a client. I went home, laid down to rest for a while and started feeling a very strong pain in the chest. I laid back down and when I got up, I felt dizzy again and the pain came back.

Source: http://www.euskalnet.net/psicosalud/respuestaestres.htm

3   Stress produces high economic costs for the company.
4   Organizations are beginning to be considered legally co-liable in Spain and Latin America for their employees' stress and the consequences that stress may have in their lives.

Nowadays, there is irrefutable evidence that stress is one of the direct causes of the most common and most lethal psychological and physiological diseases that affect the developed or developing world, including cardiovascular pathology, diabetes, asthma, cancer, hypertension, osteoporosis, anxiety, depression, insomnia, memory loss and premature aging. In the panorama of occupational health and safety, on an international level and especially at a European level, in the last few years we have witnessed the emergence of studies and analyses of what are known as "new risks", and within these, risks considered to be psycho-social in nature.

Chapter postscript

At present, work organization in most companies is still influenced by the traditional models of management where the focus is on reaching economic goals. Nevertheless, the complexity of the social, economic and cultural changes and the fight to survive is generating a new toxicology in the workplace – occupational stress. Due to globalization of the markets and tough competition, companies are realizing that the road to competitiveness requires innovation and an ability to respond in the same way to clients and employees alike, although the best way to achieve this is not always found.

In addition, workers are better trained; they have different expectations; work is no longer merely a way of earning a reasonable living. Workers expect to have jobs that are interesting, that are meaningful, stimulating and valued.[3] Increasingly more is being demanded in terms of taking part in decision-making, and an increasing number of positions have to be designed or reshaped in order to satisfy these demands.

Lastly, we are living in an age in which it is increasingly difficult to separate our working lives from our personal lives; families are split up, a greater number of people live on their own and individualism is on the rise. Therefore, the workplace has become, and will continue to become, a place where individuals have the chance to interact, to make use of their abilities, and to contribute to common objectives doing a job that gives meaning to their lives. In general, the workplace will be more and more important as a place where workers' needs in terms of affiliation and self-realization can be satisfied.

If employees are unable to satisfy their job expectations and, in addition, have to put up with an aggressive management style, increases in work-related stress and the proportion of workers who suffer from this new disease will grow. Faced with this new reality in the 21st century, we can speak of a new, colourless and odourless occupational psychological phenomenon, which is detrimental to the physical and mental health of workers. The search for a solution to this serious problem is not a luxury – it is a necessity.

From the press

Companies expect their employees to be "superman" every day of the year

It is no longer just a theory. It has been demonstrated that excessive work demands in the service sector cause illnesses that can lead to death. "Today there is a work climate that, if we don't correct it, is going to kill us. There are no symptoms; it is colourless and odourless. It is unseen and unfelt, but it is a fact that new diseases have appeared as a result of stress," says Simon Dolan, who has been Professor of Human Resources at ESADE Business School in Barcelona for the last several years. Working continually in an unpleasant working environment ultimately causes high blood pressure, heart attacks, ulcers and mental disorders such as depression and exhaustion, "that disorder called burnout: people become totally exhausted". "Companies", he adds, "expect employees to be superman every day of the year."

Thirty years ago, Professor Dolan participated in research conducted at the Mayo Clinic in the United States. He interviewed about three hundred people who had survived their first heart attack. Those who had a history of cardiovascular problems were eliminated from the sample. "Perhaps the study wasn't very scientific, but I believe it was revealing: more than 90% of the people were convinced that their heart attack was not due to difficulties with their partners or children, but to problems at work." In short, "what worries me is that companies, in defining success, only use the criterion of interest, measured in terms of the economic well-being of employees. **We need to also consider the physical and emotional well-being of those we work with: that is the new concept of success**," assures Dolan.

Until very recently, "it was considered that people with a certain level of education looked for happiness and gratification in four spheres of life: family and friends (for social and psychological support), religion (for spiritual support), leisure (for personal achievements and pleasure) and work." The theory is still valid, but we should also take a closer look at the realities of the 21st century, high degree of failed marriages that are reported in the Western world: religion rarely interests young people and older ones become frustrated (church going people seem to be declining). With reference to leisure we can also note that in spite of the fact that we have more free time for leisure, pressure from organizations and economic struggles is so overwhelming that you feel guilty if you take a holiday or don't take work home with you at the weekend at or night." All in all, of the four possible spheres of happiness, the dominant one by far is work, "and that is very dangerous. If you enjoy your work, it may very well be fulfilling and make you happy. But if this is not the case, it is worse than being in jail, because it ends up killing you."

Of course, it is not a physical risk like those faced by construction workers, "but that doesn't mean that it is no less real. In companies, sometimes due to the pressures of the stock market, such psychological climates of uncertainty are created around possible dismissals when workers end up developing a sensation of anguish that will eventually take its toll because physiological reactions build up. Neither workers nor their bosses/managers are conscious of this danger," maintains the ESADE professor. In several countries, including Spain, university research teams in which Professor Dolan has worked have offered to carry out free stress diagnoses for various companies: "They have never let us in, as they are scared of finding out the results, scared of opening their own Pandora's box."

In order to solve this problem, what first has to be done is to educate people: "Ignorance does not solve anything, instead it compounds the problem." There is still no cure for AIDS, but we have spent years investigating this disease and we now know more about it: thanks to this research we can at least take better preventative measures. We have to educate companies. In addition, "Politicians, those who make and shape employment laws, should be courageous enough to recognise that risks in the workplace do exist. In Scandinavia, strides forward have been made in that sense." A possible initiative would be to force companies to offer willing workers a medical and psychological check-up for stress. It would also be beneficial to identify the men and women who, due to their personalities or other factors, are at greater risk.

Another possible source of action would be to use suitable human resources policies. "Those who decide on the careers of employees within the company, those who dictate who moves up and to what position employees get promoted to, should make public what they use to measure performance, and help those affected bear these considerations in mind."

At the moment, the only thing that matters is that, in general, a step-up means a pay rise, that is to say, an improvement in a worker's earnings. "But what is not taken into consideration it that along with the new responsibilities come increased demands and that success is not always guaranteed: the newly promoted worker may find that he lacks training or skills, which results in a feeling of frustration and the increased demands on him may result in illness or disease. We should not forget: unhappiness, and dissatisfaction at work, leads to disease."

Before promoting a person, it is necessary for that person to be trained: "to explain his new tasks, to explain to him what the bosses expect of him, to provide him with the skills that he/she is lacking: these things should be done before, not during nor afterwards. He should be aware that he will have more money, but also face more risks. In this respect, we need to be very clear." Professor Dolan recalls that he was university professor in a Canadian university in which the position of departmental director was regularly rotated. "I never accepted taking on that responsibility: I knew it would only bring me problems and stress: the pay raise wasn't worth it."

Using and discarding people

Companies highly value and compensate only those who are successful, those who add economic value to the company. However, what happens to a person who after working hard seven years to get results ends up with an ulcer and can no longer produce the same results as before? "That person is no longer of any use to the company, and all his earlier efforts not only go unrewarded, but he gets pushed aside. Company executives in management should be concerned with making sure everybody takes the holidays that they have a right to, that they don't take *dossiers* home with them to work on at night or on the weekend: in the long run that will be good for the company," says Professor Dolan.

Protecting employees

With a decisive role to play in this is middle management, "who are in most contact with the grassroots workers. They have to be able to stand up and protect those under them. Those higher up cannot *use* their workers without consulting middle manage-ment. Middle management has to be brave and stand up to them", to reject new tasks that means an excessive amount of work over a long period of time for those who work under us. Isn't a boss who does that risking his own job? "That's part of being brave. But he has to be able to demonstrate to his boss, in turn, that in the mid-term his refusal will be good for the company: it is not a personal whim." Dolan smokes continu-ally in his office, "and it's not a whim".

Corporate anorexia

Most companies, mainly those that are on the stock exchange, are managed with the intention of satisfying economic objectives in the short-term and this can cause prob-lems. "To demonstrate economic value in the short-term and to satisfy shareholders, drastic measures and quick-fix solutions are taken that involve staff cuts, the most important budgetary item in service companies. This results in what I call "corporate anorexia".

Companies project the image that they use workers until they are no longer needed. In the past, people gave everything to the company because it was important to them: their job was guaranteed until they retired. Nowadays, from the company's point of view, there is no symmetrical attitude. To the objection that, if there are losses, action of one sort or another has to be taken, Dolan responds: "perhaps if we look at the long-term picture, perhaps there is no real crisis." Regarding this quarter's losses, or even a simple drop in profits, "management, to show that it is actually doing some-thing, trims wages: it's an easy decision to take. But, what will happen in the long-term?" In the first place, "when the company recovers from that temporary crisis and considers re-expanding, it starts rehiring people. But it won't be able to attract the best professionals who know that that company has been disloyal to its employees in the past."

In addition, "when the company starts to take anorexic measures, motivation among those who have been kept on drops: they ask themselves when the next round of job cuts will come along and if they'll lose their job when it does come. As those who had been kept on were supposedly the best workers, they will try to find better jobs at the first chance they get. Eventually the company will be left with a workforce that is increasingly less well-trained. Today few stock market companies can demonstrate that they have a high level of loyalty towards their workers."

Source: Translation into English of an Interview of Carles M. Canals with Simon Dolan entitled: "La empresa exige a sus empleados que sean 'superman' todos y cada uno de los días del año", that appeared in *Expansión (Spain)*, Monday, 13 January 2003. Used with the explicit permission of Carles M. Canals.

Interesting to know

Quality of life has three dimensions:

Quality of life has its maximum expression in quality of life related to **health**. The three dimensions that globally and integrally define quality of life are:

- **Physical dimension**: This is the perception of the physical state of health, understood as the absence of *illness* produced by disease, and the adverse effects of its *treatment*. There is no doubt that being healthy is an essential element to possessing quality of life.
- **Psychological dimension**: This is the individual's perception of the cognitive and affective states such as *fear, anxiety*, a lack of communication, loss of self-esteem and uncertainty about the future. It also includes personal, spiritual and *religious* beliefs, including the meaning of life and attitudes towards *suffering*.
- **Social dimension**: This is the individual's perception of interpersonal relationships and social roles in life, such as the need for social and *family* support, as well as the doctor-patient relationship and holding down a job.

Exercise: Test your quality of work life

Aspect	Not at all	Very little	Sometimes	Often	Constantly
1 In general I can work (including work at home)	❏ 0	❏ 1	❏ 2	❏ 3	❏ 4
2 My work (including work at home) is fulfilling	❏ 0	❏ 1	❏ 2	❏ 3	❏ 4
3 I can enjoy my work	❏ 0	❏ 1	❏ 2	❏ 3	❏ 4
4 I can balance my work with my personal life	❏ 0	❏ 1	❏ 2	❏ 3	❏ 4
5 After a normal day's work, I sleep well	❏ 0	❏ 1	❏ 2	❏ 3	❏ 4
6 The things I usually do at work are fun	❏ 0	❏ 1	❏ 2	❏ 3	❏ 4

7   I am happy with my quality
    of life at the moment   ❏ 0   ❏ 1   ❏ 2   ❏ 3   ❏ 4

8   After a day's work, I'm in
    a good mood   ❏ 0   ❏ 1   ❏ 2   ❏ 3   ❏ 4

Total score = ❏

Score and interpretation

24–32   You have an excellent level of quality of work life.

12–23   You have a good level of quality of work life.

0–11   You have a (serious) problem with your quality of work life.

REFERENCES

1   Dolan, S.L. and Schuler, R.S. (1994) *Human Resource Management: The Canadian Dynamics* (Toronto: ITP Nelson).

2   Paoli, P. (1997) *Second European Survey on Working Conditions in the European Union*. Luxembourg: European Foundation for the Improvement of Living and Working Conditions, Office for Official Publications of the European Communities.

3   Dolan, S., García, S. and Richley, B. (2006) *Managing by Values: A Corporate Guide to Living, Being Alive and Making a Living in the 21st Century*. (Basingstoke: Palgrave Macmillan).

2 Models and Concepts in Understanding Occupational Stress

Chapter outline

"Stress–A spark of life or a kiss of death?"

(Leonart Levi)

"I cannot and should not be cured of stress, but merely taught to enjoy it"
"Without stress, there would be no life."

(Hans Selye)

Stress: definitions

DEFINITION OF STRESS

The word "stress" is familiar to most of us. Almost everyone has felt "stressed out" at times or knows family and friends who complain of stress. Many people believe that we live in a particularly stressful age. But what exactly is stress? What causes it? How do we know it's affecting us? What are its consequences, both for individuals and for organizations? Given the seeming inevitability that everyone will face stress in varying amounts throughout their lives, it is important that we learn about it and learn how to manage it.

Although thousands of articles on stress appear in professional journals and popular magazines, the concept is still poorly understood by the
public. Because stress has attracted the attention of researchers in various
disciplines from medicine to management, each using its own jargon,
models, and viewpoints, there are various definitions of stress. We will
provide a general definition, but stress has meant different things to different people, and this confusion will likely continue in the future.

Interesting to know

Reactions of people participating in corporate stress training programs:

- In the face of the constant uncertainty, reduction in force, budget cuts, and reorganization facing NASA, the course is exactly what everyone needs. I wish we could
  make it mandatory for all employees... Now that would be revolutionary! Please
  feel free to refer any potential clients in industry or government to me for a rec-
  ommendation. (Miriam Glazer, MA, MPH Health Programs Manager, NASA
  Ames Research Center, Moffett Field, CA.
- NASA, IBM, Nokia, Stanford, and the U.S. Army are just a few of the organizations
  that have provided corporate stress management training to their employees.
- IBM's Global Stress Management program includes a stress intervention website,
  online manager stress intervention training, and location-specific stress management resources. Should those efforts need augmenting, additional tools are generally available through health benefits programs, which range from major
  benefits plans to services that specifically address mental health (Source:
  www.ibm.com/ibm/responsibility/people/wellbeing/ promoting-health.shtml)

Despite Hans Seyle introducing the term 60 years ago, society has
only recently begun to pay attention to the important influence stress has
on public health and the economic losses it implies for organizations and
companies.[1] Aware of this issue, studies have been carried out and strategies proposed to mitigate what was once considered laziness, reluctance
or lack of will power. From the 1970s onward, the proliferation of articles, seminars and material related to stress management reflects the
growing interest in this problem. In fact, stress management has become
top priority in companies, implying the creation of ever more workshops
designed to help employees.

A brief definition of stress is "*the non-specific response to all the demands
made*". This simple definition implies the interaction of the organism with

the environment, whether it is another organism or the environment in which we move. As such, stress can be defined according to: (a) the stimulus, (b) the response, or (c) the stimulus–response concept.

(a) *According to the stimulus*: stress is the force or stimulus which acts on the individual and which leads to a tense response.
(b) *According to the response*: stress is the physiological or psychological response which an individual manifests in a stressful environment.
(c) *According to the stimulus–response concept*: stress is the consequence of the interaction of environmental stimuli and the individual's idiosyncratic response.

We can broaden the brief definition of stress above by adding that any demand, whether physical, psychological, external or internal, good or bad, produces an identical and stereotypical biological response within the organism (Figure 2.1). This response produces quantifiable hormonal changes which can be measured by laboratory data and changes which these hormonal secretions produce in our organism and which are responsible for our reactions, whether functional or organic, when faced with stress.

Although stress is generally considered harmful, life without stimulation would be monotonous and boring; people would be missing out on the creative force which can be a source for motivation and the step prior to achieving goals.

Acute physical stressor – the explosion

Chronic physical stressors – famine, drought

Psychological-social stressors – traffic

Psychological-social stressors – relationships

Figure 2.1 **The stress mosaic**

OCCUPATIONAL STRESS

Over the years, the concept of workplace stress has evolved in its definition and scope to comprise a far more complex phenomenon. Today, workplace stress, also known as occupational stress, is seen as *the entire process in which people perceive and interpret their work environment in relation to their capability to cope with it.* Under this definition, stress is present

- **A stressor is anything that throws the body out of allostatic balance. Allostasis is a range of measures appropriate for situations (sleep vs. bungee-jumping, heat, cold, illness, injury, hunger, etc.).**
- **Homeostasis is the maintenance of single optimal level between subsystems of a larger system.**

when the environment poses (or is perceived to pose) a threat to you, either in the form of excessive demands or in the form of insufficient resources to meet your needs.

There are many types of situations that can be physically or psychologically demanding, such as a fast-paced job, getting married or divorced, having children, being fired, or even receiving a promotion or winning the lottery. Any event or situation that puts a demand on a person is called a **stressor**.

Stress generally occurs when the individual is unable to respond adequately or efficiently to the stimuli of his/her environment or when it is only achieved by affecting the organism's health. Occupational stress is, then, the imbalance between the individual's hopes and the reality of his/her working conditions or, in other words, the perceived difference between the professional demands and the individual's ability to carry them out. This definition coincides with all motivational theories in that motivation will only be present when the worker perceives that there is a chance for his/her needs to be met at work. If this were not the case, there would be no motivated behavior. Additionally, occupational stress is the individual reaction to a threatening situation related to his/her job, whether or not this is due to having the necessary means at hand to satisfy his/her needs.

An organization's results and efficiency are normally evaluated in terms of economic profit, market position, product or service quality and competitive possibilities in the medium and long-term. Well-being and an individual's illnesses are not generally seen as organizational results, not even partially. In a situation where primordial competitive advantage stems from the quality of the available human resources, offering quality of work life is one way of ensuring greater employee commitment to the organization's mission and objectives.[2]

Interesting to know

The International Labor Organization and stress

The International Labor Organization (ILO) refers to occupational stress as follows:

This disease represents a danger for the economies of industrialized and developing countries. Productivity is hampered as stress affects the physical and mental health of workers. Those companies that help their employees cope with stress and carefully reorganize the workplace based on human aptitudes and aspirations are more likely to gain competitive advantage.

Stress: different models

The first documents on stress tried to discover a common origin: doctors believed that it had a common physical, chemical or bacteriological origin; psychologists felt that the originating factors were exclusively psychological or social responses to stress. Today, it is frequently accepted that stress has its origin in a series of factors which act together, creating a series of "multi-factorial" stimuli.

THE PHYSIOLOGICAL ASPECTS OF STRESS: CANNON AND SELYE'S PIONEERING CONCEPTS

The word "stress", like many other scientific terms, existed prior to its systematic use. It was already in use in the 14th century to express toughness, tension, adversity or affliction. At the end of the 18th century, Hocke used the word in a physical context, though its use did not become systematic until the beginning of the 19th century. The word **LOAD** was defined as an external force, while **STRESS** referred to the force generated within the body as a result of the action of that external force which tended to distort it. **STRAIN** referred to the deformation or distortion suffered by the object.

The concepts of **STRESS** and **STRAIN** persisted and were incorporated into medical discourse in the 19th century as antecedents to a loss of health. The word's current use began with Dr. Hans Selye, an endocrinologist at the University of Montreal, whose work marked the first significant contributions to the systematic study of stress. In parallel (or even a bit earlier), Walter Cannon published numerous experiments based on the psychophysiology of emotions.

Selye considered stress to be a disturbance of the homeostasis when faced with situations such as the lack of oxygen, cold, a decrease in glycaemia, and so on. He concluded that this was a non-specific response to practically any harmful stimulus, calling this phenomenon the *General Syndrome of Adaptation* (or GSA) in 1936. A decade later, stress was referred to as an external force acting upon the body or the wear and tear that this action provokes.

Stress according to Cannon

The pioneering work carried out by Walter. B. Cannon is considered essential in analysing the physiological response to a psychosocial stimulus.[3] Using animals as the subject of his study, Cannon was able to elaborate a model of stress which he called the "fight or flight response". According to this model, when an animal tried to obtain the object it desired but was prevented from doing so, the animal suffered stress which was translated into emotional reactions together with sym-

pathetic and hormonal reactions. Due to these experiences, Cannon discovered the secretion of catecholamines (adrenalines and noradrenalines) in situations of stress when the animal prepared itself to either attack or flee.

Currently, there are new contributions to cognitive theory which describe four fundamental models of primary response to stress: (1) fight, (2) flight, (3) faint, and (4) freeze.

What is the biological response to stress?

The repercussions of stress have an impact on different biological systems, with their associated behavioral correlation. In this behavioral expression, different response models are included – fight, flight, faint and freeze as mentioned – mediated by the locomotive system (up to the pre-medullar system), with the prior activation of the pyramidal system and the striated nucleus. We can observe, for example, how the facial expression is mediated by the skull (trigeminal, facial). Autonomic expression, characterised by urinary or faecal incontinence, is processed by the vagal parasympathetic system (prior activation of the dorsal nucleus of the vagus vein and the medial hypothalamus). Symptoms, such as sweating, heart palpitations, high blood pressure, mydriasis and/or piloerection, are mediated by the sympathetic system (prior to the activation of the lateral hypothalamus). The hormonal response to adaptation to stress is shown in Figure 2.2, which depicts a jump situation:

As such, any external stimulus is perceived by the sensorial or sensitive cortex and it reaches the thalamic nuclei by various channels where the inputs are filtered and prioritized before activating the amygdaline circuits.

Interesting to know

The physiological changes that characterize the fight or flight response are:

- An increased blood flow to the brain and large muscle groups. This increased blood flow makes us more alert and provides us with extra strength to deal with danger.
- Vision, hearing, and other sensory processes are sharpened, so that we have heightened awareness of the stressor.
- Glucose and other fatty acids are released into the bloodstream to provide extra energy during the stressful event.
- The pupils of the eye enlarge, to improve vision in a dark hiding place.
- The palms of the hands and soles of the feet sweat, giving a better grip for running, climbing, and holding onto things.
- Digestive processes are reduced; for instance, the mouth gets dry.

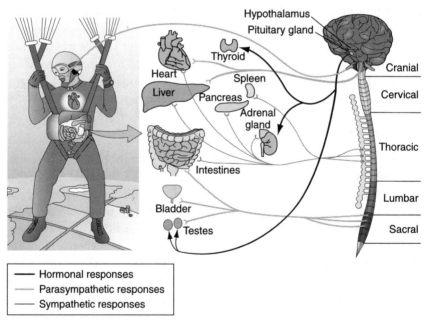

Figure 2.2 **Stress hormones during a jump situation**
Source: Rosenzweig, M.R., Breedlove, S.M. and Watson, N.V. (2004) *Biological Psychology, An Introduction to Behavioral and Cognitive neuroscience*, 4th edn (see chapter 15 "Emotions, Aggression, and Stress") figure 15.17, p. 481.
© Sinaur Associates Inc. Publishers, reproduced with permission of the publisher.

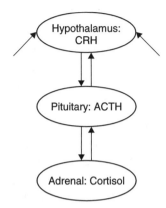

Figure 2.3 **The autonomic and endocrine responses**
Notes: Adrenocorticotropic hormone, as its name implies, stimulates the adrenal cortex. More specifically, it stimulates secretion of glucocorticoids such as cortisol, and has little control over secretion of aldosterone, the other major steroid hormone from the adrenal cortex. Another name for ACTH is *corticotropin*. Corticotropin-releasing hormone from the hypothalamus or CRH (corticotropin-releasing hormone) is secreted in response to many types of stress. Within the pituitary gland, ACTH is produced in a process that also generates several other hormones.

Visceral sensations can skip the thalamic filter. The frontal lobe cortex and the cingulate gyrus also play a part in this process and can delay the instinctive responses. It is important to recognize that they are part of the paralimbic system with a hierarchical, preventative and evaluative function. Figure 2.3 shows a schematic representation of the autonomic and endocrine responses.

Stress according to the "father" of the phenomenon: Hans Selye

Hans Selye, the great pioneer in the investigation of the physiology of stress, began his work in 1930. He studied the reaction of laboratory rats to physical stressors, such as heat, cold and physical exercise, as well as their reaction to chemical agents, such as injected hormones and steroids.

Seyle observed that, no matter what stressor he used, the animal's reaction was always the same, that is, non-specific. This led him to define stress as: the non-specific response to all stimuli.[4] Supported by his research, he formulated the theory of non-specific response which he defined as the "General Syndrome of Adaptation" (GSA).

This syndrome refers to the different changes produced within the organism as a result of the more or less constant presence of a stressor. Given that it is supposed that the organism's response is the same when faced with any stressor, all organisms when faced with stress will activate the same generalized and non-specific response. The activation produced in GSA consists of three phases:

1 Alarm is the first phase, recalling Cannon's observations, and it occurs immediately upon recognition of the threat or of the stressful situation. It is characterized by the release of corticosteroids to provoke the organism into facing and overcoming the situation. The exceptional resources mobilized are aimed at quickly overcoming the stressful situation.

2 If that does not occur, the second phase is triggered. This is the phase of resistance or defense in which activation, although less than in the previous phase, is still high and whose goal is to reduce the stressful situation. This lessened hyper-activation can now be maintained over a longer period of time and, as a result, it provides greater possibilities of overcoming the stressful situation. If this effort succeeds in overcoming the stressful situation, it marks the end of GSA.

3 Should this not occur, the previous moderate period of hyper-activation can't go on indefinitely given that the organism's reserves are being spent more quickly than the rate at which they are being produced. As such, if the stressful situation is not resolved, these resources will disappear and lead to the third phase, exhaustion, in which the organism uses up all its resources and progressively (or sometimes suddenly) loses its ability to be activated (including even normal activation). If, despite all else, the organism tries to stay activated as long as possible, the result will be complete exhaustion with all its negative consequences for the organism, including death. The intensity of the physiological responses demanded by the organism together with the latter's physical condition determine how quickly exhaustion will occur.

Seyle's GSA model encompasses a complete series of complex physiological reactions which all show common characteristics, at least in the experimental situations used by the researcher. However, reality is much more complex when Seyle's model is applied to humans given the great individual differences in the perception and standardization of alarming situations.

According to Seyle, the adrenocorticotropic hormone (ACTH) is the hormone which always increases in stressed individuals. It acts on the suprarenal cortex and produces cortisol (a neuro-endocrine response). The hypothalamus, when faced with a stressor stimulus, stimulates the hypophysis regica of the brain, thereby transmitting the stimulus to nerve endings. The central nervous system then projects it onto the rest of the organism and codifies the external and internal stress. This process is known as *heterostasis*. In heterostasis, a specific number of substances circulate within the blood, for example glucose, which contributes in increasing the consequences of stress and throwing the entire organism into a state of alert, producing a physiological change which then becomes physio-pathological.

The organism responds along three physiological axes:

1 *Neural*: the sympathetic and parasympathetic nervous systems are immediately activated. These control respiration, heart rate, muscular tension (toxicity) and movements.
2 *Neuroendocrine*: this is activated slowly and increases the activity of the spine and the suprarenal glands which release adrenaline, noradrenaline and catecholamines. This is a very important step in that it prepares the organism to respond to any external threat by either fighting or running away.
3 *Endocrine*: this is when activity is at its peak, maintained longer and is more intense. When the problem cannot be overcome, this axis controls the release of glucocorticoids (glucose and corticoids), mineralcorticoids (especially magnesium), thymus growth hormones (thymus gland and hypophysis), thyroids, vasopresina (increasing pressure) and cortisol (the hormone which produces stress).

If stress is produced due to an excess of activity or overload of the affected organs, it is normal to see this condition in the affected organs. When you learn to control a situation, which produces stress, these symptoms disappear.

Extrapolating from his animal findings to human, Selye describes the GSA model in terms of three distinct response pattern stages: stage 1 – Alarm Reaction, stage 2 – Resistance, and stage 3 – Exhaustion (Figure 2.4). He also labelled three types of stress (all associated with different hormonal reactions) in humans: **eustress, neustress and distress**. Eustress according to Selye is positive stress – it motivates, excites and energizes; distress, by contrast is negative stress – it crushes, oppresses and carries events beyond rational limits.

THE ORGANISM'S RESPONSES: THE BIOLOGICAL CONSEQUENCES OF STRESS

The organism's response will vary depending on whether or not it is in an initial phase of tension, in which there is a general activation and in which the alterations produced are easily remissible if the cause is removed or if it improves, or if it is in a phase of chronic tension or prolonged stress in which the symptoms become permanent, leading to illness. Table 2.1 lists various examples of the alterations produced.

Alarm stage
- anxiety or fear
- sorrow or depression
- shock or confusion

Self-correcting

Resistance stage
- aggression
- regression
- repression
- withdrawal
- fixation

Exhaustion stage
- physiological (ex. headaches, colds & flu)
- psychological (ex. severe depression)
- interpersonal (ex. end of relationships)
- inability to defend against stressors

Distress

Eustress

Figure 2.4 **Stages in the general adaptation syndrome and eustress vs distress in humans**

Table 2.1 **Examples of some biological consequences of stress**

Affected	Initial phases of strain	Stress consequence(s)
Brain	Clear and rapid idea	Headaches, migraines, nervous tics, insomnia
Mood	Mental concentration	Anxiety, loss of sense of humor
Saliva	Reduced	Dry mouth
Muscles	Major capacity	Muscle tension and muscle tic
Lungs	Major capacity	Hyperventilation or asthma attack
Stomach	Higher level of acids	Indigestion, throwing-up
Intestines	Spasms, peristalsis	Diarrhea, pain, colitis
Sexual	Loss of libido	Impotency, frigidity
Skin	Less humid (more dry)	Rashes, dermatitis, outbreaks
Energy	Increase in consumption of oxygen	Becoming quickly fatigued
Heart	Overuse of cardiovascular organs	Hypertension, pericardial pain

Interesting to know

Did the "GURU" of stress, Hans Selye, die from a lack of self-esteem and lots of stress in his life: a personal account

In 1977, I was a young scholar who had just completed my doctoral studies at the University of Minnesota in the United States. After having some shocking personal experience at the Mayo Clinic in Minnesota, I decided to dedicate my intellectual curiosity and energy over the next couple of years to better understanding stress in work settings. I was fortunate to encounter Prof. Paul Rohan who suggested that I join the team of interdisciplinary researchers affiliated with the Hans Selye International Institute of Stress at the University of Montreal. Paul was a personal friend of Hans Selye (they knew each other from the old continent – Vienna and Czechoslovakia). Paul introduced me to Hans Selye and the rest is history. Obviously, for me, it was a great honour and an opportunity to pursue my interest in stress research, working with the master himself. Hans Selye was commonly known as the "father of stress". I could not have known then that a few years later the overall balance of working with Selye would not be as exciting and as productive as I had imagined. Our initial contacts went very well, and within a very short time I had gained Selye's confidence and developed a very close personal relationship with him. During our many conversations, Hans shared with me his professional dreams and his personal life experiences. Our joint work continued until his death in 1982 (with the exception of a short period for reasons explained below). After Selye's death, I continued my research on stress and health at the University of Montreal for the next 20 years. In 2001, I left Montreal to join ESADE Business School in Barcelona.

After my initial excitement and the commencement of my work with Selye in 1977, I began to have some doubts about the man, especially in terms of his personality and of his own capacity to deal with stress. To quote from an old saying, "he didn't practise what he preached". What puzzled me the most was the fact that he was a very lonely man, and during his many years of leadership in stress research, he was unable (or perhaps incapable) of establishing a core team of scholars that would stay and continue working with him. On the contrary, I saw eminent names and young scholars coming and going; team rotation was very high and his style of supervision was so demanding that even those who cared and wanted to work with him ended up leaving or facing premature death (that was the case of Dr. Jean Taché). Adding salt to the wound, two of his former students and disciples ended up receiving merits and awards (including the Nobel Prize), while he was deeply hurt and disappointed for never receiving this prize (despite having been nominated on two occasions). I noticed that during later years his self-esteem was at its lowest, and he constantly needed and looked for gratification and recognition. These were by no means easy to come by.

The answer to the above puzzle was evident after getting to know the man. Hans Selye had a very demanding personality (in the work context) and was a very frightened and submissive person in the non-work context. Moreover, he did not tolerate any idea or theory that did not comply perfectly with his early research on the physiological response to stress. I, for one, tried hard to convince him that the stress mechanisms for humans worked differently than that for the cats and mice in his laboratory. I also failed to convince him that in order to understand the multidisciplinary nature of stress, an interdisciplinary team was needed. I noticed that when I mentioned these ideas he was upset and his responses at times were aggressive and antagonistic. There was no doubt in my mind why colleagues and associates decided to desert him and develop their own line of research. I ended up doing the same.

For the first 2 years (1977–79), I subjected myself to Selye's whims by thinking that it was the price that a young scholar had to pay in order to gain recognition and an opportunity to learn from the great master. During those years we had numerous mini incidents that left a bitter taste in my mouth. Selye was moody, and at times his behavior at work reflected his fear of his tyrannical latest wife. Here is a typical example. One day I received a phone call from Hans and a request to come and see him urgently. My office, located about 200 meters from his office was up the hill. I stopped what I was doing and ran to his office, arriving there breathless, to find out that the great master was in trouble with his wife because he could not return home that afternoon without bringing her new stamps for her stamp collection. While for him this signified a "real crisis", for me it meant another stupid chore that I had to put up with. These types of "false alarm" incidents became more common as our relationship grew more personal. I felt pity for the old man, and noticed how his self-esteem was getting lower and lower. Obviously, until you get to know a person very well, you will not always notice this kind of behavior.

I have to admit that, apart from these incidents, my experiences of working with Selye were not always negative. He gave me an opportunity by inviting me to participate in the 2nd International Conference on the Management of Stress that our Institute organized in Monte Carlo, Monaco, in 1979. This conference gave me a chance to share my initial thoughts about work-related stress with the world's foremost experts on stress, including several Nobel Prize-winners. Selye also asked for my editorial assistance in producing a new journal called *Stress*. For someone with limited, or no publications, revising manuscripts for this Journal and publishing two papers (with Paul Rohan) was very instrumental in my career and elevated my own self-esteem. Like many other "Selye" projects, the journal died with him; he did not prepare a successor nor did he create a structure to continue this important work. It was after the Monaco Conference and following two more incidents of "abuse of my time" that I realized that I could not count on Selye to help me develop a line of research dedicated to people in work settings, that I had to stop working with him and establish a parallel research centre at the University of Montreal. This was also the first time that I managed to receive substantial research grants from the Quebec and Canadian governments to study occupational stress.

Getting back to Selye, in 1979 we had a book project in preparation. I was supposed to provide the leadership for the book and he was supposed to guide and supervise. Once it was completed and there was no feedback from Selye, I invited another physician, Andre Arsenault, to replace Selye. My relationship with Andre Arsenault was very productive and we have jointly managed the research centre for the study of occupational stress and health for over 15 years. This collaboration also led to the publication of dozens of papers in scholarly journals (in medicine, psychology and management), which made our work known internationally. Shortly before the book was published, Selye found out about it, called me to his office and insisted that he write the preface. I accepted his offer graciously. It represented a truce in our relationship. The book was titled: *Stress, Health and Performance at Work* (in French), and it was published in 1980 by the University of Montreal; it became a best-seller in French-speaking Canada. Shortly thereafter, Selye asked me to give him a hand in organizing the 3rd International Conference on the Management of Stress to be held in Australia in 1982 and I agreed. Unfortunately, this conference was never held as Selye died just before it started. The great Hans Selye died a very lonely man, agonizing for not having received the Nobel Prize, subject to fear of his last wife and completely isolated from other people and scholars who could not work with a man who was not a team player. It is my conclusion that Selye's self-esteem at the end of his life was extremely low. The last straw which perhaps triggered the "master of stress'" death was the beginning of an inquiry by the Canadian Tax authorities into alleged tax improprieties, namely, the failure to report income received for various conferences and speeches he gave around the globe.

Note: I admit that the text written above is a biased and subjective account, representing the way I saw and interpreted the last years of Hans Selye's life. My memories are based on the period that I worked with him at the University of Montreal.

Stress, Emotions and Diseases

During the past 50 years, many scholars in psychology, management and medicine have studied the effect of emotions on human diseases. The cross-interests of psychology and medicine gave rise to the field known as psycho-somatic medicine, as well as health psychology (or behavioral medicine). In these emerging disciplines an attempt is made to explore, understand and explain the relationships between emotional stress and human diseases.

One of the dominant school of thought connects emotions and stress to human diseases via the immune system. Researchers view the immune system as an autonomic mechanism: a pathological agent in the form of a virus or bacteria that arrives on the scene can trigger the defense mechanism of the immune system. We normally react to such threats via the armoury of antibodies and other immunological devices; the immune system recognizes intruders and interacts with various organs, especially hormone systems and the nervous system. Because of the interaction of the two systems, other agents become involved, such as the endocrine system as mentioned previously. When the immune system is being "abused", in the case of chronic stress, there is enough research evidence to suggest that its function decreases and thus the susceptibility to infectious disease, cancer and

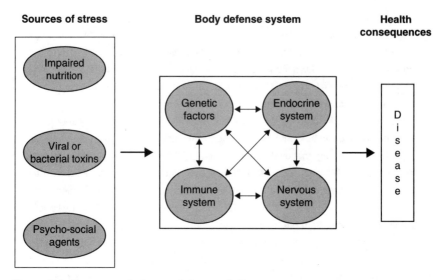

Figure 2.5 **Stress and the aetiology of disease**

autoimmune disorders increases. Figure 2.5 shows the links and the proposed interactions between, stressors, emotions, the body defense mechanisms and diseases.

But how does the immune system work? The phagocytes, a type of white blood cell in our system, are mobilized to destroy invading germs. They rely in the process on other white blood cells, namely lymphocytes, to instruct them to attack the invader. The B lymphocytes, which are called the B cells because they form in the bone marrow, produce proteins called antibodies. These latch onto antigens (the foreign molecules) such as viruses or bacteria and summon phagocytes and circulating proteins to destroy the invaders. T lymphocytes (T cells) act as a killer cells. In addition, special T lymphocytes secrete cytokines, cell-signalling proteins such as the interleukins and lymphokins, which regulate the activity of the B lymphocytes and phagocytes. These immune system cells form in the thymus gland, bone marrow, spleen and lymph nodes, and are released into the blood stream.[5]

STRESS AS A PSYCHOLOGICAL AND BEHAVIORAL CONSEQUENCE

Menninger's psychoanalytical approach

Karl Augustus Menninger was an American psychiatrist and a member of the famous Menninger family of psychiatrists who founded the Menninger Foundation and the Menninger Clinic in Topeka, Kansas.

Karl Menninger does not believe that health and illness are two separate concepts, but rather that they are psychological phenomena which make up a continuum based on an intermediate state. On either end of the continuum is the dismemberment of the person, the illness in itself. From this perspective, the ego balances the tensions posed by the superego and external reality. In this role the ego is trying to establish a tolerable level of tension, compatible with its growth, development and expression of its creativity.[6]

The Transactional Model of Stress: Lazarus' Psycho-cognitive Approach[7]

Richard S. Lazarus and his colleagues established a clear distinction between stress, the force applied on the organism, and tension, the result of that stress, which in physics corresponds to a deformation. In other words, there is a correlative internal tension to stress, the external force, which tends to disrupt the established balance. Lazarus uses this notion of stress to explain human behavior. He emphasizes the interaction between the individual and his/her environment as a generator of symptoms, and  insists on the importance of man's cognitive activity and is interested most of all in the manifestations which become behaviors. This cognitive approach relates the thought process and the mechanics behind the emission of a judgment in the subjective interpretation which the individual makes of his/her environment. As such, this subjective interpretation becomes more important and significant than the objective reality of the environment. The individual's reaction will therefore be produced by the imbalances at the core of the cognitive structure which drive the individual to act in order to eliminate those incoherencies and restore balance.

In this vision of stress there exists an implicit notion of threat, or more specifically a subjective perception of threat. As a result, the individual differences in the interpretation of what constitutes a threat invariably lead to the presence of personality factors which determine a particular vulnerability in each situation. Lazarus concludes that individual differences are not the only determinants of stress, but that cultural characteristics, personal value systems and cognitive processes also have a determinant role on behavior.

To summarize, stress, according to Lazarus and his colleagues, is a complex psycho-biological process with three main components:

1 The initial situation in which an event takes place that is potentially prejudicial or dangerous (a stressful or stressor event).
2 The event is "interpreted" as dangerous, prejudicial or threatening. The subject perceives and assesses it as such, independently of its objective characteristics.
3 The organism is activated in response to the threat.

There are two mental (and highly interrelated) processes which we use to make this appraisal:

1   **Primary appraisal**: individuals judge the meaning of a specific trans-action with respect to their well-being – if it is "irrelevant", "benign – positive" or "stressful".
2   **Secondary appraisal**: individuals assess their resources and options (physical, social, psychological and material) in order to confront the stressor.

Stress from a Cognitive and Multidisciplinary Perspective: Dolan and Arsenault's Model

Simon L. Dolan worked with Hans Selye in his laboratory at the University of Montreal from 1979 to 1982. Although Selye focused his work on tests with animals, Dolan was interested in developing a theoretical framework to apply to humans and, especially, within the workplace. In order to carry out this research, a multidisciplinary team was developed. From the 1980s onward, Dolan, a work psychologist, and Arsenault, a physician and statistician, proposed a synthetic and more holistic model which allows for a diagnosis to be made which will serve to diminish the frequency of the irreversible, long-term consequences of stress. This model sets out to answer four questions:[8]

1   What are the sources of stress in the workplace?
2   Why are workers not affected the same way by stress?
3   What are the individual consequences of stress from a physical and psychological point of view?
4   What are the consequences for the organization in terms of workers' performance (productivity, absenteeism, frequency of work-related accidents, etc.)?

The authors of this model maintain that the discordance between the individual and his/her work environment is what causes problems of adaptation. From the degree of concordance, the presence or absence of a variety of signs and symptoms of tension which make up the stress indicators can be observed.

The occupational/job stress model presented in Figure 2.6 identifies three principal components involved in the causes of stress at work:

●   *Perception of job demands.* Employees' perception of a situation can influence how (and whether) they will experience stress. For example, a manager's request that two subordinates stay an extra hour to finish important work can be perceived as stressful by one employee and have no effect on the other. Stress can originate from a single stressor or from a combination of environmental job demands.

- *Individual differences.* There are a number of individual differences that play an important role in the ways in which employees experience and respond to stress. Individual differences in needs, values, attitudes, abilities, and, of course, personality traits are important in that they may increase or reduce the perception of the harmfulness of work demands. Thus, to understand whether job incumbents will be stressed, it is critical to understand their perception about their work and their organization; what one person may consider to be a major source of stress, another may hardly notice.

- *Social support.* Compensatory mechanisms (commonly referred to as "buffers" or "moderators") that may be present or absent during stressful periods are important mediators of responses to stress. One such buffer is social support. The support of others in one's social environment includes co-workers, superiors, family and friends. The availability of such support increases confidence and strengthens the ability to cope.

The essence of the model in Figure 2.6 has been validated in different organizations, and for a variety of occupations – including hospital employees, teachers, police officers, prosecutors, executives, middle-level managers, first-line supervisors, programers, and secretaries, by researchers at the University of Montreal.[9] Notice that the consequences of job stress are labelled **strain** and are grouped along two categories: those that harm the individual's health and those that are detrimental to the health of the organization.

Similar holistic models applied to work settings have been proposed in recent years by many other scholars, and one of the most interesting models deals with Demand/Control. This model suggests that high demands plus low control contribute to strain, particularly when combined with home stress and the absence of social support. A similar model is known as the Effort/Reward Imbalance model. This model shows that high effort/low reward conditions are associated with a variety of adverse health outcomes prominent among which are cardiovascular disease and mental health problems such as anxiety and depression. There is increasing evidence that the Demand/Control model and the Effort/Reward Imbalance model are related in that high demand/low control and high effort/low reward conditions may be found in the same organizations at the same time.

The Demand/Control/Support model has stimulated much research during recent years. The model has helped to document more specifically the importance of social and psychological factors in the structure of current occupations as a risk factor for industrial society's most burdensome diseases and social conditions. Empirically, the model has been successful: a clear relationship between adverse job conditions (particularly low decision latitude) and coronary heart disease has been established.[10]

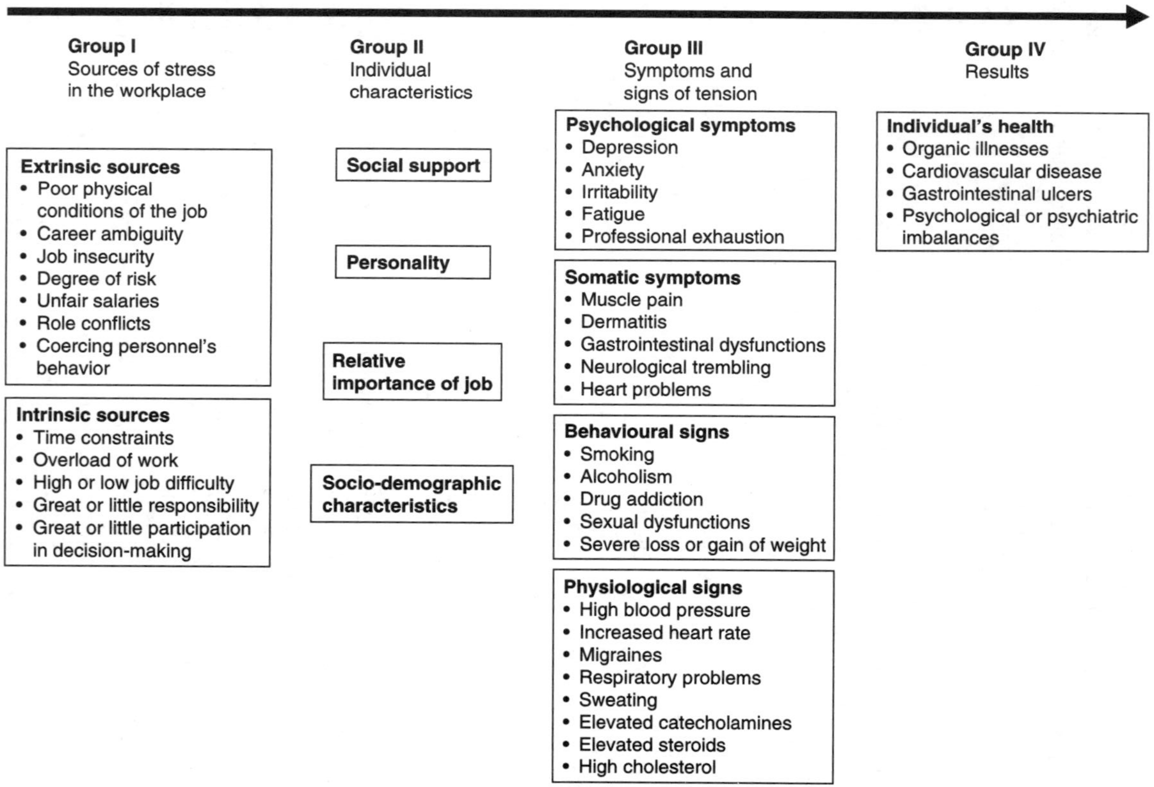

Group I
Sources of stress
in the workplace

Group II
Individual
characteristics

Group III
Symptoms and
signs of tension

Group IV
Results

Extrinsic sources
- Poor physical conditions of the job
- Career ambiguity
- Job insecurity
- Degree of risk
- Unfair salaries
- Role conflicts
- Coercing personnel's behavior

Intrinsic sources
- Time constraints
- Overload of work
- High or low job difficulty
- Great or little responsibility
- Great or little participation in decision-making

Social support

Personality

Relative importance of job

Socio-demographic characteristics

Psychological symptoms
- Depression
- Anxiety
- Irritability
- Fatigue
- Professional exhaustion

Somatic symptoms
- Muscle pain
- Dermatitis
- Gastrointestinal dysfunctions
- Neurological trembling
- Heart problems

Behavioural signs
- Smoking
- Alcoholism
- Drug addiction
- Sexual dysfunctions
- Severe loss or gain of weight

Physiological signs
- High blood pressure
- Increased heart rate
- Migraines
- Respiratory problems
- Sweating
- Elevated catecholamines
- Elevated steroids
- High cholesterol

Individual's health
- Organic illnesses
- Cardiovascular disease
- Gastrointestinal ulcers
- Psychological or psychiatric imbalances

Figure 2.6 **The cognitive and conditional model of occupational stress**

However, it is still difficult to be precise about which aspects of psychological demands, or decision latitude, are most important in the model, and for what categories of workers. Answers to these questions require more depth of explanation of the physiological and micro-behavioral effects of psychological demands, decision latitude and social support than the model's original formulation provided, and require simultaneous testing of the dynamic version of the model, including the active/passive hypotheses.[11]

Determining factors of occupational stress

During the last decade there has been increased interest in knowing about and better understanding the conditions which can make the workplace more humane and less harmful for people. It is virtually impossible, however, to provide a complete list of stressors and their consequences, especially if we bear in mind that the stressor condition depends on the assessment each individual makes of a specific condition. Nevertheless, we can establish and identify a set of stressors at different levels: organizational stressors and extra-organizational stressors.

INDIVIDUAL AND EXTRA-ORGANIZATIONAL STRESSORS

Many authors have underscored the importance of individual factors, such as personal values, needs and skills, as well as personality and personal aspirations in determining each individual's susceptibility to stress. These individual factors encompass particular characteristics on the perceptual and cognitive levels which influence both the subjective

> **Individual factors, such as personal values, needs, skills, as well as personality and aspirations determine each individual's susceptibility to stress.**

interpretation of what is considered stress as well as the reaction to stress.

Many facets of personality have been the object of study regarding stress. Typical reactions to stress vary depending on personality traits, such as neurotic anxiety, introversion and extroversion, rigidity, flexibility and ambition. A questionnaire is included in this chapter to identify a stressful person or a person with type-A behavior.

Extra-organizational stressors are those which arise beyond the work environment. They include family, political, social and economic factors, which have an impact on the individual. Though recent studies suggest that work-related stress factors outnumber family or spousal-related factors, we cannot fail to mention the existing interrelationship between the workplace and home or social relationships. Inadequate home–workplace interconnections generate psychological conflicts and mental fatigue, a lack of motivation and a decrease in productivity, as well as deterioration in family relationships.

Undoubtedly, organizational or intra-organizational problems or stressors, that is those that arise within the workplace, have an impact on the subject's personal life, provoking domestic problems which, as they increase are then fomented, generating further stress which is projected onto the workplace, creating more difficulties in job performance thereby producing a vicious cycle. Individuals spend a great deal of time at work, obtaining a substantial part of their identity and personal gratification from their tasks. However, these considerations are not always adequately assessed by companies or by the workers themselves.

INTRA-ORGANIZATIONAL STRESSORS

In order to facilitate the study and understanding of these stressors, we have grouped them into four types:

1 *Physical stressors*: light, noise, vibrations and space;
2 *Individual stressors*: work overload, conflict and ambiguity of roles, and discrepancy with career objectives;
3 *Group stressors*: lack of cohesion, conflict, climate and group pressures;
4 *Organizational stressors*: climate, size and management style, hier-archical structure, technology and irrational deadlines.

Physical stressors

These factors require double adaptation, both physical as well as psycho-logical. In this section, we will briefly outline the main physical stressors in the workplace:

- *Insufficient or excessive light* – inadequate lighting in the workplace can lead to negative consequences in terms of vision, headaches, fatigued vision, tension and frustration as the job becomes bothersome and difficult.
- *Noise* – working with noise has a negative influence on the degree of satisfaction, productivity and vulnerability to accidents, increasing the percentage of errors made. Additionally, cooperative behavior is reduced and negative attitudes are increased regarding others. Greater levels of hostility can be observed.
- *Vibrations* – being constantly exposed to vibrations leads to an increase of catecholamines, spinal injuries and neurological alterations.
- *Amount and layout of physical space in the workplace* – a lack of phys-ical space or poor layout increases the number of movements which need to be made with the resulting increase in effort and loss of time.

Individual Stressors

These factors include:

- *Work overload* – an excessive amount of work, both quantitatively and qualitatively, is a common source of stress. This overload or stress due to overstimulation can be objective or subjective depending on the individual's assessment and characteristics. On the other hand, the lack of work can also be stressful due to a lack of stimulation. This is produced by a lack of normal and physiological stimulus and allows for little or no creativity and independent thought. This situation leads to distraction, a lack of attention and an increase in work-related accidents. An overload of work generates dissatisfaction, tension, a lack of self-esteem, a sense of threat, heart palpitations, high cholesterol, and the consumption of nicotine and other addictive substances to try to respond to the over-demand.

- *Conflict of roles* – the conflict of roles can be objective or subjective. An objective conflict of roles arises when two or more people give conflicting orders. On the other hand, a subjective conflict of roles arises as a result of the contradiction between the formal orders received by the individual and the individual's own values and goals. Conflicts of roles generate a high degree of anxiety and dissatisfaction with respect to work, even more so the greater the authority of the person giving the contradictory orders. These situations lessen the individual's creativity since fear of failure provokes less satisfying job performance. On a personal level, the individual generally has high blood pressure and a high level of cholesterol.

- *Ambiguity of roles* – this refers to a lack of clarity regarding the role of the individual, the objectives of the job itself and the scope of the individual's responsibilities. Typically, there is a drop in self-esteem as a result of a lack of satisfaction from the task being carried out, as well as work satisfaction, quality and participation in decision-making. Adequate information and communication reduce this type of conflict since they improve how work-related tasks are oriented.

- *Discrepancies with career goals* – discrepancies and doubts regarding the individual's career or profession arise due to a lack of job security, doubts regarding pay rises and legitimate, frustrated ambitions. Dissatisfaction in terms of discrepancies between an individual's hopes and achievements creates anxiety and frustration, depression and stress, especially among individuals in the 40–50 age group. As well as unsatisfactory job performance, it is common to find addictions to substances, such as alcohol, drugs, coffee, tobacco, and so on.

Group Stressors

The quality of relationships is an important factor when determining their potential stress factor. A good relationship between members of the same team is a key factor for personal and organizational health. On the contrary, an untrusting relationship lacking in support and cooperation, and which is primarily destructive, can produce a high degree of tension and stress within the group or organization. The following stressful factors are included in the group stressors:

- *Lack of cohesion* – not having this bond is a characteristics that can be stressful for individuals.
- *Group conflict* – a degree of conflict is always healthy in groups or teams. In fact, it is necessary in order to achieve optimal performance. However, continued and non-constructive conflict between members of the same team can lead to emotional responses and stressful situations, such as frustration, tension, dissatisfaction, emotional exhaustion, somatic ailments, insomnia, and so on.
- *Group climate* – the climate within the team is another relevant stressor for its members. In a study carried out among teams of paramedics by Peino in 1992 in Spain (see note 2), it was found that members in teams whose climate was characterized by imbalances (between the levels of support offered to the individuals and the orientation towards the goals, and respecting the rules and an innovative orientation) suffered greater degrees of role-related stress and work tension and greater dissatisfaction than members of teams with more balanced scores.
- *Group pressure* – the pressures the groups exert on the individual members can lead to stress, especially if the object is to have the members assume values or beliefs which go against their own principles. These pressures cause various psychological and behavioral changes.

Organizational Stressors

The following are worth noting:

- *Climate within the organization* – every organization has its own personality, its own climate. This climate conditions the behavior of the individuals who make up the organization, though it is difficult to appraise since there are no scientifically valid tools available to measure it. The climate may or may not be tense, relaxed, cordial, and so on. All this produces different levels of stress in the individuals depending on their susceptibility and vulnerability.
- *Size and management style* – the most common source of stress arises from the combination of the organization's size and how formal its functioning is, in other words, bureaucracy. Many studies have shown

that highly bureaucratic organizations try to mold individuals to conform to a stereotype.

- *Hierarchical structure* – in all hierarchies where there is an unequal distribution of power, the higher the level, the greater the tendency of autocratic control of a few at the expense of others. Managers are in a good position to demand behaviors which exceed the ability of the individuals to tolerate such demands.

- *Technology* – the incorporation of new technologies has important implications for numerous work-related and organizational aspects. Changes develop in the tasks and job roles, in the supervision, in the structures and in the organizational style. These can make way for new stressors in the workplace, while eliminating others.[12]

- *Irrational deadlines* – everyone knows the impact produced by the establishment of unreachable goals given the time allotted to complete them.

So, what exactly is occupational stress?

Most would agree that occupational stress is the result of the interaction between the worker and the working conditions.

However, opinions differ regarding the importance attributed to the *worker's characteristics* compared to the importance of the *working conditions* as the primary cause of stress. These different opinions are important because they suggest different ways to avoid occupational stress.

Job stress results when the requirements of the job do not match the capabilities, resources, or needs of the worker.

According to one school of thought, the differences between personal characteristics, such as personality and how people cope with stress, are more important in predicting whether certain working conditions will result in stress. In other words, what is stressful for one person may not be stressful for someone else. This opinion leads to prevention strategies concentrated on workers and ways to help them cope with the demanding conditions of their work.

Although the importance of individual differences cannot be ignored, scientific evidence suggests that certain working conditions are stressful for the majority of people.

Chapter postscript

Stress is one of the factors directly responsible for the most common and most lethal psychological and physical illnesses affecting mankind, hence the importance of its study within organizations.

Stress means the effort required to adapt to both positive and negative changes producing stress.

- Healthy stress is the activation of the organism to adapt to a situation interpreted as a positive challenge and which is followed by the perception of achievement and deactivation.
- Harmful stress is the chronic activation of the organism to try to adapt to a situation interpreted as a threat and which is not followed by deactivation or the perception of achievement.

There are different models used to explain stress, including models based on the physiological consequences of stress, those based on the psychological and behavioral consequences, and a multidisciplinary model, the cognitive and conditional model of Dolan and Arsenault which maintains that the discordance between the individual and his/her working environment gives rise to problems of adaptation.

Occupational stress is the imbalance between the individual's aspirations and hopes and the reality of his or her working conditions. We can talk about various determining factors of occupational stress:

1 Individual stressors such as personal values, needs and skills, as well as personality and aspirations.
2 Extra-organizational stressors beyond the workplace, consisting of family, political, social and economic factors which have an impact on the individual.

3   Organizational stressors which arise within the workplace and which can be grouped into four types:

o   physical stressors: light, noise, vibrations and space;

o   individual stressors: work overload, role conflict and ambiguity, discrepancies with career goals;

o   group stressors: lack of cohesion, conflict, climate and group pressure;

o   organizational stressors: climate, size and management style, hierarchical structure, technology and irrational deadlines.

Exercise: test your stress level

How stressed are you?

The following questionnaire is designed to help you find out your stress level. Answer each question below.

Use the following scale to give your answers:

Never					Sometimes					Always	
0	1	2	3	4	5	6	7	8	9	10	

1   Are you known for seeing the positive side of life?

2   Do you feel that, in your case, you keep all your feelings locked up inside?

3   Do you ever get overwhelmed by the lack of time available to meet all of your obligations?

4   Do you ever have nothing to do?

5   Do you know how to use humor in difficult situations?

6   Do you believe your job affects your relationship with the people you most love?

7   Do you need an increasingly frequent "dose" of work to feel stimulated?

8   Does it take you a while to get your day started?

9   Do you feel you have real friends?

10   Do you ever feel "I can't take it anymore"?

11   Is it hard for you to find someone to talk to about your problems?

12   Do you want to be left alone?

13   Do you feel life is flying by?

14   Do you think you're thought of as a friendly person?

15   Do you know fun people?

16   Is it hard for you to disconnect from what's troubling you?

17   Do you have a difficult time falling asleep?

18   Do you know how to encourage yourself?

19 Is it hard for you to disconnect after a long day at work?

20 Do you know how to relax when you want to?

21 Do you have time for yourself?

22 Do you think you're "addicted" to your work?

23 Do you need to take substances (coffee, nicotine, alcohol or others) to "keep going"?

24 Do you think "if I spoke up it would only make things worse"?

25 Are you irritable or bad tempered when faced with insignificant problems?

26 Do you think you demand too much of yourself?

27 Do you have backaches, headaches, or pains in your jaws?

28 Do you laugh easily?

Score and interpretation

0–90   Not at all stressed.

91–180   A little stressed.

181–280 Very stressed:

(1) you want to take on more than you really can.

(2) you don't express your feelings or demand your rights.

(3) you don't manage your time well.

(4) you're abandoning your friends.

(5) you're hurting yourself by thinking negatively.

(6) you're not aware of what is going on around you and inside you.

(7) you're a workaholic.

(8) you're situation is very troubling; **you are extremely "burnt out" and "exhausted"**.

REFERENCES

1   For example, Selye, H. (1936). "A Syndrome Produced by Diverse Nocuous Agents", *Nature*, 138: 32; Selye, H. (1952). *The Story of the Adaptation Syndrome* (Montreal: Acta Inc. Med. Pub.); Selye, H. (1958). *The Stress of Life* (New York: McGraw Hill); Selye, H. (1955). 'Stress and Disease', *Science*, 122: s 625; Selye, H. (1975). *Tensión sin angustia* (Madrid: Editions Guadarrama).

2   Peino, J.M. (1992). *Desencadenantes del estrés laboral* (Madrid: Edudema, S.A.).

3   Cannon, W.B. (1929). *Bodily Changes in Pain, Hunger, Fear and Rage: An account of recent researches into the function of emotional excitement,* (New York: Appleton).

4   Selye (1952).

5   *Source*: Rozenzweig, M.R., Breedlove, A.M. and Watson, N.V. (2004). *Biological Psychology,* 4th edn (Sinauer Publishers): 483.

6   Menninger, K. (1954). "Psychological Aspects of the Organism Under Stress", *Journal of the American Psychoanalytic Association*, Parts 1 and 2: 67–106, 280–310.

7   Lazarus, R.S., and Folkman, S. (1984). *Stress, Appraisal, and Coping* (New York: Springer); see also: Monat, A. and Lazarus, R.S. (eds) (1991). *Stress and Coping: An anthology* (New York: Columbia university Press).

8   For example, see Dolan, S.L. and Arsenault, A. (1979). "The Organisational and Individual Consequences of Stress at Work: A new frontier to human resource administration", in V.V. Veysey and G.A. Hall Jr. (eds), *The New World of Managing Human Resources* (Pasadina: California Institute of Technology); Dolan, S.L. and Arsanult, A. (1980). "Stress, santé et rendement au travail", Montreal, École de relations industrielles, monographie no.5, Université de Montréal; Rohan, P. and Dolan, S.L. (1980). "The Management of Occupational Stress", *Stress*, 1(2): 13–18; Dolan, S.L. and Arsenault, A. "Occupational Stress", *Quality of Working Life*, Part I: 1981, vol. 4 (1): 6–9 and Part II: 1981, vol. 4(2): 10–15.

9   See for example, Dolan, S.L. (1987). "Job Stress among College Administrators: An empirical study", *The International Journal of Management*, 4(4): 553–60; van Ameringen, M.R., Arsenault, A. and Dolan, S.L. (1988). "Intrinsic Job Stress as Predictor of Diastolic Blood Pressure among Female Hospital Workers', *Journal of Occupational Medicine*, 30(2): 93–7; Dolan, S.L. and Tziner, A. (1988). "Implementing Computer-based Automation in the Office: A comparative study of experienced stress", *Journal of Organizational Behavior*, 19: 183–7; Dolan, S.L. (1990). "Case Illustration of Proneness to Stress among Hospital Workers," in L.E. Miller and J. Seltzer (eds), *Innovations in Research and Teaching*, Proceedings of the 27th Annual Meeting of the Eastern Academy of Management, Philadelphia, EAM: 308–11; Dolan, S.L. (1995). "Individual, Organizational and Social Determinants of Managerial Burnout: Theoretical and empirical update", in P. Perrewe (ed.), *Occupational Stress: A handbook* (New York: Taylor & Francis): 223–38.

10   *Source*:   http://www.ilo.org/encyclopaedia/?doc&nd=857100006&nh=0 &ssect=6

11   See for example, Karasek, R.A. and Theorell, T. (1990). *Healthy Work* (New York: Basic Books).

12   http://www.mercantil.com/soluciones/bibliotecacontenido.asp?News_ Code=5001&lang=esp)

3 Self-Esteem and Stress: A Critical Analysis*

"Unlike the virtuous, far removed from mediocrity, men of action, whose happiness resides in standing out, seek honour only to convince themselves of their own worth."

(Aristotle)

What is self-esteem?

Self-esteem is one of the most popularized psychological concepts of our times, probably due to its practical use in understanding a good part of our journey through life in search of happiness.

---

* This chapter is heavily inspired by a chapter written in Spanish by the author of this book and two other Spanish colleagues. The material borrowed, which is copy-righted by the authors, is used with the permission of the two other authors, Salvador García and Miriam Díez-Piñol. *Source*: Dolan, García and Díez-Piñol (2005) *Auto-estima, estréés y trabajo* (Madrid: McGraw-Hill) mainly chapter 3.

Intuitively, we know that "self-esteem" is something desirable and positive, especially if it is balanced and does not end up as self-hate or narcissism.

> **Human beings are blessed with an essential and originating self-esteem, which, little by little, is lost as they navigate the seas of mistrust and the desire to control variables beyond themselves, no matter how well the individual has learned to navigate through the Internet in the so-called era of knowledge and information.**

SELF-ESTEEM AND PURPOSE IN LIFE

"Self-esteem" according to Webster's *New Collegiate Dictionary* (G. & C. Merriam Co., 1981), is defined as (1) a confidence and satisfaction in one's own self: self-respect; and (2) self-conceit.

At a deep, existential level we assess ourselves depending on where we see ourselves on our journey through life, or if we are on the right path. The final destination on this road, what everyone is searching for throughout life, is to be happy. Happiness, the Hellenic *eudaimonia*, is to find the correct destiny and be comfortable with it. Happiness consists of savouring one's freely chosen path in life. Self-esteem, then, is absolutely necessary to be happy.

Self-esteem is at the centre of a loop: It depends on what each individual does with their life based on, and as a consequence, of their private appraisal of what life is. The real moral task is to become everything one can possibly be with what one is (Aranguren, 1994).[1]

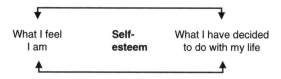

Human beings are blessed with an essential and originating self-esteem, which, little by little, is lost as they navigate the seas of mistrust and the desire to control variables beyond themselves, no matter how well the individual has learned to navigate through the Internet in the so-called era of knowledge and information.

Part of life's mission is to assume the responsibility for creating greater health, greater happiness, greater commitment and greater endeavour in the world around us and in ourselves. When this occurs, we increase our real self-esteem.

Self-love is the source of self-conservation and survival as well as awareness of oneself and others. Personal dignity, our own honour, is the *axioprepia*; the final goal, *par excellence*, is making the right values fit together. Loving oneself (self-love) has its biological foundation based on our natural survival instinct and on our quest to constantly improve. Everyone must love himself or herself above or at least in equal measure to any other person or thing. From this stems that some might want their own failure as a dysfunctional form of self-affirmation (Polaino-Lorente, 2003).[2] It would also explain the golden rule found in most religions, to "love others as you love yourself". The coincidence among different cultures and religions regarding this essential bit of wisdom, to treat and love others, as you would have them treat and love you, is nevertheless surprising.

Regardless, people see themselves as valid or non-valid, as "good" or "bad", they love themselves or not to a greater or lesser degree, and they have a higher or lower opinion of themselves depending on their positive or negative experiences and the way they react to the events in their lives. All this occurs with varying degrees of pathology, sobriety, arrogance and drama, depending on individual differences.

APPARENT, FANTASIZED AND PROFOUND SELF-ESTEEM

One thing is apparent, self-esteem derives from the portrayal of a character more or less appreciated by oneself and others. Another matter is real self-esteem, the connection with the essential and authentic *ego*.

The first type is fragile and volatile, the second, solid and permanent, and allows many defense mechanisms against the anxiety caused by feeling fake or vulnerable to be eliminated. One of these not so uncommon defense mechanisms is the obsessive, active and exhausting accumulation of professional and materialistic achievements.

> **One thing is apparent, self-esteem derives from the portrayal of a character more or less appreciated by oneself and others. Another matter is real self-esteem, the connection with the essential and authentic *ego*.**

There is also another dimension to self-esteem, which is based on our fantasies and desires about what we would like to do.

THE EGO CHARACTER, WISHFUL EGO AND THE EGO CONSCIENCE

We can identify three types of egos amongst managers and enployees normally found in an average organization (see Figure 3.1):

1 the *Ego Character* – a pragmatic adaptive person who generates an "apparent" self-esteem;
2 the *Wishful Ego* – the hopeful, creative person who generates fantasized self-esteem (sometimes feels to be acting in a dreamland); and

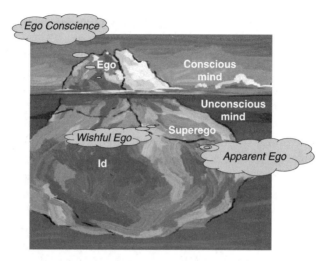

Figure 3.1 **Self-esteem and the "ego" dimensions**

3   the *Ego Conscience* – a truly concerned individual, ethically oriented
     who generates the deepest and most fundamental self-esteem.

These characters can be connected very well to the Freudian psychodynamic
model, where the assumptions about human behavior are based on the
following:

- The *Id* – contains a reservoir of unconscious psychic energy; strives to
  satisfy basic sexual and aggressive drives; and operates on the pleasure
  principle, demanding immediate gratification.
- The *Superego* – the part of personality that presents internalized ideals;
  provides standards for judgement (the conscience) and for future
  aspirations.
- The *Ego* – the largely conscious, "executive" part of personality; it
  mediates among the demands of the id, superego, and reality; operates
  on the reality principle, satisfying the id's desires in ways that will realistically bring pleasure rather than pain.

Thus, extrapolating from Freud's view of the struggle between our conscious and unconscious mind, the internal struggle can be reflected in the
type of ego adapted. The *Ego Character* or *Apparent Ego* is the character
we play in our daily interactions with others, the conventional mask of
our true wishes and human essence in our efforts to survive. It is associated
to what is known as the sound judgement or practical reasoning. It is our
mental identity, standardized, rational and prudent. Psychodynamic theory
would easily identify it with the controlling superego, formed basically by

the interaction with authority figures in our childhood, namely our parents and teachers.

This adaptive mask is superficially calming and is conventionally designed to interpret a socially accepted and reinforced role, approved by our groups of reference and the groups we belong to, those we would like to emulate and in those groups we feel we are included. It conforms to a life script which often limits real possibilities, whether practical, emotional or ethical. When we talk about the utopian principle, that the person is the end in itself, we refer to the person in all their fullness.

The *Wishful Ego* is the dimension of our being which responds to the "poetic" impulses of life (*poiesis* = generate, give birth to): creation, spontaneity, madness, pleasure and Dali's "*rauxa*". In psychodynamic theory it corresponds to the libidinous impulse which, as we shall see, is conventionally modulated and even repressed during our conventional education. It corresponds to the "pre-conventional" phase in the evolution of moral consciousness according to Kohlberg's theory.[3]

The *Ego Conscience* is the real, essential and characteristic person. It is the home of the being, the deepest ethical instance of our moral character (*ethos* = abode and character). Its existence is especially serene, inspirational, and it is the generator of self-esteem well beyond conventionalisms. An excess of externalization and stimuli derived from the desire to control and the fear of boredom and social rejection makes it difficult to access this essential asset and source of freedom, goodwill and vital wisdom which we all have inside us.

On a more conventional basis, Freud's ego-defense mechanisms can be connected to self-esteem issues in the following manner:

- **Compensation**: the process of masking perceived negative self-concepts, or of developing positive self-concepts to make up for the perceived negative self-concepts. For example, if someone thinks they are an idiot they may work at becoming physically more fit than others to make up for this shortcoming.
- **Denial**: this is the subconscious or conscious process of blinding oneself to negative self-concepts that we believe exist, but that we do not want to deal with. It is "closing our eyes" to the negative self-concepts about people, places, or things that we find too severe to deal with. For example, a family may pretend and act as if the father is only sick when it is obvious that he is an alcoholic.
- **Displacement**: this is when we express feelings to a substitute target because we are unwilling to express them to the real target. And the feelings expressed to the substitute target are based on our negative self-concepts about the real target. "Crooked anger" or "dumping" on another are examples of displacement. In these examples, we let out

our anger and frustration about the negative self-concepts we are feeling about someone else onto a safer target: such as someone below us, someone dependent on us, or someone under our control.

- **Identification**: this is the identification of oneself with heroes, stars, organizations, causes, religions, groups, or whatever we perceive as good self-concepts. This is a way to think of oneself as associated with good self-concepts. For example, we may identify with a crusade to help starving children so that we can incorporate into our ego some of the good self-concepts associated with that crusade.

- **Introjection**: this is the acceptance of the standards of others to avoid being rated as negative self-concepts by their standards. For example, a person might uncritically accept the standards of their government or religion in order to be accepted as good self-concepts by them.

- **Projection**: this is the attribution to others of our own negative self-concepts. This occurs when we want to avoid facing negative self-concepts about our behaviors or intentions and do so by seeing them, instead, in other people. For example, a person might be mad at their spouse but think, instead, that their spouse is mad at them.

- **Rationalization**: this is the process of explaining why, this time, you do not have to be judged as negative self-concepts because of your behaviors or intentions. It is sometimes referred to as "sour grapes" when, for example, you rationalize that you do not want something that you did not get because "it was lousy anyway". Rationalization can also take the opposite tack, or what is sometimes referred to as the "sweet lemon". In this case one might justify, for example, an error in purchasing by extolling some of the insignificant good points of the product.

- **Reaction formation**: this is the process of developing conscious positive self-concepts in order to cover and hide opposite, negative self-concepts. It is the making up for negative self-concepts by showing off their reverse. For example, a person might hate their parents, but go out of their way to show care and concern for them.

- **Regression**: this is the returning to an earlier time in one's life when we were not so threatened with becoming negative self-concepts. We return to thoughts, feelings, and/or behaviors of an earlier developmental stage in order to identify ourselves as we used to back then. For example, we might be being criticized as an adult and feeling horrible about it, and to escape this revert back to acting like a little child because we did not own criticism then as meaning we had negative self-concepts.

- **Repression**: this is the unconscious and seemingly involuntary removal from awareness of the negative self-concepts that the ego finds too painful to tolerate. For example, you may completely block out thoughts of killing a parent. This is not the same as suppression, which is also the removal from consciousness of intolerable negative self-concepts, but by conscious choice.

- **Ritual and undoing**: this is the process of trying to undo negative self-concept ratings of oneself by performing rituals or behaviors designed to offset the behaviors that the negative ratings were based on. For example, a millionaire might give to charities for the poor to make up for profiting from the poor. Or, a parent may buy their child a lot of gifts to make up for not spending time with them.
- **Sublimation**: this is the process of diverting feelings about the negative self-concepts one might have of oneself or others into more socially acceptable activities. For example, if you generally hate people, you might be an aggressive environmental activist, an aggressive political activist, or join a fighting army. This way you can get some approval for the feelings that you disapprove of.

THE PYTHAGORAS TRIANGLE

According to Brian Bacon, a global management consultant and author of numerous publications on Management and Leadership,[4] Pythagoras theorized the existence of a wise, triangular relationship between self, others and truth (Figure 3.2). Habitually, we try to base our self-esteem on others giving us what we need in life: admiration, money, a job well done, support, affection, fun, and so on. In fact, we spend life getting it one way or another, trying at the same time to be reciprocal.

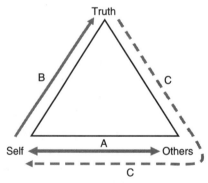

A: Normal exchanges and influences between self and others
B: Possible connections with the "real" truth
C: Consequences connected with relative truth in order to
   maintain relationships with others

Figure 3.2 **The Pythagoras triangle**
Source: Modified from Dolan, García and Díez-Piñol (2005) *Autoestima, estrés y trabajo* (Madrid: McGraw-Hill): 48. Used with permission.

However, there is another way for others to end up giving us what we need: not trying to get it directly, but by connecting our essential ego to a truth greater than ourselves, valid on its own. Like "magic" or something unexpected and without any logical cause and effect, life ends up giving us what we really need in order to achieve this truth or existential purpose, producing a full and deep construction of our self-esteem.

Interesting to know

Excerpt from an interview with Brian Bacon
(Founder of the Oxford Leadership Academy, an executive development
institute promoting values-based leadership)

"In a world of massive choices, we've got endless opportunities for pleasure but very few opportunities for joy. In 300 BC Epicurus talked about the three fundamentals of happiness: a sense of belonging in a community of friends, freedom and the feeling that the choices and decisions of one's life are in one's own hands, and time to reflect about the meaning and direction of one's life. Those fundamentals are just not accessible when we are working and living the way we are. As a consequence, there is a feeling of despair, hopelessness, and emptiness.

People just have a dry existence. They seek meaning by going shopping, and they avoid having meaningful conversations by going to a movie or renting a video. We're afraid that if we talk about things that are meaningful and moving, it might create conflict, so we don't go there any longer. And we don't have time to reflect and process our feelings and fears"

"64 per cent of employees say they are depressed, anxious, and wished they worked elsewhere. Seventy-four per cent of workers are disengaged clock watchers who can't wait to go home. People are working harder, longer, and getting less out of it. Their bosses are struggling as well. The average length of tenure of a CEO is 4.6 years. Twenty-two European CEOs were fired in 2003. A recent EU study shows that 45 per cent of top management are currently looking for a new position. Executives are getting burned out, pissed off, and fired."

Source: www.iwandarmansjah.web.id/attachment/at_Fieldnotes%20Bacon.pdf.

Definition of Self-esteem

Abraham Maslow, one of the best-known humanist psychologists of the 20th century, defined self-esteem as a vital need of intermediate priority, preceded only by the basic needs of safety and affective links, and ahead of self-realization. From his point of view, the search for self-esteem is a driving force generating motivation. According to Maslow, once the "lower" physiological and social needs are met, people need to experience achievements to foment their self-esteem, taking them closer to a feeling of existential plenitude.[5]

Other authors have regarded self-esteem differently:

- Experiencing one's own competence and the feeling of self-efficacy which arises from it (White, 1963).[6]
- A positive or negative attitude towards a particular object: oneself (Rosenberg, 1979).[7]
- The appraisal made by the individual about himself and which is generally maintained and expresses either approval or disapproval, indicating the degree to which the individual considers himself capable, important, successful and valuable (Coopersmith, 1967).[8]
- It is the conviction of how worthy a person is of his or her own love and, as a result, of others' love, independently of what one is, has or appears to be. It is the capacity with which the person is endowed to feel intrinsic self-worth, independently of their personal characteristics, circumstances and achievements that, in part, also define and identify the individual (Polaino-Lorente, 2003).[9]

For Branden (1969),[10] self-esteem counts in two, interrelated aspects: it links the feeling of personal efficacy to a sense of personal merit. It is the integrated sum of self-confidence and self-respect. It is the conviction that one is competent to live and to merit living. It is the experience of being competent to face the basic challenges in life and to be worthy of happiness. It consists of two components:

(1)   To consider oneself effective, to trust in one's ability to think, learn, choose and make correct decisions, and, by extension, to overcome challenges and produce changes;
(2)   To respect oneself, the confidence in one's right to be happy and, by extension, the confidence that people are worthy of the respect, love and self-fulfilment appearing in their lives (Branden, 1994).[11]

SELF-EFFECTIVENESS, SELF-CONCEPT, RESILIENCE AND "HARDINESS"

Among the many psychological concepts related to self-esteem, the following are worth noting: self-effectiveness, self-concept, resilience and resistance to stress, or "hardiness".

Self-effectiveness was defined by Bandura (1999)[12] as the belief in one's own abilities to organize and execute the actions necessary to manage all possible situations; individuals are seen as products and producers of their own environments and social systems.

Self-concept is the sum of a series of attitudes individuals have about them-selves and which can predict the actions individuals carry out to maintain this concept, whether the content is positive or negative, like a "self-fulfilling prophecy" (Burns, 1990).[13]

Resilience can be defined as an individual's or group's ability to project themselves into the future despite destabilizing events, difficult life condi-tions or sometimes severe traumas. Its appearance is at times incompre-hensible and even psychopathic, but it indicates a healthy response to adversity. The possibility of achieving self-esteem at any price has a lot to do with its development (Bonanno, 2004)[14], as if it were a survival mechanism more than a defense mechanism.

Hardiness. There are relatively few studies regarding the positive antecedents of health, most dealing with the negative precedents. The resistant to stress personality, or "hardiness", as defined by Kobasa (1979)[15] in relation to protection against life stressors, has three essential dimensions: the sense of jovial and spontaneous commitment, the interpretation of stressful events as natural, life challenges, and the openness to changes interpreted as challenges. Like a cause and effect relationship, this pattern of resistance to stress is also undoubtedly related to self-esteem.

Antecedent and consequential variables of self-esteem

As we have seen, self-esteem is complex, the result of numerous, antecedent variables and the generator at the same time of diverse individual and organizational consequences (Figure 3.3).

AFFECTIVE PLOTTING IN INFANCY AND ADOLESCENCE

Parents' availability, accessibility, credibility, tenderness, stimulus and rein-forcement are essential for a child's self-esteem, the undeniable base on which the adult's self-esteem depends.

Affective plotting or mapping consists of the early relationships of affection occurring within the home (Carballo, 1977),[16] espe-cially between children and their parents, but also with sib-lings, grandparents and other members of the family who more or less accept the child

> The parents' availability, accessibility, credibility, tenderness, stimulus and reinforcement are essential for a child's self-esteem, the undeniable base on which the adult's self-esteem depends.

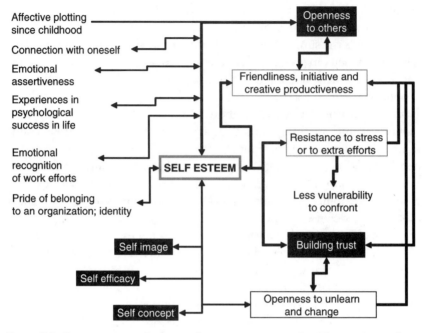

Figure 3.3 Some antecedents and consequences of self-esteem and occupational stress

Source: Modified from Dolan, García and Díez-Piñol (2005) *Autoestima, estrés y trabajo* (Madrid: McGraw-Hill): 50. Used with permission.

unconditionally, just by virtue of existing, while at the same time establishing limits as to what is correct or incorrect behavior. Feeling loved is essential to knowing how to love others and to be able to love oneself. It is very difficult for children to trust themselves if they haven't first trusted their parents. One of the best sources of self-esteem is having parents who exemplify good self-esteem (Coopersmith, 1967).[17]

Parents who generate self-esteem adopt a series of values and conducts with respect to their children:

- They raise them with love and respect;
- They allow them to feel a coherent and benevolent acceptance of themselves;
- They offer a support structure which includes reasonable rules and adequate expectations;
- They do not bombard their children with contradictions;
- They do not resort to ridicule, humiliation or physical abuse to control them; and
- They demonstrate that they believe in their children's competence, goodwill and responsible autonomy.

AUTONOMY AND THE MANAGEMENT OF ONE'S OWN SELF

As Fernando Savater outlines in his book, *La tarea del héroe* (*The Hero's Task*):[18]

> When man loses his creative autonomy, he begins to live himself from without, precisely because he has furnished his interior – his nothingness, his empty night – with the external, causal order. The technical ease of managing the world is accompanied by the unequivocal conviction experienced that he is no longer in charge: Theoretical king of this world, his familiarity with things has removed him from the throne. The price of forced normalization with the trade of objects is compliance with death, in the least biological and more "spiritual" sense of the word.

Interesting to know

James Allan used the following thoughts in the anatomy of one's own self thoughts:

- A man is not rightly conditioned until he is a happy, healthy, and a prosperous being; and happiness, health, and prosperity are the result of a harmonious adjustment of the inner with the outer of the man with his surroundings.
- All that you accomplish or fail to accomplish with your life is the direct result of your thoughts.
- Man is made or unmade by himself. By the right choice he ascends. As a being of power, intelligence, and love, and the lord of his own thoughts, he holds the key to every situation.

Source: http://www.brainyquote.com/quotes/authors/j/james_allen.html

---

These ideas are based on the idea that the external world is not only dominated by technology and material objects, but that its dominion has also reached the very essence of human beings. Perhaps the technology and money that dominate the world are nothing more than the expression of our pre-existing levels of inner consciousness.

How many people control material fortunes yet do not control themselves, their emotions, their inner conscience, their being, or, simply, something as important as their health and continue smoking, for example? How many people go through life playing a part or reacting impulsively or more or less capriciously, without stopping to think first or decide for themselves, from within their very core? Not being aware of what is going on around and inside you is tantamount to living your life alienated, out of control.

Is it possible to obtain a high degree of professional performance while being aware of what is going on around and inside us? Of course. In fact, being incompetent in terms of self-management and being unaware of what is going on around and inside us is the source of mistakes, errors, oversights, accidents and work-related conflict, all of which act as inhibitors of self-esteem at the same time.

> How many people control material fortunes yet do not control themselves, their emotions, their inner conscience, their being, or, simply, something as important as their health and continue smoking, for example?

Being aware not only means feeling or thinking. It is contemplating from within what is valued: what is felt and thought and being able to freely choose another feeling or thought. Emilio Lledó writes:[19]

But, what man is interesting; the one who thinks or the one who thinks about the one who is thinking?... Above and beyond the real conditions in which life evolves while "feeling and thinking it", we have the ability to rise above the level at which we perceive those elemental and essential moments. Being is not only feeling or thinking, but feeling the feeling and thinking the thought. Being is, then, overcoming the saturation which thinking with the previous thought implies. But this transcends the limits placed on us by objects and takes us to a place in which man reaches his own freedom. This state allows him to contemplate and choose himself, observe and overcome himself.

As Ortega y Gasset[20] warned in his wonderful essay, "Regarding Galileo", more than fifty years ago, "in modern times, we live hither and thither!" The sonorous Spanish word he used, estricote, is a definite precursor to the now worn-out word, stress.

I am myself...and my circumstances. Too many people have lost control and internal peace. They are overwhelmed by too many "circumstances" in their environment, by too many thoughts and emotions lived as inevitable internal bonds or unavoidable external controls. By being so intent on controlling variables beyond themselves, they end up spiralling out of control. In the end, we think we burnt the rice (or any other domestic accident) because of the "environment" or "globalization", and not due to our "character" (or the lack of character, more than likely).

SELF-ESTEEM, LEADERSHIP AND THE SUCCESS SYNDROME

A great portion of contemporary business literature deals almost exclusively with success stories. A lot can be learned from them, naturally, but we must understand the root causes of that success in order to learn the right lessons.

Mark Twain once said that if a cat jumped on a hot stove, it would never jump on any stove again, hot or cold. Success, then, can lead to conservatism, which, in a highly competitive and ever-changing environment, can lead to failure. Is this inevitable?

Authors define the following series of causal relationships behind the "Success Syndrome": When companies become successful and dominate the market, they are convinced that they are right. This in turn makes them stop paying attention to the important changes taking place in the outside world. From this they deduce that they have nothing to fear or learn from their competitors. Besides, they reject any ideas or strategies not produced within the company (the NIH syndrome, "Not Invented Here").

For Kurt Lewin[21], one of the founders of social psychology, however, the most important success is psychological success, the consequence of having established and recognized one's own adequate achievements, neither too difficult nor insufficiently challenging.

SELF-ESTEEM = SUCCESS/PRETENSIONS

According to James,[22] self-esteem is determined by the relationship between our reality and our expectations. As such, self-esteem can increase or decrease according to the values assigned to the numerator or the denominator in the equation above. Self-esteem is a finalist definition, described as "utilitarian pragmatism or efficiency-ism" by some scholars, and is based on the results more than on the principles or the qualities of personal dignity. According to James, the person esteems or disesteems based on what the individual obtains more than on how he acts. On the other hand, reality is always the perceived reality, and the potentialities perceived within oneself are always subjective and changing. There can be no doubt that this is an interesting approach to the phenomenon at hand.

The esteem, recognition and admiration perceived from those relevant individuals we establish relationships with throughout our lives are the essential source of our perception of psychological success and self-esteem. That is why the emotional recognition for a job well-done is so important in the work context, something that occurs less frequently than it should.

SELF-ESTEEM AND ONE'S OWN LIFE SCRIPT

The life script is a type of musical score or theatrical role to be performed in life, written basically in our childhood and adolescence, depending on

- "Numero uno"
- Mr/Ms "you can never have enough"
- Mr/Ms success or failure
- The one who's always in a hurry
- The great, lone leader
- Mr/Ms seriousness
- The great practical realist
- Poor little me
- The good boy/girl
- The all business businessman
- The super dad
- The super, sacrificing mother
- The eternal jokester
- The grey bureaucrat
- The playboy
- The barbie
- The aggressive executive

Figure 3.4 **Examples of limiting life scripts**

our dependent relationship with family authority-figures and teachers. Detecting it and being able to overcome it is one of life's most significant acts. In order to achieve this task, introspection, honesty and courage are fundamental (Figure 3.4).

SELF-ESTEEM AND THE BALANCE OF ACHIEVEMENTS AND VALUES

Self-esteem comes about as the result of the adequate combination of the essential values needed for psychological success: humility, in order to recognize one's own limits and avoid failures, and valour, to strive to reach goals and have successful experiences. This polarity is generative, unlike that occurring between humiliation and arrogance, which are two negative emotional states and are adaptively dysfunctional.

James distinguishes between three types of self-esteem:

1 *material*: vanity, pride in wealth;
2 *social*: social and familiar pride, professional pride; and
3 *spiritual*: a feeling of moral superiority.

Axiology, or the study of values, has its origins in the Greek word *axios*, meaning *axis*. Values are the axes around which our actions revolve. Based on these categories but developed within the triaxial model (García, 2002[23] and 2005[24]; Dolan 2003[25], Dolan, García and Díez-Piñol, 2004[26]; Dolan, García and Richley, 2006[27]). From the thoughts of Pérez López (1998)[28]

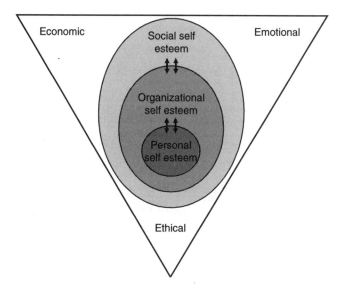

Figure 3.5 Triaxial model of self-esteem
Source: Modified from Dolan, García and Díez-Piñol (2005) *Autoestima, estrés y trabajo* (Madrid: McGraw-Hill): 56. Used with permission.

(see Figure 3.5), we can identify three axes of interrelated values upon which to build balanced self-esteem:

1 **The axis of material achievement and social status, the "praxis" axis or utilitarian axis**
   This is the most conventionally developed axis in our capitalist-consumer societies, ruled politically and culturally by the pragmatism of our economy and businesses. *Praxis* means to act, or carry out, and it is the root of the word *prose*. The most adequate prosaic values for the development of the economical-practical axis of self-esteem are discipline, hard work, adaptability to change, savings, being results-orientated, efficacy and efficiency.
2 **The emotional and creative achievement axis, "poietic" axis or generative axis**
   As seen with the discussion on the Wishful Ego, *poiesis* means to generate or to give birth, from which comes the word *poetry*. Closely related theoretically to the previous bidirectional cause and effect, the emotional-creative or "poietic" axis has its own identity, so much so that on occasion it is disassociated and almost always overshadowed in the business world by the previous axis. The pragmatic imperative tends wrongly to annul the often-fragile poetic imperative.

Emotional and creative achievements are very similar. Does the production of a new idea generate dejection or enthusiasm? The values associated with emotional achievement are openness, happiness, imagination, daring, harmony, aesthetic experience, friendship (*filia* or deep trust) or illusion regarding new projects.

Emotional self-esteem originates from our self-perceived ability to overcome adversity, generate positive thoughts, be imaginative, create physical and affective harmony around us, and, in general, live life with commitment, illusion and even enthusiasm and passion, even at the risk of getting hurt.

3   **The ethical and social achievement axis or transcendent axis**
John Stuart Mill (1997),[29] one of the precursors of the best liberal school of thought, used to say that there were three types of pleasures: solitary, gregarious and shared pleasures, the latter being the greatest producer of true happiness.

The values or principles of action to develop the ethical-social axis of self-esteem are authenticity with oneself, dignity, philanthropy or love for the human being, altruism/alterity (the recognition of others), and benevolence or well-wishing for others.

Self-esteem, according to this triaxial model, is the degree of internal perception regarding how competent we are to work, live and share, fully developing as balanced individuals. In other words, it is the result of the perception of material, emotional and ethical achievements based on one's own efforts and on the confidence we place in ourselves and in others. It is based on the self-confidence in our ability to dream, care, think and manage to be efficient and to be able to cope with the challenges posed by life, both positive and negative. It is also based on the trust or belief in others, as well as on the trustworthiness that we inspire in others.

> **Self-esteem, according to this triaxial model, is the degree of internal perception regarding how competent we are to work, live and share, fully developing as balanced individuals.**

Just as humility and bravery are virtuous extremes generating self-esteem, humiliation and arrogance are their behavioral and adaptively negative extremes. Depression and narcissism (or manias) are their psycho-pathological extremes.

Self-esteem and confidence

It is one thing to have confidence or a belief in oneself (self-confidence). It is a separate matter altogether to have trust in others, in the future of humanity, in our political leaders, or in the company's project we may be participating in (hetero-confidence). Yet another matter is the confidence or trustworthiness we inspire in others.

Both people and social systems are more likely to be trusting if they have inner security, a positive self-esteem and confidence in themselves, if they are actively aware of what is going on within and around them.

We generate confidence when we are integral, wish the best for others, show an ability to fulfil our needs, adopt a positive emotional tone, and maintain positive self-esteem.

The organizational and social consequences of this confidence are notable: dialogue, stable relationships, mutual support and learning, creative initiative and building what could be called "organizational self-esteem", which will be examined in more detail in the final chapter of this book. Confidence acts as a *cohesive glue* for the relationships between individuals, groups, organizations and societies. Without this confidence, there is interpersonal separation, disintegration and fragmentation, both organizationally and socially.

Continuing with the ideas outlined by Kenneth Joseph Arrow, a Nobel Prize-winner, the lack of confidence, or *lubricant*, makes the gears screech in the social system made up of different interest groups within the company: owners, employees, clients, unions, financial backers, publicity agents and suppliers. Without it, it is much more difficult to make all the sub-systems work in a coordinated, synergetic and effective manner. As Arrow affirms, confidence acts as a facilitator or lubricant for social systems. Daring to build up this confidence in social systems is the critical lubricant necessary in order to avoid conflict and manage change.[30]

There is also a third, suitable analogy for this confidence: it is the *voussoir*, or wedge-shaped keystone used in arches and vaults, (Figure 3.6) for all long-lasting human projects, so that these are fluid, happy and effective. Without it, the entire building would crumble, and the structure would have to be reinforced with unsightly and inefficient support structures, implying great emotional, economic and even aesthetic costs. Can you imagine the world-famous aqueduct in Segovia, a splendid, Roman structure supported by metal girders? Self-esteem and confidence, or a belief in oneself, are very similar concepts. When others trust us and give us freedom to act, our self-esteem improves and we tend to become more productive. This is, as we shall see further on, the basis of *empowerment* initiatives within companies.

On the other hand, we tend to trust others (hetero-confidence) and judge them depending on how much we trust ourselves and on our own self-esteem. Thirdly, it is easier to trust someone who has high self-esteem, which in turn creates vicious or virtuous circles.

However, self-confidence and self-esteem are not synonymous concepts. Confidence is an important value, it is pure value and very valuable.

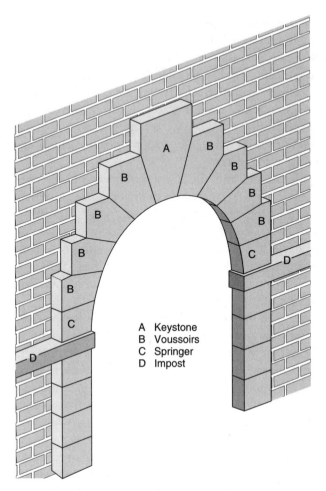

A Keystone
B Voussoirs
C Springer
D Impost

Figure 3.6 **Confidence: key support for the system**
Note: The various parts of an arch have specific names, as shown, which ensures the stability of the final structure.

Confidence is a brave, strategic choice. The need to trust arises when we decide to risk making ourselves vulnerable to the consequences of others' or our own behavior without feeling intimidated, without an inhibiting fear of consequences.

When others trust us and give us freedom to act, our self-esteem improves and we tend to become more productive. This is, as we shall see further on, the basis of *empowerment* initiatives within companies.

The belief in the predictability of one's own or another's behavior generates a positive feeling, one that anticipates a future without threats and which favours the conditions for the construction of self-esteem.

Confidence is the generalized expectation that others will responsibly manage their own freedom, and potential to affect our well-being, for their own sake and for ours. This will lead to the belief in their goodwill, or *bene-volence*, towards us. The need for confidence only arises in situations of risk. Our will to make us vulnerable to the actions of others is based on the expectation that their actions will be important for our own interests, independently of our ability to monitor or control those actions. The importance of the confidence concept arises from the need to reduce the control mechanisms and increase interaction in management models based on autonomous work groups and empowered employees.

The word *confidence* is derived from Latin but, in fact, it should be "without guarantee", bond or "instrument" which the contracting party offers to secure the fulfilment of their obligations. Without this confidence or joint faith, no project or delegation is possible. Instead, there is a lot of stress due to an overload of work and social isolation.

The Greek word for confidence is *empistosini*, "to have faith or believe in". To be convinced, have faith, believe in oneself, in others or in an ideal, is the basis to live with credibility, security and happiness.

Interpersonal trust is the expectation of an individual or group of individuals that another word or written declaration can be taken seriously.

Confidence is expressed at many levels within companies:

- individuals' self-confidence;
- employees' confidence in the company's leadership and future;
- clients' trust in the company;
- owners' trust in company management;
- trust between members of the company, individuals and the functional units; and
- the company's trust in its suppliers (and vice versa).

> **The coercive techniques of persuasion used by sects are based on the elimination of self-esteem in order to then offer the possibility of its reconstruction within a new system of possible actions.**

The freedom of choice to trust is a continuum, which ranges from profound confidence to active mistrust. This deep trust, or meta-confidence, generates the creation of solid and stable human bonds. It is the principal source of commitment and faithfulness in interpersonal relationships or the relationship between the individual and the organization they work for. Without real trust, there is no freely chosen commitment. In any case, a contract is needed to avoid opportunistic behavior by either party.

Superficial trust refers to the familiarity or camaraderie of the relationship, which, as it eases social interaction, makes life more pleasant.

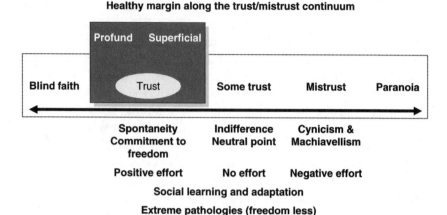

Healthy margin along the trust/mistrust continuum

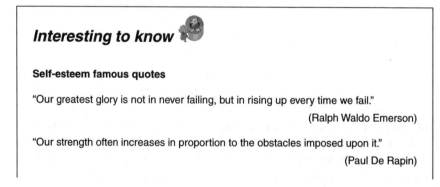

Figure 3.7 **The confidence/trust continuum**
Source: Modified from Dolan, García and Díez-Piñol (2005) *Autoestima, estrés y trabajo* (Madrid: McGraw-Hill): 61. Used with permission.

CONFIDENCE AND BLIND FAITH

On one pathological extreme of the confidence continuum, and therefore not free, is blind faith in the leader (Figure 3.7), a sadly frequent situation in destructive sects and even in certain organizations that use a discourse of values in a manipulative and coercive manner to maintain unbreakable commitments, even in cases where individuals adopt certain behaviors that they would consider unethical if they were able to think freely. It is well-known that the coercive techniques of persuasion used by sects are based on the elimination of self-esteem in order to then offer the possibility of its reconstruction within a new system of possible actions. As the playwright, George Bernard Shaw, once wrote: "It is easy, terribly easy, to shake the confidence a man has in himself. However, taking advantage of this in order to disturb a person's spirit, is the devil's work."

Interesting to know

Self-esteem famous quotes

"Our greatest glory is not in never failing, but in rising up every time we fail."
(Ralph Waldo Emerson)

"Our strength often increases in proportion to the obstacles imposed upon it."
(Paul De Rapin)

"Courage is resistance to fear, mastery of fear, not absence of fear. Except a creature be part coward it is not a compliment to say it is brave."

(Mark Twain)

"Success doesn't come to you…you go to it."

(Marva Collins)

"Criticism may not be agreeable, but it is necessary. It fulfils the same function as pain in the human body. It calls attention to an unhealthy state of things."

(Winston Churchill)

"No one can make you feel inferior without your consent."

(Eleanor Roosevelt)

"The people who get on in this world are the people who get up and look for the circumstances they want, and, if they can't find them, make them."

(George Bernard Shaw)

Source: http://www.coolnurse.com/self_esteem2.htm

CONFIDENCE AND PARANOIA

The word *paranoia* stems from the Greek word *para*, meaning on the side or parallel, and *nous*, referring to the idea of spirit and thought. Perhaps it could be translated as meaning a parallel thought or an un-centred spirit. The paranoid personality is characterized by a series of factors:

- rigidity;
- a hypertrophied ego;
- erroneous, passionate judgements;
- justice and fanaticism;
- defense mechanisms, especially negation and projection;
- mistrust, in other words, permanent suspicion, at times hidden and apparently just the opposite.

These individuals have an exaggerated belief in the aggressive and scheming possibilities of others, and they are easily provoked or alluded to. They maintain a distant attitude with respect to their social relationships, which is manifested basically in two ways: exaggerated courtesy mixed with resistance or a directly manifested aggressiveness that may be disguised by projection.

The less confidence there is, the greater the need to control. The conventional, hierarchical company is based on an excess of the desire to control based on fear and insecurity. Without confidence, fear hypertrophies the control structures and generates systems that are not very fluid, making them bureaucratic, slow, disheartening, repetitive, predictable, and definitely inefficient and emotionally draining.

The obsession for control is generally based on mistrusts, the lack of real self-esteem, insecurity, and the fear of doubt and freedom. Taken to an extreme, it implies that aversion to risk, resistance to change, and the inhibition of one's own creativity and that of others. The obsession for control arises from the inability to recognize and appreciate the value of spontaneity and happiness. This would explain why the machine and the army are the best concepts for human organizations from the military-economist perspective, dominating the most conventional companies' mental maps.

Confidence is a basic attitude to enable individuals to flow through life and face doubts and complexities with a certain degree of emotional success. Without it – as Luhmann states[31] – we would not be able to get up in the morning, much less project towards the future. Without confidence, there is no hope, no freedom, no tolerance, and no possibility of learning from mistakes, making the construction of self-esteem very difficult.

Confidence is daring; it requires a certain degree of bravery in the sense of courage and valour. Daring to trust, to assume one's own freedom and that of others, being open to their ideas, being creative, making mistakes and learning from them, is the basis for a full and well-lived life. Lack of confidence in oneself inhibits the will to take risks and take on new projects, face changes or "simply" unlearn and evolve.

Keys to developing self-esteem from the perspective of self-confidence include:

- positively risk giving yourself power;
- be open to questioning your own prejudices and to unlearn;
- exercise your freedom responsibly;
- know your personal values and beliefs; and
- live with personal integrity.

Self-esteem: between depression and narcissism

We can talk about a *continuum* between depression as an affective disorder and what psychiatrists occasionally observe as a hypo-maniacal, over-evaluation or narcissistic personality disorder (Figure 3.8).

Without becoming pathological disorders, there are a series of personality traits associated to an apparent excess of self-esteem, such as arrogance

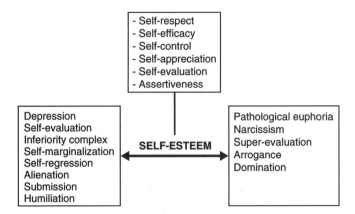

Figure 3.8 **Self-esteem, depression and narcissism**

and conceit. In the end, both are a consequence of a lack of deep-rooted and sincere self-esteem.

The arrogant individual is jealous and insatiable, demanding they be treated as they feel they should be treated. Saint Gregory the Great synthesized arrogance and conceit well. Conceit is a disorderly appetite for perverted grandeur, leading to susceptibility, impatience, demand, inflexibility, aloofness, and the exaggerated defense of one's rights.

Under-esteem, by contrast, leads to resentment (Polaino-Lorente, 2003)[32] and self-marginalization, and is characteristic in cases of depression. It is clear that depressed individuals do not love themselves, and constantly blame, punish and torment themselves by selecting the negative aspects of life and themselves. Their sadly selective memory has a clear neuro-biological base.

Exaggerated self-esteem leads to narcissism and the search for unconditional acceptance. Narcissists see themselves as the centre of the universe; in the mirror they only see themselves reflected. They see themselves as if they were the only reality worthy of esteem, the rest being mere generators of their supposed grandeur and worth. Narcissists are always talking about their supposed greatness and worth, about their uncommon, marvellous experiences, their extremely interesting projects, about how much they have done to improve in life, and even to help others. Narcissists are actors who need an audience to recognize and unconditionally and enthusiastically affirm their brilliant achievements and personal worth beyond any shadow of a doubt, especially their deepest and most personal doubts. Their lives are a histrionic hell, salvageable only by the heaven of apparent death.

72

The DSM-IV criteria for manic episodes:
(DSM is the Diagnostic and Statistical Manual of Mental Disorders of the American Psychological Association)

A   A distinct period of abnormally and persistently elevated, expansive or irritable mood, lasting at least 1 week (or any duration if hospitalization is necessary)

B   During the period of mood disturbance, three (or more) of the following symptoms have persisted (four if the mood is only irritable) and have been present to a significant degree:
   (1)   inflated self-esteem or grandiosity
   (2)   decreased need for sleep (e.g., feels rested after only 3 hours of sleep)
   (3)   more talkative than usual or pressure to keep talking
   (4)   flight of ideas or subjective experience that thoughts are racing
   (5)   distractibility (i.e., attention too easily drawn to unimportant or irrelevant external stimuli)
   (6)   increase in goal-directed activity (at work, at school, or sexually) or psychomotor agitation
   (7)   excessive involvement in pleasurable activities that have a high potential for painful consequences (e.g., engaging in unrestrained buying sprees, sexual indiscretions, or foolish business investments)

C   The symptoms do not meet criteria for a Mixed Episode

D   The mood disturbance is sufficiently severe to cause marked impairment in occupational functioning or in usual social activities or relationships with others, or to necessitate hospitalization to prevent harm to self or others, or there are psychotic features.

E   The symptoms are not due to the direct physiological effects of a substance (e.g., a drug of abuse, a medication or other treatment) or a general medical condition (e.g., hyperthyroidism)

The DSM-IV criteria for a state of serious depression:

A   Five (or more) of the following symptoms have been present during the same 2-week period and represent a change from previous functioning; at least one of the symptoms is either (1) depressed mood or (2) loss of interest or pleasure

Note: Do not include symptoms that are clearly due to a general medical condition, or mood-incongruent delusions or hallucinations

    (1) depressed mood most of the day, nearly every day, as indicated by either subjective report (e.g., feels sad or empty) or observation made by others (e.g., appears tearful). Note: In children and adolescents, this can be an irritable mood.

    (2) markedly diminished interest or pleasure in all, or almost all, activities most of the day, nearly every day (as indicated by either subjective account or observation made by others)

    (3) significant weight loss when not dieting or weight gain (e.g., a change of more than 5% of body weight in a month), or decrease or increase in appetite nearly every day. Note: In children, consider failure to make expected weight gains.

    (4) insomnia or hypersomnia nearly every day

    (5) psychomotor agitation or retardation nearly every day (observable by others, not merely subjective feelings of restlessness or being slowed down)

    (6) fatigue or loss of energy nearly every day

    (7) feelings of worthlessness or excessive or inappropriate guilt (which may be delusional) nearly every day (not merely self-reproach or guilt about being sick)

    (8) diminished ability to think or concentrate, or indecisiveness, nearly every day (either by subjective account or as observed by others)

    (9) recurrent thoughts of death (not just fear of dying), recurrent suicidal ideation without a specific plan, or a suicide attempt or a specific plan for committing suicide

B   The symptoms do not meet criteria for a Mixed Episode

C   The symptoms cause clinically significant distress or impairment in social, occupational, or other important areas of functioning.

D   The symptoms are not due to the direct physiological effects of a substance (e.g., a drug of abuse, a medication) or a general medical condition (e.g., hypothyroidism)

E   The symptoms are not better accounted for by Bereavement, i.e., after the loss of a loved one, the symptoms persist for longer than 2 months or are characterized by marked functional impairment, morbid preoccupation with worthlessness, suicidal ideation, psychotic symptoms, or psychomotor retardation.

Interesting to know

The DSM-IV criteria for diagnosing a narcissistic personality:

An all-pervasive pattern of grandiosity (in fantasy or behavior), need for admiration *or adulation* and lack of empathy, *usually* beginning by early adulthood and present in various contexts. Five (or more) of the following criteria must be met:

- Feels grandiose and self-important (e.g., exaggerates achievements and talents **to the point of lying, demands** to be recognized as superior without commensurate achievements)
- Is **obsessed** with fantasies of unlimited success, **fame, fearsome** power or **omnipotence, unequalled** brilliance **(the cerebral narcissist), bodily** beauty **or sexual performance (the somatic narcissist),** or ideal, **everlasting, all-conquering** love **or passion**
- Firmly convinced that he or she is unique and, being special, can only be understood by, **should only be treated by,** or associate with, other special or unique, or high-status people (or institutions)
- Requires excessive admiration, adulation, **attention and affirmation – or, failing that, wishes to be feared and to be notorious (narcissistic supply)**
- Feels entitled. Expects unreasonable or special and **favorable priority** treatment. Demands automatic **and full** compliance with his or her expectations
- Is "interpersonally exploitative", i.e., **uses** others to achieve his or her own ends
- **Devoid** of empathy. Is **unable** or unwilling to identify with **or acknowledge the** feelings and needs of others
- Constantly envious of others or believes that they feel the same about him or her
- Arrogant, haughty behaviors or attitudes **coupled with rage when frustrated, contradicted, or confronted**

Self-esteem and hetero-esteem: bene-volence

Hetero-esteem is the positive or negative appraisal we make of others. Positive well-wishing or an attitude of benevolence, from the Latin *bene-volere*, wanting the best for others, searching for mutual benefit. Benevolence comes from the sequence between positive self-esteem and hetero-esteem. In fact, it is practically impossible without it and essential in order to establish deep and mutual bonds with others, whether with our life partner, clients, suppliers or friends. Wanting the best for another person means wanting them to become the best person possible in all senses, and it is an attitude with important economic, emotional, and, of course, ethical consequences (Figure 3.9).

As proposed earlier, the bene-volence is like a religion where the point of "to love others as you love yourself" is pushed to the limit. The antonym of love is hate. What is unknown cannot be loved (Figure 3.10). As such, we must know others and ourselves if we want to have self-esteem and be benevolent. Those who do not love themselves cannot love anyone else. It is the "existential tantrum" described by Aquilino Polaino-Lorente (2003, p. 80)[33], one of the leading experts on self-esteem.

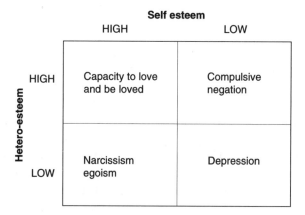

Figure 3.9 **Combining self-esteem with hetero-esteem**

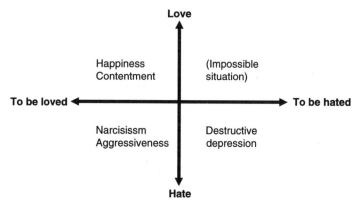

Figure 3.10 **Love, hate and consequences**
Source: Modified from Dolan, García and Díez-Piñol (2005) *Autoestima, estrés y trabajo* (Madrid: McGraw-Hill): 68. Used with permission.

People with appropriate self-esteem experience themselves better; they are and feel alive; they are proud of it and are more willing to go beyond themselves and take care of others. They establish certain interpersonal bonds easily, they don't feel alone, and they have that *joie de vivre* which is so important to manage their lives with ease and are relaxed towards their own destiny, towards their own happiness.[34]

> People with appropriate self-esteem experience themselves better; they are and feel alive; they are proud of it and are more willing to go beyond themselves and take care of others.

Self-esteem and youth

Self-esteem goes through many cycles in the course of a lifetime. Adolescence, being fifty-something and old-age are critical periods for one's self-esteem. Teenagers, busy building their identity, don't have the necessary experience yet to be serene and appraise their achievements and how these have come about. Their self-esteem is "*under construction*", just like many of the webpages in the Internet, which they are so adept at using.

Fifty-something individuals, when they feel they have reached their ceiling of personal and professional achievements, begin to question if it was worth the effort and if they journeyed towards the right goal or if they reached the peak, all of which begins to undermine their self-esteem and their perception of happiness, running the risk of feeling washed-up.

Fifty-something is a critical age range for crisis and illness to develop as it is dominated by a certain depressive state, occasionally a real depression, and fighting inertia and a desire to have taken control in the past decades. The organism enters a phase of extreme psycho-biological vulnerability. The immunological defenses decrease and hormones and cerebral and neurotransmitters begin to sway. Heart problems and other internal disorders can be disconcerting. All this induces the shutdown of the mechanisms designed to maintain homeostasis and health (Henry and Stephens, 1977).[35]

In old age, the individual is devitalized after their desire has been consumed and consummated. They give up exploring and taking risks, entering into a vegetative phase of esteem, living off a more or less glorious past, a more or less valuable past.

However, in order to avoid depression affecting our self-esteem when we're no longer twenty years old, it is worth reading Fontana Tarrats (1979)[36] on youth and old age:

> **The years wrinkle the skin; giving up on our ideals wrinkles the soul. The youth is someone who is surprised and fascinated, the one who asks questions like an insatiable child: "And now what?"**

Youth is not a period in life, but rather a spiritual state, an effect of a will, a quality of imagination, an emotive intensity, a victory of valour over shyness, a taste for adventure over love and comfort. The years wrinkle the skin; giving up on our ideals wrinkles the soul. The youth is someone who is surprised and fascinated, the one who asks questions like an insatiable child: "And now what?" A youth is someone who challenges events and is happy in the game of life. You are as young as the confidence you have in yourself. If one day your heart is on the verge of being gnawed by pessimism and annihilated by cynicism, may God have mercy on your old soul.

Self-esteem and gender

Men and women tend to put self-esteem and stress at risk differently. The different levels of catecholaminergic activation between the sexes and mediated by cultural differences have been known for decades (Frankenhauser, 1976).[37] Men tend to activate themselves and stress more when their abilities and competitive achievements are at risk, whereas this occurs in women when they are induced to implicate themselves in specific roles culturally considered as "theirs", such as taking care of children (Table 3.1).

Table 3.1 **Possible gender differences in self-esteem**

Sources of self-esteem	Women	Men
Body aspect	Younger	More mature
Existential orientation	A greater orientation to intimacy and emotional bonds than to transforming the world	A greater orientation towards conquering territory and transforming the world than to emotional bonds
Sensorial dominance	Sound and touch	Sight and space
Hand specialization	Caressing, signalling, gesturing, communication; Delicate handling	Capturing, transport; Rough handling
Temporality	Maintenance and waiting	Instantaneousness and fugacity
Concrete-abstract	Motivated by the concrete	Motivated by the abstract
Attention paid to one's own body	Greater attention paid to one's own body	Less attention paid to the body
Attitude towards relationships	Welcoming and caring	Intervention and treatment
Emotional life	Capacity to colour emotional experiences	Tendency to separate the emotional from action
Intellectually	Capacity for memory, intuition and integration	Capacity for logic, visualization and periodic formal thought

Source: Based on Polaino-Lorente (2003)[38]

Self-esteem and stress

As Ortega y Gasset said more than fifty years ago in his wonderful essay, "Regarding Galileo",[39] a precursor to the idea of "*stress*" in modern life when talking about living *al estricote*, hither and thither:

> In modern times, we live hither and thither; we've lost the ability for contemplation and being self-absorbed in thought. Self-absorption in

thought is the opposite of living life maltreated, when the things around us dictate what we do, push us mechanically one way or another, and take us hither and thither.

Effectively, we've been living unaware of the things around us and within us for decades , which, as we've already seen, makes it difficult to build true self-esteem.

Our fast-paced, tense and agitated lifestyle, overwhelmed by an excess of commitments and activities beyond our real possibilities of adaptation, control and calm, has become a source of dissatisfaction, a low sense of self-esteem and collective unhappiness. In the pretentiously called "Information Age", we lack the necessary wisdom to live in peace and harmony with others, our environment and ourselves.

> In the pretentiously termed "Information Age", we lack the necessary wisdom to live in peace and harmony with others, our environment, and ourselves.

Just as Aristotle warned 24 centuries ago, "the excess of work makes the adequate contemplation of beauty and truth impossible...it deforms the human body".

Positive self-esteem works, in reality, like the immune system of the conscience, offering greater resistance, strength and a regenerative capacity when coping with the traumas of life. Those with low self-esteem tend to feel more influenced by the desire to avoid pain than by the desire to feel happiness. And nothing they do will feel sufficient (Branden, 2001).[40] This makes them, like the Sisyphus of myth, carry out titanic efforts to senselessly achieve impossible goals, without ever recognising their own merit and with insufficient reward.

A lot of people, apparently successful both socially and professionally, so sure of themselves that they even seem perfect, have a low level of deep-rooted self-esteem. Perhaps that is why they try so hard to show their worth as individuals. Real self-esteem has been substituted by individualism as the cardinal value (Lipovetsky, 1986[41]). This hyper-competitive individualism is especially fomented within the efficientist paradigm, which tries to obtain greater profit by reducing costs without thinking about other values and results. Stressed individuals submit themselves conformingly and conventionally to this pressure, feeling trapped like a victim and agent in a world without meaning that continually demands more from them and offers less reward.

Self-esteem based on being is much more solid, deeper and longer-lasting than self-esteem based on doing and accumulating. Tense individuals do not feel satisfied with their lives; they are not comfortable with themselves. They become *strange* in the sense defined by Polaino-Lorente

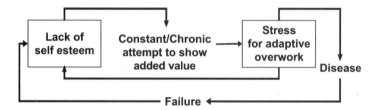

Figure 3.11 **Low self-esteem, stress and disease**

(2003):[42] it becomes difficult to talk to them; they close themselves off inside their shell; they have problems with their life partner; they don't have real friends. They are suffering from an identity crisis similar to a tormented teen.

> **Self-esteem based on being is much more solid, deeper and longer-lasting than self-esteem based on doing and accumulating.**

Lack of self-esteem throws the individual into a labyrinth of stress and failure to adapt with no way out (Figure 3.11).

The more confident the individual, the less they will need material things to affirm themselves in their own eyes and in the eyes of others. This also means they have less likelihood of suffering states of perceived uncontrollability and stress, and they will be less vulnerable to the pathogenic accumulation of uncontrolled life events, thereby benefiting their health.[43] (Figure 3.12).

EMOTIONS, SELF-ESTEEM AND STRESS

Chronic, professional or the so-called white-collar stress, may be defined as the adaptive overload occurring ever more commonly in the technologically and economically prosperous countries than in developing countries. At the heart of this situation is an important strategic disorientation in terms of where we are going, why, and with what values. It comes about as the result of an excess of work-related and personal commitments (externally and internally conditioned), associated to a lack of psychological controls or situational coping mechanisms and not taking care of creating strong, long-term social support.

In order to make it easier to understand and remember, Dolan, García and Díez-Piñol (2005)[44] proposed the acronym "CRASH" (Figure 3.13), in allusion to the dramatically negative consequences of chronic stress. It is worth noting that self-esteem works as a buffering variable along with social support. By the same token, humor stands out as one of the most human and efficient resources for coping.

Self esteem & perception of control

	HIGH	LOW
HIGH	Activation	Stress
LOW	Relaxation	Depression

(left axis label: Adaptation effort for controlling the situation)

Figure 3.12 **Self-esteem and perception of control**

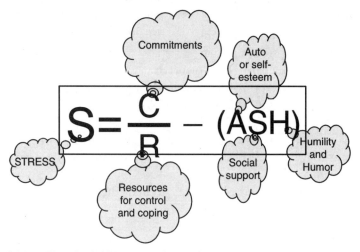

Figure 3.13   **The CRASH, stress formula**
Source: Modified from Dolan, García and Díez-Piñol (2005) *Autoestima, estrés y trabajo* (Madrid: McGraw-Hill): 75. Used with permission.

The "CRASH" formula also highlights the importance of humility as a virtue and highly valuable as a de-stressing agent. There is no doubt that knowing one's limit, being open to learning and coping with excessively over-demanding life scripts, is recommended to avoid excessive stress. As already noted, humility and valour are necessary complements for good self-esteem, unlike their negative versions, humiliation and reckless arrogance.

With respect to the very human value of a good sense of humor, often ignored or even criticized by rationalist and pragmatic thought, Antonio Gala writes:[45]

Against conceited imbeciles who, in general, tend to self-consecrate themselves as managers of mystery, there is no better response than laughter, not as a sound made in vain, but as a manifestation of happiness, a manifestation of our privileged human condition, since man is the only animal capable of laughing ... Hooded Muslims who sentence certain writers to death have forgotten that the Koran says: "He who makes his companions laugh merits Paradise". And dry Calvinists and their friends have perhaps forgotten that Luther said: "My laughter is my sword, my happiness, my shield ... I do not want wearisome and baleful sufferers by my side. I know that he who laughs will never be too great a danger and will end up winning the wars of this world concocted by the constipated and by the critics."

From the existential point of view, the most important psychological resource of situational control, other than good humor, is the bravery to decide to live the way one really wants, beyond what is conventionally considered "normal" by society, as Ortega and Gasset[46] would say, living "hither and thither", having lost the ability to be "self-absorbed in thought".

Stress from a self-esteem perspective is pure fear and a fundamental mistrust of the future; fear of not being worthy, of not being able to cope with adaptative demands, of not being loved, of not being recognized, of deciding not to decide, of fearing life and death ... a fear of losing existential control. Leadership, by contrast, no matter how it is defined, involves coping, activation, dominion, pleasure, achievement, enthusiasm, and certainly, adaptative success (or understanding success in relative terms); it is the pure perception of existential controllability.

From the psycho-biological perspective (Figure 3.14), there are four basic emotions resulting from the different adaptative efforts and perceptions of control: happiness, sadness, placidity and rage. There are also four possible opposing and basic psycho-biological states: serenity-fear and activation-defeat. Self-esteem is generated in the psycho-biological dimension of serenity-activation, where the adaptative effort to control the situation is low or moderate. In either case, it is associated with a sense of controllability and a perception of achievement and self-control.

When individuals feel placid, they perceive controllability without needing to make an effort to control anything. It occurs within relaxed contexts or during meditative contemplation, and it is absolutely necessary to rest or relax and achieve high-performance intellectual production. Serenity is a vital experience between placidity and happiness, in which there is no fear of tension. It evokes tenderness, far-removed from aggression and close to activation, life and existential meaning. Happiness is an emotional asset associated to achievement, pleasure, generosity and vital fluidity. It is the opposite of sadness and existential neurosis.

As individuals need to make efforts to control multiple situations, they begin to activate themselves for a fight. Rage, hostility, fury and irritability are the manifestations when a person enters a state of fear, anxiety and

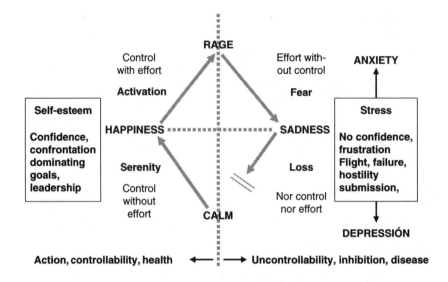

Figure 3.14 **Emotional, health and leadership dimensions**
Source: Modified from Dolan, García and Díez-Piñol (2005) *Autoestima, estrés y trabajo* (Madrid: McGraw-Hill) 76. Used with permission.

lack of control: when their adaptative resources are insufficient, entering a state of vulnerability to disease.

Fear (Table 3.2) is a vital experience between rage and sadness, where there is anxiety, inhibition and mistrust. It is close to aggression and cynicism, depression, disease and defeat, a lack of existential meaning, and, eventually, death.

For Aristotle, fear is the expectation of an evil. There are evils which must be feared to avoid being reckless or shameless.[47] For him, among those evils to be feared are vileness (if you don't want to be shameless) and a lack of friends (if you don't want to be reckless). Evils that a brave individual should not fear are poverty or illness and especially death. But that's nothing! Plato went as far as stigmatizing fear as a vice, contrary to the "noble warrior virtues" which would rule his "utopian" Republic.

FATIGUE FROM NOT BEING ONESELF

Never-ending activity as a result of a lack of self-esteem is a limitless source of chronic stress. The excessive adaptative effort made in search of efficiency as the final objective, relatively disdainful as regards feelings, without real awareness of one's own identity

> "I've had every success in life. Now I'm going to make sure my life is a success," said a wise, albeit belated, optimist on his eightieth birthday.

Table 3.2 **Principal fears to be overcome in the construction of self-esteem**

- Fear of dreaming
- Fear of not being able to materialize what is dreamt
- Fear of trusting oneself, others and the future of humanity
- Fear of cooperating and sharing
- Fear of living and enjoying
- Fear of losing control of the situation
- Fear of being marginalized from the system
- Fear of thinking differently
- Fear of not being understood and being abandoned
- Fear of feeling guilty for not always being busy
- Fear of making a fool of yourself
- Fear of being absorbed in thought
- Fear of losing security
- Fear of failure
- Fear of change
- Fear of being free
- Fear of being

and personal worth, is extremely alienating and disconcerting, removing and distancing the individual from their centre. The person feels guilty and empty inside and conventionally successful on the outside. "I've had every success in life. Now I'm going to make sure my life is a success", said a wise, albeit belated, optimist on his eightieth birthday.

The guilty fear of not having found are adequate, personal and collective destiny is one of the deepest sources of the occupational stress pandemic that we face today.

People with Type A behavior pattern which will be discussed later, are predisposed to suffering coronary problems. They have interiorized a very demanding sense of obligation. They are perfectionists, which makes them highly involved in their work, with a chronic case of urgent deadlines, and, what's worse for their health, high levels of hostility and easily infuriated in their personal relationships, leaving them in a chronic state of vegetative violence.[48]

Doing things out of a sense of obligation and being compulsively perfectionist amputates imagination, sensitivity, spontaneity and the pleasure derived from the journey itself.

SELF-ESTEEM, ENTREPRENEURSHIP BEHAVIOR, STRESS AND ORGANIZATIONAL EFFECTIVENESS

Juxtaposed to the stressing Biblical condemnation of "you will earn your bread by the sweat of your brow" which represents work as suffering or submission, in 1486, the Renaissance thinker, Pico de la Mirandola,

> **Self-esteem is a necessary preceding condition for initiative, amiability and creative productivity, all the variables necessary for a successfully competitive company.**

published a work titled *Oratio*, later called the *Manifesto of Humanism*. It contains an interesting, new and enterprising version regarding the inevitability of occupational stress, corresponding to an anthropocentric and Renaissance ethos forging a new and collective self-esteem:

> Man is at the centre of everything he does. When all was created and the world was complete, man emerged, and God said to him: I have not given you a place, task or plan; you can take on any enterprise and occupy any place you choose. Everything else that exists will be subject to the laws you dictate. You alone are capable of determining what you are.

As we shall see in the final chapter, an adequate degree of self-esteem in the people who make up an organization is fundamental for its effectiveness. Firstly, self-esteem is a necessary preceding condition for initiative, amiability and creative productivity, all the variables necessary for a successfully competitive company. These variables are necessary in and of themselves, but also because they increase the resistance to stress and the resistance to illness. Secondly, self-esteem increases the openness to processes of unlearning and change, two absolutely necessary factors for organizational adaptability in complex environments.

However, self-esteem is made more difficult by the fear found in the workplace. People are afraid at work, more than it may seem at first glance. They are afraid to give their opinions to their bosses, to question the system, afraid of being sacked, sanctioned or mistreated at any given point. They are afraid to be themselves, to decide to take the time to take care of their family and friends, or "simply" to give full meaning to their lives.

As we discuss in the final chapter, an essential change is needed in leadership style and company management practises if we aim to aspire and achieve true self-esteem and happiness as human beings.

Keys for developing individual self-esteem and avoiding stress

While there are no universal "turn-key" recepies to boost self esteem and lower stress, an amalgamation of advices taken from different sources might include the following:

1   **Centre yourself, calmly learn to be aware of what is going on within**. The habitual practice of contemplative meditation allows us

to be in touch with the never-changing essence of ourselves, with the best we have, with the purest, essential instance of our nature. It is an experience of serenity and essential centring to build true self-esteem, security and confidence in ourselves and others. It is especially important for those people who have influence over others, such as parents, managers, political leaders, judges, doctors or teachers.

The aim is to reflect on oneself, looking in from the outside in order to truly see our inner self and contemplate our feelings, ideas and actions. Being aware of what we think, feel and do is very important in order to adopt the position of neutral observer with respect to our self-esteem, thereby changing it rationally and effectively for our own happiness and that of those around us.

Who we are is what we do. First comes *being*, and then comes *doing*. The things a person does gives added value to their *being*. From this idea comes Aristotle's concept of habit. The good person is one who transmits goodwill to the things they habitually work on. Interiorization is essential for true knowledge and awareness of one's own reality. Without knowing who we are, it is very difficult to love oneself. Nobody can love what he or she does not know. At the same time, by meditative reflection, reflecting on oneself, it is easier to redesign the real values and life purposes that will help appreciate oneself better, beyond the iconic or representative *ego*.

We need to try to be interesting to ourselves; if not, others won't find us interesting. If someone stops being interested in their own self, they cannot appreciate themselves and it will be difficult for others to appreciate them. Most likely, others won't be interesting to them either. Being able to have fun with your self is fundamental to avoid being jealous. The effervescence inside has to be creative and fun for a deep and long-lasting self-esteem to be experienced.

2   **Remember and rebuild as much as possible the love and trust with parents in childhood and adolescence**. As reminded by Polaino-Lorente (2003)[49] a person's life is worth what their love is worth. Especially, we could add, a person's life is worth what their love is worth, just as they perceive, remember and rebuild it.

It is clear that affective plotting in childhood and adolescence is constructed more or less objectively. However, at times there are cognitive filters, which minimize or negatively distort our memories of having been loved and accepted by our parents and others in the first stages of our lives. It is very important, in this sense, for our self-esteem to try and rationalise to make cognitive filters positive, by attempting to choose and retain positive scenes, dialogues and other memories which remind us we were loved.

3   **Try to be honorable and coherent with professed values, living wholesome and not dissociated nor inconsistent lives**. Congruity or integrity between what you say and what you do is essential for self-esteem. This is especially true regarding moral values. The problem often lies in the fact that the values we profess to hold, according to Maturana[50], are relegated to mere "lip service".

The anonymous negative value of integrity is corruption. It is very difficult for someone corrupt, someone broken on the inside, to experience authentic self-esteem.

4   **Set projects with psychological successes in mind**. We have to project our aims with perseverance and determination until we achieve psychological success. Without a project and without celebrating the results of the project there is no self-esteem. It is very important to celebrate both quantitative and qualitative achievements. We must reward ourselves based on real events, both quantitative and qualitative, but always based on truth. It is impossible to lie to one's deeper-most inner-self.

It is important not to forget that true psychological success is obtained when we incorporate and balance material, emotional and ethical achievements.

(a) *Emotional achievement*: make the effort to try to generate your own positive thoughts and emotions in daily life, as well as modulate your reactive emotions when confronted by negative events. By the same token, being able to love and be loved is, obviously, the most important and general emotional achievement in life.

(b) *Ethical achievement*: make the effort to be the best person possible, savouring the actual putting into practice of values, such as integrity, generosity or authenticity.

(c) *Material achievement*: make the effort to be economically self-sufficient, enjoying the material things you obtain from your own efforts through a blend of ingenuity, determination and luck.

5   **Transcend, go well-beyond yourself**. Real self-esteem goes well-beyond the material and emotional achievements that everyone has. As mentioned when discussing the origins of self-esteem, it is based on the perception of utility for others, beyond individual utilitarianism. It is also very improbable that we will reach elevated goals, either personal or social, if we don't give back a part of what we receive, if we do not share with others. If we are like a TV channel transmitting what we've learned, we have to leave room to continue learning to be alive. "Trans-mission" is the aim of transmitting.

6   **Go beyond conventional beliefs and values**. Real self-esteem is based on the adoption of judgements and behaviors which arise from one's

own conscience regarding what is appropriate to do and say, well-beyond the predominant cultural beliefs and values in the group we belong to and use as a reference.

If we want to build healthy, "post-conventional" (Kohlberg, 1992)[51] self-esteem, we have to grant ourselves the freedom to:

(a) *Be ourselves*: we have to dare to discover our own reality, our weaknesses and strengths, well beyond the computer postulates of the "Information Society".

(b) *Come out of the emotional closet*: we have to express ourselves, be spontaneous, show our feelings, pains and joys, as well as our own principles and criteria: aesthetic, ethical, political, etc. But, especially, we have to be able to give ourselves the freedom for an adequate expression of these emotions and rights. We have to overcome the fear of making a fool of ourselves and adopt an expressive style which is neither passive nor aggressive, which allows us to express ourselves politely and at the right time let others have the opportunity to participate and help us build our own reasoning (basic emotional rights of self-esteem).

(c) *Really achieve what we visualize* by maintaining our intention over time and transferring energy where we project it. We have to get rid of the fear of failure and fear of success. As Brian Bacon says, "Where attention goes, so flows life".

(d) *Enjoy learning* about everything from everyone.

(e) *Savour* what life offers every single moment.

(f) *Accept our own body and self-image*: the body manifests the *ego* to the world. For example, one of the best indicators of self-esteem and mental health is to elegantly accept those little extra kilos.

(g) *Be happy.*

7 **Dare to trust**. We have to trust or believe in ourselves and in our potential. We have to believe that our mental processes work correctly (analysis, comprehension, sequencing, learning, choice, and decision). We have to believe in our ability to objectively observe the facts. And we have to believe in our own intuitive abilities and ethically adequate actions.
We have to trust in life and that beauty and truth are possible.
We have to trust that others are going to help us achieve our goals, which we have set honestly and passionately.

8 **Make adequate comparisons**. Satisfaction in life is subjective, depending on the comparisons we make with our own and others' references, past, present and future:

"How is your husband?"
"With respect to whom?" – answered a woman with astute self-esteem.

9   **Develop pride in belonging**. We have to love the country where we were born and the organisations we work for. Our origin and work should not be seen as a source of arrogant identity, but as a valued root and source of legitimate pride and differentiated culture. We have to try to make this a reality.

10   **Decide to have time**. The decision to have time to dedicate to essential human tasks, such as playing, reading, thinking, putting ideas in order, having friends, living or "simply" being, is necessary to make life human. And it has to be legitimated politically and enabled on a practical level from the different strata of power and management that each of us has in our lives.

    And, especially, we have to know that no one will magically appear to make us happy and rescue us from our existential void. We have to be the ones who decide to live life with a purpose and be ourselves, with all of the consequences that may entail.

Interesting to know:

The basic emotional rights of self-esteem, which should be assertively expressed and executed, are:

- The right to say "no";
- The right to say "I don't know";
- The right not to do anything or have time for yourself, regardless of work-related, family or other type of obligations;
- The right to take risks and make mistakes (whether that's cooking, shopping or playing your favourite sport);
- The right to change your opinion or criteria about people and things;
- The right to change your appearance or even life style;
- The right to ask for help when you think you need it;
- The right not to have to put up with meaningless commitments or relationships;
- The right to interrupt to ask a question or ask for clarification;
- The right not to always have to be witty and funny;
- The right to be sad when you're not happy;
- The right to have a job well done formally recognized;
- The right to look for new roads in life;
- The right not to accept advice (*including, of course, the advice mentioned in this chapter*).

Chapter postscript

Psychological stress is the internal/biochemical response to perceived threat. Subconscious perceptions, or thoughts, of the individual caused his or her stress at work and elsewhere. If we subconsciously think that a "life or work event" is threat-

> People with high self-esteem are significantly happier than others. They are also less likely to be depressed. If you feel out of control you are more likely to have negative thoughts. Combined, stress and low self esteem can have you spiralling in a vicious cycle.

ening, then we have this internal/biochemical response. Our self-concept influences our subconscious thoughts or perceptions. Self-esteem, which is our general opinion of ourselves as capable of coping with perceived threats. If we have "lower" self-concepts, we are more likely to perceive actual or imagined events in our lives (life events) as causing stress. To reduce stress, therefore, we (in part) need to increase the accuracy of our self-esteems, and consequently, our subconscious thoughts.

Study after study has found that increasing someone's self-esteem will reduce the relative amount of stress they experience, especially in work settings. The jury is still out, however, about whether increasing someone's job chronic stress (without giving them time to relax and recharge) will reduce their self-esteem levels. There is anecdotal evidence that, if a person starts with high self esteem, stress does not seem to affect it If, however, the person's self-esteem levels start out low, stress will often reduce them even further.

The question then becomes, if we know that raising our self-esteem is going to help us manage our stress, what do we do to boost it? How do we go about building our self-esteem to the level that we are in the optimum state possible to manage all those work stressors, before they affect our health? As with every complex topic, there are many theories – some have been reviewed in this chapter; some may seem more logical to you than others. There seems not to be a quick fix.

And finally, we need to remember that gauging the value of self-esteem requires, first of all, a sensible way to measure it. Most investigators just ask people what they think of themselves. Naturally enough, the answers are often coloured by the common tendency to want to make oneself look good. Unfortunately, psychologists lack any better method to assess the phenomenon of self-esteem.

Exercise: Test your self-esteem

Give a numerical value to the following:

Question	Never 1	Sometimes 2	Almost always 3	Always 4

1. I feel happy.
2. I feel uncomfortable with people I don't know.
3. I feel dependent on others.
4. Challenges are a threat to me.
5. I feel sad.
6. I feel comfortable with people I don't know.
7. When things go wrong, it's my fault.
8. I think I'm nice to others.
9. Making mistakes is good.
10. If things go well, it's due to my best efforts.
11. Others don't like me.
12. A wise man corrects himself.
13. I feel like the least important person in the world.
14. I need to do what others want in order to feel accepted.
15. I feel like the most important person in the world.
16. Everything I do turns out wrong.
17. I feel like the whole world laughs at me.
18. I can take constructive criticism.
19. I make fun of everybody.
20. Nothing bothers me.
21. I'm happy with my height.
22. Everything I do turns out great.
23. I can talk openly about my feelings.
24. I feel my height is wrong.
25. I only accept the praises I get.
26. I have fun laughing at my mistakes.
27. I keep my feelings to myself.
28. I'm perfect.
29. I laugh when others fail.
30. I'd like to change how I look.
31. I avoid new experiences.
32. I am really shy.
33. I accept challenges without thinking.
34. I find excuses to not accept changes.

35. I feel that others depend on me.

36. Other people make more mistakes than I do.

37. I consider myself highly aggressive.

38. I'm terrified of changes.

39. I love adventure.

40. I'm happy when others succeed.

Total in each column

Grand total

Score and interpretation

Total the number of times you selected the value in each column and then multiply that total by the number of that column. For example, if you chose the column "Always" ten times, multiply 10 × 4 for a total of 40 points in that column. When you've finished this process for all of the columns, add up the respective totals and check your results against the following table:

160–104	High self-esteem (negative)
103–84	High self-esteem (positive)
83–74	Low self-esteem (positive)
73–40	Low self-esteem (negative)

REFERENCES

1 Aranguren, J.L.A. (1975). *Ética* (Madrid: Alianza Editorial).

2 Polaino-Lorente, A. (2003). *En busca de la autoestima perdida* (Bilbao: Desclée de Brouwer).

3 Kohlberg, L. (1992). *Psicología del desarrollo moral* (Bilbao: Desclée de Brouwer).

4 See: http://www.shambhalainstitute.org/2005/cm_bacon.shtml

5 See the first chapter in "Motivarás y reconocerás el esfuerzo", in Dolan, S.L. Martín, I. and Soto, E. (2004). *Los 10 mandamientos para la dirección de personas* (Barcelona: Gestión 2000).

6 White, R. (1963). "Ego and Reality in Psychoanalytic Theory: A proposal regarding independent ego energies", *Psychological Issues*, 3(3): 125–50.

7 Rosenberg, M. (1979). *Conceiving the Self* (New York: Basic Books).

8 Coopersmith, S. (1967). *The Antecedents of Self-Esteem* (San Francisco: Freeman & Company).

9 Polaino-Lorente, A. (2003).

10 Branden, N. (1969). *The Psychology of Self-Esteem.* (New York: Bantam).

11 Branden, N. (1994). *El poder de la autoestima* (México: Paidós).

12 Bandura, A. (1999). *Auto-eficacia: cómo afrontamos los cambios de la sociedad actual* (Bilbao: Desclée de Rrouwer).

13 Burns, R.B. (1990). *El autoconcepto. Teoría, medición, desarrollo y comportamiento* (Bilbao: Edicions Ega).

14 Bonanno, G.A. (2004). "Loss, Trauma and Human Resilience", *American Psychologist*, 59(1): 20–28.

15 Kobassa, S.C. (1979). "Stressful Life Events, Personality and Health: An inquiry into hardiness", *Journal of Personality and Social Psychology*, 37(1): 1–11.

16 Carballo R. (1977). *Violencia y ternura* (Madrid: Prensa Española).

17 Coopersmith (1967). *op.cit.*

18 Savater, F. (1983). *La tarea del héroe* (Madrid: Taurus), free translation from the original text in Spanish.

19 Emilio Lledó (n.d.). *Un ser para la vida*, cited in http://www.aea.es/revista/43/dos.htm, translated from the original in Spanish.

20 Ortega y Gasset first published the essay on "En torno a Galileo." in Spanish in 1933. The book was republished in 2005 by Editorial Biblioteca Nueva, S.L.

21 Lewin, K. (1935). *A Dynamic Theory of Personality* (New York: McGraw-Hill).

22 James, W. (1989). *The Principles of Psychology* (Cambridge: Harvard University Press).

23 García, S. (2002). "La Dirección por Valores", in *Management español: los mejores textos,* chapter 8, pp. 225–65 (Madrid: Ariel).

24 García, S. (2005). La Empresa 'Utopica': el equilibrio económico, ético y emocional', unpublished manuscript.

25 Dolan, S.L. (2003). "Making a Life or Making a Living", ESADE MBA *Business Review*, vol. 1: 8–11.

26 Dolan, S.L., García, S. and Díez Piñol, M. (2004). "Validation of 'Triaxial' Model of Values-Based Management: Towards new perspectives to manage culture in organisations", *Proceedings of the 9th International Conference of Work Values and Behavior*, New Orleans, 3–6 August 2004.

27 Dolan, S.L., García, S. and Richley, B. (2005). *Managing by Values* (London: Palgrave Macmillan).

28 Pérez López, J.A. (1998). *Liderazgo y ética en la dirección de empresas* (Bilbao: Deusto).

29 Mill, J.S. (1997). *Sobre la libertad* (Madrid: Alianza Editorial).

30 Arrow, K. J. (1970). *Social Choice and Individual Values*, 2nd edn. Cowles Foundation Monographs Series, Yale University.

31 Luhmann, N. (1996). *Confianza* (Barcelona: Anthropos).

32 Polaino-Lorente (2003).

33 Polaino-Lorente (2003).

34 Polaino-Lorente (2003).

35 Henry, J.P. and Stephens, P.M. (1977). *Stress, health and the social environment: a sociobiologic approach to medicine* (New York: Springer Verlag).

36 Tarrats, F. (1979). *Dos trenes se Cruzan en Reus* (Barcelona: Acervo). The quote is a translation from the original text in Spanish.

37 Frankenhaeuser, M., Dunne, E. and Lundberg, U. (1976). "Sex differences in sympathetic-adrenal modularly reactions induced by different stressors". *Psychopharmacology*, vol. 47: 1–5.

38 Polaino-Lorente (2003).

39 Ortega y Gasset, J. (1947). *En torno a Galileo* (Madrid: Revista de Occidente).

40   Branden, N. (2001). "Answering Misconceptions About Self-Esteem". *National Association for Self-Esteem* [On-line]. Available: http://www.self-esteem-nase. org/journal01.shtml.

41   Lipovetsky, G. (1986). *La era del vacío. Ensayos sobre el individualismo contemporáneo* (Barcelona: Anagrama).

42   Polaino-Lorente (2003).

43   García Sanchez, S. (1990). "Estrés laboral, percepción de control sobre el trabajo y número de visitas al médico". Medicina de Empresa vol. 23. 3:5–14.

44   Dolan, S.L., García, S. and Díez-Piñol, M. (2005). *Autoestima, estrés y trabajo.* (Madrid, McGraw-Hill), p. 75.

45   Gala, A. (1995). "Un valle de risas". *El Pais*, December, p. 122.

46   Ortega y Gasset J. (1947). *En torno a Galileo* (Madrid: Revista de Occidente).

47   Aristotle (1997). *Ética nicomáquea* (Madrid: Santillana).

48   Valdes M. de Flores and García Sánchez, S. (1988). *Estrés y cardiopatía isquémica.* (Barcelona: Almax).

49   Polaino-Lorente (2003).

50   Maturana, H.R. and Varela, F.L. (1980). "Autopoiesis and cognition: The Revolution of the Living". *Boston Studies in the Philosophy of Science.* vol. 42, Reidel, Boston.

51   Kohlberg, L. (1992). *Psicología del desarrollo moral* (Bilbao: Desclée de Brouwer).

4 Why Does Occupational Stress Occur? Antecedents and Consequences

"I'm an old man and I've had many troubles, most of which never happened."

(Mark Twain)

"Future Shock is the shattering stress and disorientation that we induce in individuals by subjecting them to too much change in too short a time."

(Alvin Toffler)

Stress as a difficulty in adapting to the environment

Stress is a normal part of our daily lives. It is generally associated to a negative state or detrimental experience, which must be eliminated at all cost. But this isn't always the case. Stress becomes negative when this experience becomes *excessive*, *uncontrolled* or *uncontrollable*. In the workplace, an insufficient amount of work as well as an overload of work can lead to the worker feeling inhibited, with the resulting physical and mental consequences. Depending on the type of job and the organizational and cultural characteristics of the job, work-related stress can take many forms.

From this perspective, stress, in general, means an *effort to adapt*. Faced with an excess of environmental demands (*over-stimulation*) related to the person's very source of satisfaction, the person feels unable to resolve them. However, there can also be a lack of environmental stimulation (*under-stimulation*), which produces boredom and fatigue within the individual. Both in over and under-stimulation the action necessary to cope with the situation is inhibited. Thus, the traditional Performance–Stress Relationship Curve, looks like an inverted "U" (see Figure 4.1), At zero arousal, the person has zero performance – which means that he/she is either sleeping or inactive. At maximum arousal, the person *also* has zero performance – here, being overwhelmed incapacitates the person. Curiously enough, the only way to have any performance is to have *some* level of arousal. At the same time, specific areas of the brain are activated producing an inhibition of the body's defense mechanisms, along with reduced mobility and a lack of exploratory behaviors. This leads to greater vulnerability to disease and infection. Only with a level of moderate activity do behaviors such as friendliness, creativity and professional commitment arise.

In order to find out if someone adapts well to the stress in an environment, researchers have developed a tool called "Stressful Life Events". Any change in the routine of our lives – even welcome changes – can be stressful, both in terms of the ways we perceive them and in terms of the increased incidence of physical illness and death that occur during the 12 months following the changes. The Holmes–Rahe Scale assigns values (based upon the sample being told that marriage represents 50 points) attributed by a sample of 394 individuals to the life events concerned.[1]

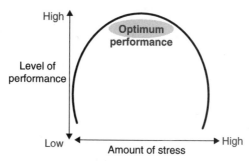

Figure 4.1 **Stress and performance: the inverted-U stress curve**

Exercise: assess your life stress and adaptation

This is a list of stressful events in your life which have different number values to show the pressure, that they add to your life. Sit back, take a moment, and review your life over the past 1 to 2 years. Go through the following list. Place a check mark on the box of those stressful events that have happened or are taking place in your life. When you are done calculate your total score and see the general interpretation. Note that in life additional events can generate stress. However, the following is based on the original work of Holmes and Rahe.

100 ☐ Death of a spouse	73 ☐ Divorce
36 ☐ Change to different line of work	37 ☐ Death of a close friend
65 ☐ Marital separation (or separation from any major intimate relationship)	63 ☐ Jail term
63 ☐ Death of a close family member	53 ☐ Personal injury or illness
44 ☐ Major change in health or behavior of a family member	47 ☐ Being fired from work
40 ☐ Sexual difficulties	45 ☐ Marital reconciliation
39 ☐ Gain of new family member through birth, adoption, or remarriage	45 ☐ Retirement
39 ☐ Business readjustment	40 ☐ Pregnancy
38 ☐ Major change in finances	50 ☐ Marriage
35 ☐ Increase in number of arguments with spouse	23 ☐ Trouble with boss/superior
31 ☐ Mortgage or loan for major purchase (i.e. home, etc.)	30 ☐ Foreclosure of mortgage or loan
29 ☐ Changes in responsibility at work	29 ☐ Son or daughter leaving home
28 ☐ Outstanding Personal Achievement	26 ☐ Spouse stops work outside of home
29 ☐ Trouble with in-laws	26 ☐ Going back to school
25 ☐ Change in living condition (rebuilding, remodelling)	20 ☐ Change in residence
20 ☐ Change in work hours or responsibilities	20 ☐ Change in school
24 ☐ Revision/change of personal habits	19 ☐ Change in recreational habits
19 ☐ Change in church/spiritual activities	18 ☐ Change in social activities
17 ☐ Purchase of major items (auto, computer, etc.)	16 ☐ Change in sleeping habits
15 ☐ Change in number of family get-togethers	15 ☐ Change in eating habits
15 ☐ Vacation	12 ☐ Christmas
11 ☐ Minor violations of the law (e.g., traffic tickets, misdemeanours)	

Your overall stress score is ☐☐☐☐

Interpretation of the scores

0–149   Relatively low susceptibility to stress-related illness.

150–299   Medium susceptibility to stress-related illness (you need to learn and practice stress management skills and adaptation techniques in order to pursue a healthy life style).

300 and over High susceptibility to stress-related illness. (Daily practice of stress management skills are called for. It is very important for your well-being. Take care of it now before a serious illness erupts or an affliction becomes worse.)

In the workplace, **occupational stress** consists of the imbalance between the individual's aspirations and the realities of the person's work conditions. It is the perceived difference between the professional demands and the person's ability to carry out the demands. As such, the perception of a lack of control over the situation and a feeling of over-exertion beyond the individual's resources leads to feeling run down due to excessive activation. This wear and tear has consequences at different levels: it generates a state of irritability, a feeling of adaptative failure in controlling the situation, and a initiation of biological processes which favor the appearance of illnesses (mood, cardiovascular and immunological disorders primarily).

The specialized literature offers many theoretical models to explain and understand work-related stress. The model proposed by Dolan and Arsenault (1980),[2] for example, allows for a diagnosis to be made so that the long-term, irreversible consequences of stress can be reduced. The authors maintain that problems of adaptation are produced by the discordance between the person and the person's work environment. Depending on the degree of discordance, a variety of signs and symptoms of strain (i.e. the stress indicators) will appear. The relationship established between the individual and the person's work environment evolves depending on the adaptation cycle. This is subject to variation depending on time-related issues and changes either in the organization or in the individual. A general description of this model is available in Chapter 2 of this book; however, there are six blocks of relevant variables in studies regarding occupational stress.

- **Environmental variables (stressors and resources)**. Environmental variables are basically conceived as a discrepancy or as an imbalance between the environmental demands and the available resources

> **Stress appears when the demands of adaptation imposed on us, whether by others, or ourselves, begins to overwhelm our resources to control them. We begin to feel frustrated and anxious, and our well-being is threatened.**

(personal and environmental). It has been demonstrated that control, decision-making ability and social support can work as moderators or shock-absorbers affecting results and consequences.

Interesting to know

Professor Robert Karasek is well-known for his Job Demand Control (JD-C) model, which is the leading model in the field of work stress. The model has been widely tested in research. He formulated the JD-C model in the late seventies while working on his doctoral dissertation. The model combines epidemiological views on the relationship between work demands and health complaints on the one hand, with studies on job satisfaction and motivation on the other (Karasek, 1979). Central to the model is the interaction between job demands and job control. The model assumes two main hypotheses: (1) the combination of high job demands along with low job control precipitates psychological and physical strain ("high strain" jobs); (2) jobs in which both demands and control are high lead to well-being, learning and personal growth ("active" jobs) (Karasek and Theorell, 1990).

Sources: (1) Karasek (1979) "Job Demands, Job Decision Latitude and Mental Strain: Implications for Job Redesign", *Administrative Science Quarterly*, 24: 285–306; (2) Karasek and Theorell (1990) *Healthy Work: Stress, Productivity and the Reconstruction of Working Life* (New York: Basic Books).

- **Personal characteristics**. Various stress models have emphasized the importance of individual characteristics and their differences regarding the processes of stress. The type-A personality, the resistant personality, neuroticism, cognitive styles, self-efficacy, the locus of control, values, and other more or less stable characteristics play a modulating role over the different influences which appear during the stress process (stressor–appraisal, appraisal–confrontation, appraisal–results–consequences, appraisal–coping). We will elaborate these concepts later in the book.
- **The subjective experience**. This block distinguishes between the appraisal and the coping processes. Some scientists distinguish between primary appraisal (the evaluation of an event as benign, irrelevant or negative) and a secondary appraisal (the evaluation of the necessary

resources once the event has been categorized as negative). Coping refers to the cognitive and behavioral efforts to control, reduce or eliminate the effects of the situation perceived to be negative.

- **Individual responses: coping strategies**. This is directly related to the previous block and takes into consideration the individual's coping strategies and the appraisal regarding whether or not these strategies have been successful.
- **The result of stress**. This block defines the physiological, cognitive and behavioral reactions which take place when an individual faces a stress stimulus.

Work-originated stress affects millions of European workers across all sectors. For example, in the *Second European Survey of Working Conditions, 1997* carried out by the European Foundation of Dublin, 28 percent of workers reported health problems related to stress (the second most common problem after backache). This figure translates into 41 million EU workers affected by occupational stress each year and represents many millions of days not worked.

The health and safety authorities of the European Union member countries have identified occupational stress as one of the most significant emerging risks. In the last few decades, life, in general, has become more fast-paced and restless, creating more pressures. According to the European Agency for Health and Safety at Work, work-related stress implies an annual expense of at least 20 billion euros. Besides this economic cost, less tangible costs exist which affect society, businesses and individuals.

Antecedents of stress

The first studies on stress were aimed at finding a single definition, either focusing on physical factors or on psychological and/or social factors. However, I share the current school of thought that stress is an illness with various and diverse causes (it is a multifactorial and dynamic concept) including: individual characteristics, psycho-social working characteristics, organizational characteristics, and social and cultural aspects, among others.

It is virtually impossible to provide a single and complete list of stressors and their consequences, especially if we bear in mind that the definition of stressor depends on the individual appraising a specific situation as such. However, we can establish and identify series of stressors based on their source:

- Intrinsic sources; and
- Extrinsic sources.

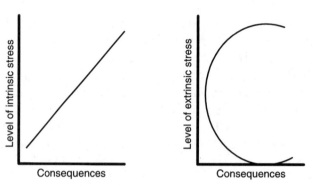

Figure 4.2 **Intrinsic and extrinsic stress**

What is truly interesting is that these two sources of stress are related differently to the negative consequences of stress. *Extrinsic sources* of stress, for example, are related linearly (that is, directly) in that these sources accumulate (see Figure 4.2). Extrinsic means that these sources of stress have a common denominator – they are related to the work context (for example, salary, timetable, company policies, benefits, and so on). On the contrary, *intrinsic sources* of stress are related to the specific job content (responsibilities, decision-making, and so on), and they have an inverted-U relationship with the negative consequences generated by stress, as can be seen in Figure 4.2.

To help understand the differences between these two sources of stress, we shall use the example of job responsibility. The individual's level of responsibility at work (the real or perceived) is an intrinsic stressor. An excessive amount of responsibility can accentuate the negative consequences due to over-stimulation. By contrast, having a job without any responsibility can also be stressful and foment negative consequences. In addition, there are individual personality differences which allow for different people to have optimal levels of responsibility with which they feel good and are unstressed. The distinction between intrinsic and extrinsic sources of stress is very important in order to understand the aetiology, or causes, of occupational stress; it is also important in the sense that addressing stress in a work setting will differ in focus and scope depending if the stress is caused by an intrinsic or by an extrinsic source.

SOME TYPICAL INTRINSIC ANTECEDENTS IN WORK SETTINGS

- *Opportunity to control.* A characteristic that can produce stress or, on the contrary, psychological well-being is the degree to which a work environment allows the individual to control the tasks at hand. This characteristic can be described as: autonomy, participation in decision-making, influence, power, and so on. First, it is important to distinguish between intrinsic and extrinsic control. Intrinsic control has a clear relationship with work satisfaction when it neutralizes other factors (pay, security, etc.). A lack of intrinsic control implies a series of negative psychological and somatic consequences (insomnia, headaches, anxiety, exhaustion, coronary disease, etc.). Excessive control also implies negative consequences. Extrinsic control seems much less related to mental health as it is often in the hands of unions and company representatives.

- *Opportunity to use one's skills.* Another important characteristic of psychological well-being is the opportunity the job provides for us to use and develop our skills. It seems that the higher the position within the organization, the greater the opportunity to use skills at work. As with other characteristics, it seems that intermediate levels are the most adequate since little or very elevated opportunities produce stress. There have been problems reported with anxiety, insomnia, and indigestion, among others.

- *Variety of tasks.* This characteristic refers to novelty and change within a specific job or work environment. As such, it is important to distinguish between the intrinsic and extrinsic variety of tasks. The intrinsic variety may be defined as the degree to which the job requires different activities in order to be carried out, implying the worker's use of different skills and talents. The extrinsic variety refers to the aspects not related to the task as such, but rather to the work environment (music, lighting, windows, etc.).

- *Feedback.* The feedback received on an employee's actions and results is, up to a point, a valued aspect. It has been demonstrated that workers whose job has this characteristic are more motivated and enjoy greater job satisfaction.

SOME TYPICAL EXTRINSIC ANTECEDENTS IN WORK SETTINGS

The environment in which people live influences their health and their physical, psychological and social well-being. Their environment can be a source of problems, restrictions and discomforts, putting to the test their capacity to adapt. An individual's expectations and needs regarding the characteristics of their work environment (location, size, etc.) are basically similar to those regarding where they live. In terms of work, the possibility of choosing a company that meets their expectations is often very limited. However, the need or desire for the company to fulfil certain characteristics (pleasant setting, close to home, positive social image, pleasant work place, etc.) does not diminish.

The lack of these characteristics can turn into additional pressures to the demands of the job, thereby aggravating the psycho-social problems

> The stressors originating in the workplace affect the individual's personal and professional life, creating problems within the family on both the personal and professional levels.

the individual already has. The stressors originating in the workplace affect the individual's personal and professional life, creating problems within the family on both the personal and professional levels. This turns into a vicious cycle, the stressful work situation affecting the worker personally, and the personal situation affecting work... We spend a great deal of our time at work and a large part of our identity stems from the jobs we do. For this reason, professional-work stressors very important.

Interesting to know

Some jobs are more stressful than others. A great deal of stress is found in jobs with changing shifts, those with a demanding pace and those with little or no control over one's job. However, both the executive under pressure to meet short-term goals and financial results as well as the worker who has to carry out a great deal of work at low pay are at risk of suffering stress due to work.

The University of Manchester Institute of Science and Technology (UK) carried out a study analysing stress levels in different jobs, using a scale of 1 to 10. The results indicated a higher degree of stress among professionals within the mining, construction and service sectors (police, journalists, dentists, doctors, etc.) than that found in management positions:

- Miners 8.3
- Police 7.7
- Construction workers 7.5
- Journalists 7.5
- Dentists 7.3
- Doctors 6.8
- Nurses 6.5
- Ambulance drivers 6.3
- Teachers 6.2
- Personnel managers 6.0

Changes which take place in companies are a widely recognized, general source of stress. If these changes imply technological change or moving offices, they can be a very important source of stress, especially when there are doubts or little participation in the process of such changes.

Source: The University of Manchester Institute of Science and Technology (UK).

Stress and personality

To a certain degree, people's reactions to the different stressors affecting them are conditioned by their personality profiles. Not all people respond the same way, bearing in mind that a great deal of our responses to stress depends on psychological factors. Additionally, not everyone develops the same adaptation disorders when faced by persistent stress conditions. We will look at this relationship in this section.

PERSONALITY TYPES A, B AND C

While the factors causing stress may be the same, the way people react is linked to their degree of vulnerability and their psychological profile. As such, a person's behavior is subject to their personality traits, attitudes, beliefs, manifest behavior and a certain psycho-physiological activation. Everybody is different and responses differently to stressors. What causes one person to stress out can be a relaxation aid for another. People are unique. Some years ago two cardiologists (Drs Friedman and Rosenman)[3] discovered a pattern between personality types and their reactions to stress. Doubtless you have heard of these "types" of people – they relate to how people deal with stress that comes into their lives.

People defined as **Type-A** personalities have a psychological profile in which an excessive response predominates. They appear hyperactive, irritable, ambitious, aggressive, hostile, impulsive, chronically impatient, tense, and competitive. Their interpersonal relationships are problematic and they tend to be dominant. People with a type-A pattern of behavior, with an autonomous response to stress, have a greater predisposition to suffer cardiovascular pathologies due to the activation of catecholamines. At the same time, these people frequently have a high degree of LDL cholesterol and reduced HDL cholesterol, while accumulating other risk factors such as obesity, high blood pressure and an addiction to nicotine.

People with a **Type-B** pattern of behavior are generally calm, trusting and confident, relaxed and open to their emotions, including hostile emotions. The role of adaptative mechanisms when coping with stress in the event of failure is clear, provoking and leading to neurotic and depressive processes.

The **Type-C** pattern of behavior occurs in people who are introverted, obsessive, passive, resigned and placid, extremely cooperative, submissive and conformist, who interiorize their response to stress and always control their hostility, desiring social approval. Although the type-C patterns were not discovered initially by Drs Freidman and Rosenman, published research suggests that by and large people with type-C behavior are statistically more predisposed to rheumatism, infections, allergies and various dermatological ills, including cancer, the latter is associated to the immunological inhibition which these individuals suffer from.

Exercise: assess your type A/B personality

Answer YES or NO based on your immediate reaction to the following questions. That is to say, after reading each item you need to respond instantly without spending too much time thinking about your response. If you do not follow this guideline, the validity of the assessment will not be as good.

1   I talk fast and really stress the key words.
2   I tend to walk, move and act fast.
3   I always get impatient and angry with how most events take place because they don't go fast enough or they're too tiresome.
4   I tend to steer conversations to topics and matters that are really important to me.
5   I feel guilty when I'm resting or have free time.
6   I tend not to notice new details that show up in my environment.
7   I'm more concerned with what is worth *having* than what is worth *being*.
8   I tend increasingly to plan more and more in less time.
9   I feel I'm competing against people who are also under time deadlines and pressures.
10   I have developed nervous tics or gestures, such as making fists or hitting the table while speaking.
11   I think success is doing things faster than anyone else.
12   I tend to perceive and evaluate my personal activities and those of others' in terms of numbers.

Results and interpretation

If you answered YES to most of the questions, you have a Type-A personality. Type-A behavior is understood as the "speed disease". People with this type of behavior display the behaviors outlined in the questionnaire. In high-pressure jobs centred on success, Type-A behavior is admired – even unconsciously. By contrast, Type-B personalities are relaxed and easy to deal with, and it is less likely that they will react in a hostile or aggressive manner.

Source: Dolan and Martín (2000) *Los 10 Mandamientos para la dirección de personas* (Barcelona: Gestión 2000). Used with the permission of the author (Dolan). This test was inspired by the work of Friedman and Roseman (1974) but was adapted and validated by the author in numerous studies with diverse samples.

LOCUS OF CONTROL

Control is one of the most important variables in coping with stressful situations. Having or perceiving control over stressor situations or events increases the degree of stress tolerance and reduces the severity of its negative effects.

People who perceive themselves as having a low capacity for controlling their environment tend to be more vulnerable when coping with stressor events. The concept developed by Rotter (1966) regarding the locus of control, referring to the causal attributions people make with specific results, is widely used to evaluate the variable of controlling their environment.[4] Julian Rotter observed people in therapy and noticed that:

- Different people, given identical conditions for learning, learn different things.
- Some people respond predictably to reinforcement, others less, and some respond unpredictably.
- Some people see a direct and strong connection between their behavior and the rewards and punishments they receive.

The core of his approach is called Expectancy Value Theory: the basic assumption is that your behavior is determined not just by the presence or size of reinforcements, but by the beliefs about what the results of your behavior are likely to be; that is, how likely you are to get the reinforcement.

Those with an external locus of control attribute the results to external forces beyond their control. Those with an internal locus of control establish a direct connection between their behavior and the reinforcements and results they obtain.

Exercise: are you in control of your work?

Indicate how often the following situations occur at work. Use only one number value, from 1 to 4, for each situation:

1 = Always	*2 = Often*	*3 = Rarely*	*4 = Never*

1　I can decide how I do my job.	☐
2　I can decide what to do in my job.	☐

3	I have a lot of say in the decisions made regarding my job.	☐
4	Others make decisions about my job.	☐
5	I can play a part in determining the speed of doing my job.	☐
6	My time schedule can be flexible.	☐
7	I can decide when to take breaks.	☐
8	I can choose who I work with.	☐
9	At work, I can play a part in planning.	☐
10	I have to do different things.	☐
11	My job offers me a variety of interesting things to do.	☐
12	My job is fun.	☐
13	I can learn new things at work.	☐
14	My job requires a lot of skill and experience.	☐
15	My job requires me to take the initiative.	☐

Results and interpretation

Questions 1–9 evaluate the degree of authority one has in decision-making. A low score (between 9 and 18 points) indicates a high degree of authority in decision-making at work, implying an internal locus of control. By contrast, a high score (more than 27 points) indicates a low degree of authority at work, in other words, an external locus of control.

Questions 10–15 measure the degree of professional competencies required for the job. A low score (between 6 and 12 points) indicates a more internal locus of control, in which the job requires personal skills and abilities in order to carry it out. By contrast, a high score (more than 18 points) indicates a more external locus of control, in which a job requires few personal skills.

DOLAN AND ARSENAULT COMBINED PERSONALITY MEASURE

In the previous sections I have described the commonly used measures of personality in stress research. In Canada, a team of us working with a huge sample of employees in different sectors, discovered that combining the type A/B personality description with the locus of control adds significant value in explaining how people perceive their work environment and how they respond to it. Using a

Dr. André Arsenault

median-split method, each personality scale was split at the 50 percent percentile point to yield four categories of personality. Labels were also attributed to personality types using the following arguments. The type-A personality was labelled (HOT – comes from "hot temper" or "hot reactors"), while the type-B personality was labelled COOL (named after

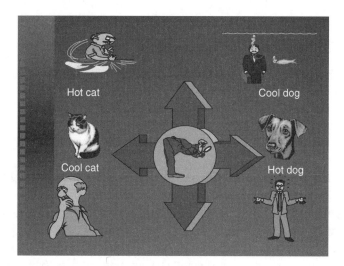

Figure 4.3 **The Dolan and Arsenault typology**

Fonzy from the Happy Days TV series in the 1980s – a "cool dood", takes things easy). Animal labels were used to describe the locus of control, where the internal locus of control was called CAT (if you own or know a cat you know that cats are very independent); external personalities were labelled DOG (if you own a dog you know that dogs are very dependent on external stimuli). Figure 4.3 shows this typology.

In combining the two dimensions, we get the following four categories of personalities described by Dolan and his colleagues:[5]

- The HOT-CATs are competitive, preoccupied with control of their territory, must engage in immediate action and exert control over their emotional reactions. They see themselves as formal and authoritative leaders, the so-called dominants of the social structure. They strive in order to maintain control.
- The HOT-DOGs are hyperactive optimistic individuals who feel guided by external events. They are restless individuals who find satisfaction in the demonstration that they have kept themselves busy doing whatever has to be done. They are more devoted than faithful; and formal roles in an organized social structure do not interest them. They strive and don't always believe in control.
- The COOL-CATs have a tendency to be overwhelmed by their analytical mind. Being extremely critical, they have a tendency towards pessimism. It is difficult to determine if they are solitary by choice or if others avoid them because of their retreating behavior. They like to feel unpredictable and do not like to be controlled or directed. They don't strive or compete but believe in control.

- COOL-DOGs never act hastily. Their domain is more of quiet reflection and slow paced jobs. They are quite sensitive to all sorts of joys and mishaps, yet do not search and even prefer not to have control of such happenings. They appear more faithful than devoted. They neither strive nor believe in control.

PROFILE OF THE STRESS-RESISTANT PERSONALITY

The models developed by Kobassa (1982) and Antonovsky (1987)[6] are the best-known models regarding the stress-resistant personality. *Kobassa's model* centres around the concept of "hardiness" or the "hardy personality", a personality type with three dimensions: commitment or implication, control and challenge. A resistant personality corresponds to a committed person identifying with their specific task, convinced that they can act and maintain control of their results, they clearly focused towards change and new situations marked by challenge and novelty. *Antonovsky's model* especially focuses on the cognitive variables, which, in daily tasks and events, look for a comprehensive framework within a cognitive context, the ability to manage events and the meaning these have within their framework and hierarchy of values and beliefs. Operatively, the model is identified with comprehensibility, manageability and significance. The different studies carried out on both models in terms of health have shown that resistant personality and a sense of coherence are associated to a lower level of both psychological and physical symptomatology. As such, these people are characterized by a high degree of health and less vulnerability to stress.

Resistance to change is greatly related to the Resistant Personality concept. It is a personality style, a source of resistance to stress, with three attributes: commitment, control and challenge. *Commitment* is the ability to believe in what you are doing and the tendency to get involved in what you do; *control* is the tendency to believe and act with the supposition that you can influence the course of events, and responsibility in your actions; *challenge* is based on the belief that change more than stability is the norm in life. Individuals motivated by challenge look for changes and new experiences, flexibly and tolerantly coping with ambiguity. Undesirable events are seen as possibilities, not as threats.[7]

TYPE "R" PERSONALITY: SENSATION SEEKERS

Marvin Zuckerman's landmark 1971 article on "Sensation Seekers" ranks as one of the 50 most influential works in the history of psychology – along with work by such researchers as Sigmund Freud, B.F. Skinner, Jean Piaget and others.[8] In more recent publications he developed a personality-assessment tool known as the "Sensation-Seeking Scale (SSS).[9] By prompting respondents to agree or disagree with such statements as, "I sometimes like to do things that are a little frightening" and "I like doing things just for the thrill of it", the SSS helps psychologists gauge sensation-seeking tendencies. A personality category first identified by Zuckerman in 1964, the sensation-seeker personality craves "varied, novel, complex and intense sensations and experiences". Zuckerman's studies of sensation seekers have had a profound impact on our understanding of personality traits.

The first version of Zuckerman's Sensation-Seeking Scale, created more than 30 years ago, was designed to predict an individual's response to sensory deprivation. Since then, the personality-assessment tool has been refined to gauge four key tendencies: thrill and adventure seeking; experience seeking; disinhibition; and susceptibility to boredom. "Thrill seekers" get a kick out of activities or sports that provide unusual sensations and experiences – even if they involve risk. Motorcycle racing or water-skiing, for example, might appeal to this category of sensation seekers. "Experience seekers" enjoy novel experiences such as travelling to exotic locations, listening to unusual or exciting music, experimenting with drugs and living a "non-conformist" lifestyle. "Disinhibitors" are constantly searching for opportunities to lose their inhibitions at "wild" parties involving heavy drinking and sexual activities with strangers. Finally, sensation seekers are very easily bored by repetitive, predictable experiences and people, and by routine work assignments.

In general, Zuckerman said, men usually demonstrate a stronger overall sensation-seeking tendency than women. People who have been divorced score higher, on average, than married or single people. Sensation-seeking behaviors seem to peak among people in their late teens and early 20s, and they decline with age in both men and women. People who regularly practice a conventional religion are more likely to be classified as low sensation seekers. The Sensation Seeking Scale has been used to identify teenagers who may be jeopardizing their health and safety by using drugs, engaging in frequent sexual activity with many partners and driving recklessly or under the influence of alcohol. Zuckerman's analytical techniques might also be used to develop teaching methods to best suit children's individual learning styles, or to match job assignments with employees' personality traits. For example, high sensation seekers like risky or even periodically stressful vocations, like air pilots, air-traffic controllers, emergency-room hospital workers or occupations providing a great deal of varied social contacts; they're dissatisfied and bored by routine, repetitious jobs that don't involve social interaction or challenging and changing activities.

THE BIG-FIVE PERSONALITY TRAITS

In 1981 in a symposium in Honolulu, four prominent researchers (Lewis Goldberg, Naomi Takamoto-Chock, Andrew Comrey and John M. Digman) reviewed the available personality tests of the day, and decided that most of the tests which held any promise seemed to measure a subset of five common factors. They include: extraversion, emotional stability, agreeableness, openness to experience, and conscientiousness.

The big five personality traits can be summarized as follows:

- **Neuroticism** is defined as a tendency to easily experience unpleasant emotions such as anxiety, anger or depression. Neuroticism refers to the tendency to experience negative feelings. Those who score high on neuroticism may experience one specific negative feeling such as anxiety, anger or depression primarily, but are also likely to experience several of these emotions at the same time. People high in neuroticism are emotionally reactive. They respond emotionally to events that would not affect most people, and their reactions tend to be more intense than normal. They are more likely to interpret ordinary situations as threatening, and minor frustrations as hopelessly difficult. Their negative emotional reactions tend to persist for unusually long periods of time, which means they are often in a bad mood. These problems in emotional regulation can diminish a neurotic's ability to think clearly, make decisions, and cope effectively with stress.

  At the other end of the scale, individuals who score low in neuroticism are less easily upset and are less emotionally reactive. They tend to be calm, emotionally stable, and free from persistent negative feelings. Freedom from negative feelings does not mean that low scorers experience a lot of positive feelings; frequency of positive emotions is a component of the extroversion domain.

- **Extroversion** is defined as energy, surgency, and the tendency to seek stimulation and the company of others. Extroversion is marked by pronounced engagement with the external world. Extroverts enjoy being with people, are full of energy, and often experience positive emotions. They tend to be enthusiastic, action-oriented individuals who are likely to say, "Yes!" or "Let's go!" to opportunities for excitement. In groups they like to talk, assert themselves, and draw attention to themselves.

  Introverts lack the exuberance, energy and activity levels of extroverts. They tend to be quiet, low-key, deliberate, and disengaged from the social world. Their lack of social involvement should not be interpreted as shyness or depression; the introvert simply needs less stimulation than an extrovert and prefers to be alone.

- **Agreeableness** is defined as the tendency to be compassionate and cooperative rather than suspicious and antagonistic towards others. Agreeableness reflects individual differences in concern with cooperation and social harmony. Agreeable individuals value getting along with others. They are considerate, friendly, generous, helpful and willing to compromise their interests with others. Agreeable people have an optimistic view of human nature. They believe people are basically honest, decent and trustworthy.

  Disagreeable individuals place self-interest above getting along with others. They are generally unconcerned with others' well-being, and therefore are unlikely to extend themselves for other people. Sometimes their scepticism about others' motives causes them to be suspicious, unfriendly, and uncooperative.

  Agreeableness is obviously advantageous for attaining and maintaining popularity. Agreeable people are better liked than disagreeable people. On the other hand, agreeableness is not useful in situations that require tough or absolute objective decisions. Disagreeable people can make excellent scientists, critics or soldiers.

- **Conscientiousness** is defined as the tendency to show self-discipline, act dutifully and aim for achievement. Conscientiousness concerns the way in which we control, regulate and direct our impulses. Impulses are not inherently bad; occasionally time constraints require a snap decision, and acting on our first impulse can be an effective response. Also, in times of play rather than work, acting spontaneously and impulsively can be fun. Impulsive individuals are seen by others as colourful, fun-to-be-with and zany. Conscientiousness includes the factor known as *Need for Achievement* (NAch).

  The benefits of high conscientiousness are obvious. Conscientious individuals avoid trouble and achieve high levels of success through purposeful planning and persistence. They are also positively regarded by others as intelligent and reliable. On the negative side, they can be compulsive perfectionists and workaholics. Furthermore, extremely conscientious individuals might be regarded as stuffy and boring. Unconscientious people may be criticized for their unreliability, lack of ambition, and failure to stay within the lines, but they will experience many short-lived pleasures and they will never be called stuffy.

- **Openness to experience** is defined as the appreciation for art, emotion, adventure and unusual ideas; and such individuals are after imaginative and curious. Openness to experience describes a dimension of cognitive style that distinguishes imaginative, creative people from down-to-earth, conventional people. Open people are intellectually curious, appreciative of art and sensitive to beauty. They tend to be, compared to closed people, more aware of their feelings. They tend to think and act in individualistic and nonconforming ways. People with low scores on openness to experience tend to have narrow, common interests. They prefer the plain, straightforward and obvious to the complex, ambiguous, and subtle. They may regard the arts and sciences with suspicion, regarding these endeavors as abstruse or of no practical use. Closed people prefer familiarity to novelty; they are conservative and resistant to change.

Openness is often presented as healthier or more mature by psychologists, who are often themselves open to experience. However, open and closed styles of thinking are useful in different environments. The intellectual style of the open person may serve a professor well, but research has shown that closed thinking is related to superior job performance in police work, sales, and a number of service occupations.

These traits are usually measured as percentile scores, with the average mark at 50 per cent; so, for example, a conscientiousness rating in the 80th percentile indicates a greater than average sense of responsibility and orderliness, while an extroversion rating in the 5th percentile indicates an exceptional need for solitude and quiet.

The following are some of the important characteristics of the five factors:

- First, the factors are dimensions, not types, so people vary continuously on them, with most people falling in between the extremes.
- Second, the factors are stable over a 45-year period beginning in young adulthood.
- Third, the factors and their specific facets are heritable (i.e., genetic), at least in part.
- Fourth, the factors probably had adaptive value in a prehistoric environment.
- Fifth, the factors are considered universal, having been recovered in languages as diverse as German and Chinese.
- Sixth, knowing one's placement on the factors is useful for insight and improvement through therapy.

Consequences of occupational stress

What consequences does stress have for workers? And for organizations? In today's world, organizations have to be able to give quick and effective responses to change, this pressure is passed on to the workers and creates a stressful situation at both the organizational and personal levels. A stressed organization is an organization where there is an imbalance between its objectives and its internal and external realities (corporate strategy, technology, human resources, culture, values, economic results, competitors, etc.). At the same time, the stressed worker suffers from an imbalance, in this case between his or her expectations and professional interest and the reality of his or her individual work conditions (responsibilities, autonomy and control, incentive programs, career plans and professional development, etc.).

According to the European Agency for Health and Safety at Work based in Bilbao (Spain), stress is a problem already affecting one-third of all EU workers. The European Agency has published a report regarding research on work-related stress, offering a general review of the most recent scientific conclusions on topics ranging from the measurement of stress, to strategies for coping with stress and risk management. A summary and the complete report are available online at http://agency.osha.eu.int/publications. The high level of work-related stress in European workplaces is the main challenge and reason for concern, not just in terms of its effects on workers' health, but also in terms of the economic costs and repercussions for companies and the social costs for European countries.

PERSONAL CONSEQUENCES

Not everyone feels the same degree of stress nor shows similar reactions to a specific type of stress factor. Obviously, the previous section, which describes different types of personalities suggest that some people are more prone to stress than others. If, for example, the demand is matched by the person's abilities, knowledge, health and personality, stress will tend to diminish, and there will be positive, stimulating signals which will let the person advance in the professional arena while achieving greater achievements in terms of personal, spiritual and material gratification. Depression, anxiety, irritability and somatic problems are the more typical manifestations of stress, as well as various forms of addictions (i.e. to nicotine, alcoholism, drugs and others). In terms of the physiological consequences of stress, researchers have detected an increase in the secretion of catecholamines (adrenaline and noradrenaline) and steroids, as well as an increase in blood pressure, all symptoms appear prior to the development of stomach ulcers and cardiovascular disease.

Physical Health Consequences

The symptomatology produced by occupational stress is, in great measure, psychosomatic and related to: migraines, gastrointestinal problems, virus-related processes, sleep disorders, dermatological problems, and so on. This leads to the problem being treated more often than not as a common illness and not as a work-related pathology.

Although Science has not been able to demonstrate a concrete connection between stress and disease in humans, this section presents various scientific views and explanations of hypothesized relationships between stress and disease. Taking together the thousands of papers and scientific articles published in various journals, disciplines and geographical locations, one can conclude that 70 to 80 per cent of health-related problems may be precipitated or aggravated by stress. Stress and illness in general has been studied with a focus on three subsystems: the endocrine subsystem, the immune subsystem, and the nervous subsystem.

Interesting to know

Being exposed to physical risk at work, the intensity of this risk, and flexible employment practices are the main cause of health problems for workers in the European Union. The most frequent, work-related health problems in the EU are:

- Backaches (mentioned by 33% of those surveyed)
- Stress (28%)
- Muscular pain in the shoulders and neck (23%)
- General fatigue (23%).

Source: *Ten Years of Work Conditions in the European Union*, The European Foundation for Improving Life and Work Conditions (EFILWC), 2001.

Borysenko has developed an interesting framework to connect stress and diseases,[10] and summary of the continuum proposed by Borysenko is exhibited in Table 4.1.

A word of caution: In order to understand the stress–disease/mind–body phenomenon, we need to consider individuals as greater than the sum of their physiological parts.

Table 4.1 Borysenko's framework connecting stress and disease

Autonomic dysregulation (overresponsive autonomic nervous system)	Immune dysregulation
Migraines	Infection (virus)
Peptic ulcers	Allergies
Irritable bowel syndrome	AIDS
Hypertension	Cancer
Coronary heart disease	Lupus
Asthma	Arthritis

In the workplace, the physical problems suffered by workers are easier to quantify than psychological effects, although both are equally important. Table 4.2 describes some of the pathologies which may be produced by stress.

Table 4.2 **Most frequent physical pathologies derived from stress**[11]

Gastrointestinal disorders	Peptic ulcer
	Functional dyspepsia
	Irritable bowel syndrome
	Ulcerous colitis
	Aerophagia
	Slow digestion
Cardiovascular disorders	High blood pressure
	Coronary disease (angina, myocardium)
	Arrhythmia
Respiratory disorders	Asthma
	Hyperventilation
	Dyspnoea
	Feeling pressure in the thorax
Endocrinal disorders	Hypoglycaemia
	Diabetes
	Hyperthyroidism
	Hypothyroidism
	Cushing syndrome
Sexual disorders	Impotence
	Premature ejaculation
	Vaginism
	Painful intercourse
	Alterations in the libido
Dermatological disorders	Itches
	Atypical dermatitis
	Excessive sweating
	Alopecia
	Trichotillomania
Muscular disorders	Tics and spasms
	Rigidity
	Muscle pain
	Alterations in muscular reflexes (hyperreflexia, hyporreflexia).
Others	Migraines
	Chronic pain
	Insomnia
	Immunological disorders (flu, herpes,...)
	Loss of appetite
	Rheumatoid arthritis

Interesting to know

According to the European Commission (Levi, 1993), approximately 30% of all Europeans have suffered from physical symptoms derived from stress. Stress (in all its forms, including burnout) is the second most important health problem relating to work in the European Union. In the former 15 member countries, the economic costs derived from these health problems total approximately 265 billion euros annually.

Source: European Foundation, 1998.

Stress, when accumulated and experienced over time, can cause serious physical diseases. Some research even suggests that stress can trigger cell mutations and produce cancer. Although cancer is multifactorial (genetic, eating habits, sedentary life, etc.) the impact of the psychological factors is non-negligible. In a similar manner to the exposure of certain chemicals causing cancer, so is the chronic exposure to the psychological work environment. Moreover, stress is also causing sleep deprivation that is known to reduce our immune function and expose us to a variety of disease contaminations. Figure 4.4 shows the relationships between stress and the immune system.

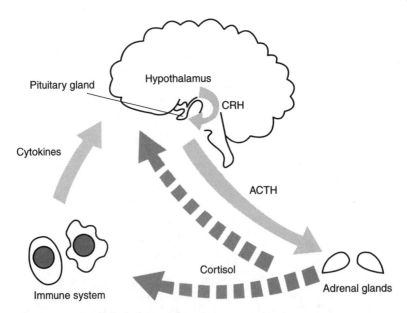

Figure 4.4 **Stress and the immune system at the molecular level**[12]

Stress promotes transcription of cytokines including pro-inflammatory IL-6, which increases the release of glucocorticoids and increases the severity of illness.[13] Catecholamine binding decreases IL-12 and IFN-γ production and increases IL-10; this causes a shift from TH1 cells to TH2 cells and the lack of TH1 cells causes a decrease in cell-mediated immune responses.

Studies also show that negative mood (anxiety, depression, hostility) characteristic of some people during acute stress, leads to fewer cytotoxic and suppressor T cells, and thus leads to more outbreaks of all forms of herpes.

Stress and its relation to ulcers is another recent discovery. Research suggests that 66 per cent of people under stress eat *more* than usual (*hyperphagic*) and eat fast. During prolonged stress digestion shuts down; there is decreased acid release, decreased mucus which protects the stomach, and decreased thickness of the stomach living.

But obviously not every person has the same proneness to develop certain diseases during stress. The importance of coping capacity is demonstrated in Figures 4.5a and 4.5b.

Mental Health Consequences

A large number of emotional disorders dealt with by primary healthcare centres mask cases of occupational stress. People suffering from stress habitually consult their healthcare centre more often than those who do not show this type of problem. These people are normally treated therapeutically for the disorders but not for the underlying stress. This situation, without a doubt, leads to short-term remission of some of the stress-related symptoms, though in the mid and/or long term the individual will either feel the same or worse than before.

Below is a list of some of the mental and emotional consequences of stress:

- *Irritability.* Being in a bad mood, irascible, and the person feeling like "snapping at the slightest provocation" may be the consequence of a case of chronic stress.

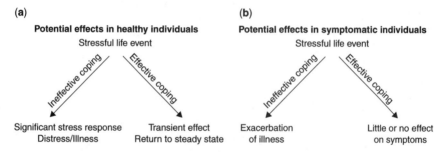

(a)

Potential effects in healthy individuals

Stressful life event

Ineffective coping / Effective coping

Significant stress response
Distress/Illness

Transient effect
Return to steady state

(b)

Potential effects in symptomatic individuals

Stressful life event

Ineffective coping / Effective coping

Exacerbation
of illness

Little or no effect
on symptoms

Figure 4.5 **Stress and coping capacity**

- *Emotional exhaustion.* The person feels exhausted, without the vital energy necessary to carry out daily activities, especially those outside of the office and related to the family (partner, children) and friends, among others.
- *Forgetting important things.* There are frequent lapses in memory, especially with important life events (wedding anniversary) or those related with people we are very close to (meeting with a child's teacher, calling a friend, etc.).
- *Wanting to radically change our lives.* A stressed person tends to have polarized and inflexible thoughts, limiting the ability to see things relatively. This makes the person tend to overexert himself to adapt to work or life in general. Feeling stressed implies wanting a radical change in life, partner, and profession, among other things. Stressful thoughts, such as "This can't go on" or "I need to separate", are common.
- *Repeatedly postponing planned actions.* A stressed individual tends to postpone the actions and tasks considered important. For example: "one of these days I'll give up smoking" or "I need to make more time to be with my kids". However, getting round to finding those days and making more time never materializes.
- *Sense of a lack of time.* People suffering from stress tend to feel that there isn't enough time to take on the tasks and objectives before them. This feeling makes them uncomfortable and unhappy with themselves. They may have a low appreciation of what they do as they focus more on what they haven't been able to finish rather than on what they've accomplished.
- *Cynicism and mistrust.* The stressed individual tends to be pessimistic, frustrated and suspicious towards others. This type of behavior is generally a consequence of repressed aggression within the individual.

ORGANIZATIONAL CONSEQUENCES

The effects of stress can be found not only on the personal level, but also within the organization. A prolonged situation of negative stress leads to a deterioration in the work environment, fewer and poorer interpersonal relationships, as well as a loss in productivity and job performance.

Interesting to know

- The European Foundation for Improving Life and Work Conditions (EFILWC) located in Dublin, highlighted in its 2000 report that the professional sectors

affected by the greatest psycho-social risk are: Public Administration, Education, Health, Restaurants and Hotels, Transportation, Commerce, and Defense.
- Scandinavian countries have been pioneers and efficient at studying work-related risk factors (occupational stress, moral harassment, burnout, etc.).
- In the Netherlands, the percentage of workers receiving disability compensation due to stress-related disorders rose from 21% to 50% between 1981 and 1999.

Below are some estimates of the possible costs and consequences of stress regarding the different indicators within the organization. It is well-known that the direct and indirect costs of work-related accidents are on the rise. Research carried out by the National Safety Council and the National Institute for Occupational Safety and Health (NIOSH) in the United States has revealed that between 75 per cent and 85 per cent of all industrial accidents are caused by workers' inability to cope with stress. For US industries, this represents a cost estimated at 3.2 billion dollars per year.

- According to a survey organized by the compensation board regarding compensation for work-related accidents, the number of compensation claims for work-related stress filed with the Work Accident Commissions across Canada stands at 9,000, with an associated average cost of 178 million dollars per year.
- The American Psychological Association claims that 43 per cent of adults suffer from stress.
- It is estimated that absenteeism and stress-related illness cost the British economy the equivalent of 10 per cent of its GDP, while in Scandinavia the figure ranges from 2.5 per cent in Denmark to 10 per cent in Norway.
- A survey carried out among various financial entities in Spain in 1992 by the Spanish trade union (Comisiones Obreras), revealed that more than 60 per cent of staff confessed feeling unmotivated; the workers who identified themselves as such showed above average values in terms of stress symptomatology, including headaches, insomnia, fatigue and so on, and at the same time demonstrated a high level of personal frustration with negative feelings in terms of their dreams and fulfilment.
- According to a third study on working conditions carried out by the European Foundation for Improving Life and Work Conditions, intimidation in the workplace is, at 47 per cent, the most frequent cause of stress suffered by workers and would explain the 34 per cent rate of absenteeism at work.

- A Mori poll of 112 top UK companies revealed that 65 per cent believed stress was a major factor in ill-health in their organizations. Every day 270,000 people take time off work for stress-related illness and absenteeism cost the UK £10.2 bn in 2001.

Although the precision of the above figures is subject to debate, the message is very clear: the cost of stress in the workplace is enormous, and, if opportune measures are not taken, there is no doubt that this cost will steadily rise. This is why any program focused on stress with the aim of reducing the costs of stress will be extremely beneficial for the company.

Interesting to know

Workplaces "getting more stressful"

Britain's workplaces are becoming increasingly stressful and few managers are accepting responsibility for the problem, a new survey has shown.

The report, commissioned by the UK's biggest private sector union, Amicus, has been released at the start of a TUC campaign to combat stress and bullying. The survey of 2,000 union health and safety representatives from across the economy found half believed stress was a bigger problem than five years ago, and a similar number said it had got worse in the last 12 months. Amicus said three out of four of the officials it surveyed had raised stress-related issues with their employers, but only one in three firms accepted responsibility of tackling the problem. Most employers would rather deal with the symptoms rather than the causes, with few offering to reduce hours or introduce flexible work programs the survey found.

Source: http://news.bbc.co.uk/1/hi/business/2325307.stm

Chapter postscript

In this chapter we have summarized the main causes of work-related stress and their consequences and effects at the personal and organizational levels. Without a doubt, personal and organizational self-esteem are related to different levels of stress. When the working environment fosters an optimal level of activation, it helps promote self-esteem. On the other hand, inhibitive organizational environments provoke a loss of personal and organizational self-esteem.

We have also discussed different types of personalities in order to understand how people interpret the work environment and how they react to it. All personality types are connected to the theme of self-esteem, which is

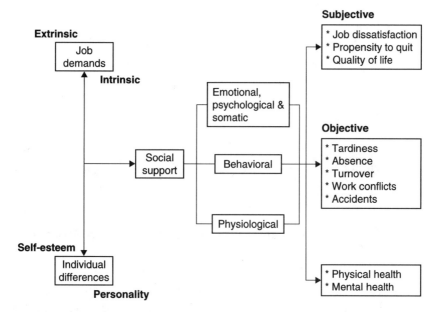

Figure 4.6 **A prototype model of stress (antecedents and consequences)**

a cardinal concept in this book. Self-esteem at work is directly related to the clarity and precision with which the organization is capable of defining and communicating its objectives, values and cultural principles, among others. It is important to understand how certain organizational contexts are perceived by the workers as risk factors for work-related stress.

Figure 4.6 provides an overall view on how to link the antecedents while the individual differences (that is, personality and social support) and the consequences, while Figure 4.7 illustrates the interactions and the dynamics of the aetiology of stress consequences.

Three concepts are important in understanding the relationships described in Figure 4.6:

1 Stress is an interaction between individuals and any source of demand (stressor) within their environment.
2 A stressor is the object or event that the individual perceives to be disruptive. Stress results from the perception that the demands exceed one's capacity to cope with the said demand. The interpretation or appraisal of stress is considered an intermediate step in the relationship between a given stressor and the individual's response to it.
3 Appraisals are determined by the values, goals, individual commitment, as personal resources (e.g., income, family, self-esteem), and coping strategies that employees bring to the situation.

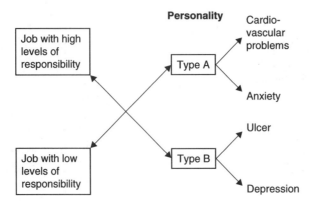

Figure 4.7 **Antecedents, personality and consequences: an illustration**

Reciprocally, elevated stress levels in an organization are associated with increased turnover, absenteeism, sickness, reduced productivity and low morale.

Extrapolating from the Person–Environment (P–E) Fit model, developed in the early 1970s by researchers at the University of Michigan,[14] Figure 4.7 states that the negative consequences of stress develop when there is a discrepancy between the motives of the person (i.e. personality) and the supplies of the environment (job), or between the demands of the job and the abilities of the person to meet those demands. In the figure only one job dimension is illustrated (i.e. level of job responsibility) in its interaction with one personality trait (type A/B behavior). The results suggest the following:

1   A type-A personality combined with relatively high job responsibility constitutes a relatively good fit, and therefore no negative stress consequences are expected. However, if a type-A person will be placed in a job with no or low job responsibility, this will increase the likelihood of misfit, which may result in physical diseases connecting with the hyperactive system (adrenaline, noradrenalin) and can eventually develop into hypertension and cardiovascular problems. At the mental end, this type of misfit can lead to high levels of anxiety.

2   A type-B personality, by contrast, placed in a relatively low responsibility job, will lead to a good fit. On the other hand, a type-B person placed in a job with a high level of responsibility will produce a situation of misfit. The latter will lead to different outcomes. The type-B misfit will increase the likelihood of the person to develop peptic ulcers (on the physical health side) or depression (on the mental health side).

Thus, understanding the origins and consequences of stress is critical in one decision (in an individual form or organizational form) to do something about it. This chapter was intended to create an awareness of the real threat to one's life (and organizational life) if stress is not addressed both in a life context and in a work context. Some managers do not feel stress themselves, but in their acts they generate stress to other people (colleagues and subordinates) working with or/for them and producing situations of misfits; this chapter might, I hope, educate, provoke and elicit instrumental remedies on the part of those managers. Trust, proximity, clarity and precision are all values which favour the construction of "healthy" working environments, reducing stress and professional burnout among workers. We will learn about reducing stress and burnout in the remaining chapters.

Exercise: a quick stress audit[15]

Please read the following questionnaires. If you have experienced a sign or a symptom described within the last three months, place a check mark in the box.

Psychological symptoms

Inability to concentrate ☐

Not thinking clearly ☐

Difficulty in making simple decisions ☐

Loss of self-confidence ☐

Being vague or forgetful ☐

Frustration ☐

Feeling out of control and helpless ☐

Depression ☐

Difficulty making rational judgements ☐

Getting things out of perspective ☐

Undue mental tiredness ☐

Feeling there's never enough time ☐

Diminished sex drive ☐

Loss of sense of humor ☐

More arguments with spouse or children ☐

Emotional symptoms

Feelings of anxiety or worry ☐

Irritability ☐

Angry outbursts ☐

Feelings of guilt ☐

Feelings of hostility ☐

Defensive and over-sensitive to criticism ☐

Feeling isolated from colleagues and friends ☐

Fear of rejection ☐

Fear of failure ☐

Fear of success or promotion ☐

Panicky feelings or panic attacks ☐

Nightmares or disturbing dreams ☐

Feelings of impending doom ☐

Feelings of worthlessness ☐

Feelings of hopelessness ☐

Feel lonely or sad ☐

Physical signs

(Place a mark in the box if you experience the following symptoms

    frequently or severely) ☐

Sweaty, clammy hands ☐

Shaking hands ☐

Knot in the stomach ☐

Butterflies in the stomach ☐

Hyperventilation ☐

Erratic breathing ☐

Palpitations ☐

Rapid pulse ☐

Dizziness ☐

Faintness ☐

Ringing in the ears ☐

Difficulty in swallowing ☐

Lump in the throat ☐

Sore throat or hoarseness ☐

Enlarged glands in the neck ☐

High-pitched voice ☐

Talking faster than usual ☐

Jelly legs ☐

Cramps ☐

Restless leg syndrome ☐

Physical tiredness ☐

Feeling of being drained ☐

Insomnia ☐

Waking up in the middle of the night or too early ☐

Still tired after a night's sleep ☐

Headache ☐

Dry mouth ☐

Muscle tension ☐

Tight neck or shoulders ☐

Teeth grinding ☐

Sexual difficulties ☐

Stiff jaw ☐

Constipation ☐

Diarrhea ☐

Nausea ☐

Abdominal pain or indigestion ☐

Loss of appetite ☐

Excess hunger ☐

High or low blood pressure ☐

Frequent urination ☐

Women only:

Difficult menstruation ☐

Premenstrual syndrome ☐

Menopausal or pre-menopausal difficulties ☐

Men only:

Weak or slow urine stream ☐

Prostate trouble ☐

Trouble with erections ☐

Behavioral signs

Smoke more than usual ☐

Drink more alcohol than is generally

accepted is good for health ☐

Eat more sweets, chocolate or pastries than usual ☐

Take antidepressants, tranquilizers, sleeping pills, narcotics,

pain relievers, marijuana or other street drugs ☐

Eat less than usual ☐

Eat more than usual ☐

Bingeing on foods or alcohol ☐

Taking laxatives or purging to control weight ☐

Becoming a workaholic with no time for

relaxation or pleasurable activities ☐

Absenteeism from work ☐

Avoidance of certain people or places ☐

Withdrawal from social gatherings ☐

Obsessive or compulsive behavior; for example, checking and

re-checking you have locked the doors, switched the lights off,

washing your hands over and over again, etc., pulling your hair out,

e.g. hair on head, eyebrows, arms, etc. ☐

Results and interpretation

(A) *Psychological manifestations*. If you marked more than 8 symptoms in this category, you are likely to suffer from significant stress and you manifest it psychologically. If you marked between 5–7 you are experiencing medium-high stress, and below 4 is more or less normal.

(B) *Emotional symptoms*. If you marked more than 8 symptoms in this category , you are likely to suffer from significant stress and you manifest it emotionally. If you marked between 5–7 you are experiencing medium-high stress, and below 4 is more or less normal.

(C) *Physical signs*. If you marked more than 9 signs in this category, you are likely to suffer from significant stress and you show physical signs of it. Between 5–8 marks medium-high stress, and below 4 is more or less normal.

(D) *Behavioral signs*. If you marked more than 9 signs in this category, you are likely to suffer from significant stress and you show physical signs of it. Between 5–8 marks is medium-high stress, and below 4 is more or less normal.

Note: Repeat the same audit but answer the same questions for the three previous months (if you can remember). If the patterns of your responses are similar it means that you are suffering from chronic stress, and if you marked many categories it indicates your incapacity to manage the stress in your work/life. It also means that you might be better off to consult a health professional who may help you manage your stress and reduce your chances of serious health problems.

REFERENCES

1   Holmes, and Rahe, R. (1967). "Holmes-Rahe Life Changes Scale", *Journal of Psychosomatic Research*, 11:213–18.

2   Dolan, S.L. and Arsenault, A. (1980). *Stress, santé et rendement au travail* (Montreal: University of Montreal, Press).

3   Friedman, M. and Rosenman, R.H. (1974). *Type A. Behavior and your Heart?* (New York). Also: Rosenman, R.H. Friedman, M. Straus R. *et al.* (1964) "A Predictive Study of Coronary Heart Disease: The Western Collaborative Group Study," *Journal of the American Medical Association*, 15–22.

4   Rotter, J.B. (1966). "Generalized Expectancies for Internal versus External Control of Reinforcement", *Psychological Monographs*, 80. (whole issue no. 609).

5   Dolan, S.L. and Arsenault, A. (1984). "Stress, Personality and Samples of Work Attitudes and Behavior: Analysis, Beyond a Single Level of Aggregation", in R. Burke (ed.), *Current Issues in Occupational Stress: Research and Intervention* (Toronto: University of Toronto Press): 53–78; Van Ameringen, M.R., Arsenault, A. and Dolan, S.L. (1988). "Intrinsic Job Stress as Predictor of Diastolic Blood Pressure among Female Hospital Workers", *Journal of Occupational Medicine*, 30(2): 93–7; Dolan, S.L., van Ameringen, M.R. and Arsenault, A. (1992). "The Role of Personality and

Social Support in the Etiology of Workers' Stress and Psychological Strain", *Industrial Relations* (Canada), 47(1).

6   Kobasa, S. (1982). "The Hardy Personality toward a Social Psychology of Stress and Health" in Sanders, G.S. and Suls, J. (ed.). *The Social Psychology of Health and Illness* (Hillsdale, NJ: Erlbaum).

7   To learn more about the resilient personality, visit: http://www.hardiness-institute.com

8   Zuckerman, M. (1971). "Dimensions of Sensation-Seeking", *Journal of Consulting and Clinical Psychology*, 36: 45–52.

9   Zuckerman, M. (1979). *Sensation Seeking: Beyond the optimal level of arousal.* (Hillsdale, NJ: Erlbaum); Zuckerman, M. (1994). *Behavioral Expressions and Bicycle Bases of Sensation Seeking* (New York: Cambridge University Press).

10   Borysenko, J. (1988). *Minding the Body, Mending the Mind* (New York: Random House).

11   Ministerio de Trabajo y Asuntos Sociales. Instituto Nacional de Seguridad e Higiene en el Trabajo. *Estrés laboral.* Informational documents.

12   Figure borrowed from: http://www.nih.gov/news/WordonHealth/oct2000/stressfigure.htm

13   Cohen, Sheldon, *et al.* (1999). "Psychological Stress, Cytokine Production, and Severity of Upper Respiratory Illness." Psychosomatic Medicine. March/April; 61(2): 175–180; O'Leary. (1990). "Stress, Emotion, and Human Immune Function." *Psychological Bulletin.* Nov; 108(3): 363–82; Padgett, David and Glaser Ronald, (2003). "How stress influences the immune response." *Trends in Immunology.* Aug; 24(8): 444–448.

14   Caplan, R.D., Cobb, S., French, J.R.P., Van Harrison, R., Pinneau, S.R. (1975). *Job demands and worker health.* Cincinnati, OH: National Institute for Occupational Safety and Health. (Publication No. 75–168); French JRP, Caplan R.D., Van Harrison R. (1982). *The mechanisms of job stress and strain.* (New York: Wiley); Van Harrison R. (1978). "Person-environment fit and job stress". In Cooper, C.L. and Payne, R. (eds), *Stress at work* (Chichester: Wiley).

15   The stress audit is a modified version and adaptation of the original measures used by Dolan and Arsenault in several studies conducted during the 1980s and the 1990s. For more details consult: Arsenault, A. and Dolan, S.L. (1983). *Le stress au travail et ses effects sur l'individu et l'organisation.* Notes et rapports scientifiques et techniques. L`institut de recherche en santé et en sécurité du travail du Québec; Arsenault, A. and Dolan, S.L. (1983). "The role of Personality, Occupation and Organization in Understanding the Relationship between Job Stress, Performance and Absenteeism", *Journal of Occupational Psychology*, 56(2): 227–40; Dolan, S.L. and Arsenault, A. (1984). "Job Demands Related Cognitions and Psychosomatic Ailments", in R. Schwarzer (ed.), *The Self in Anxiety, Stress and Depression* (Amsterdam: North-Holland Elsevier Science Publishers) 265–82; Arsenault, A. and Dolan, S.L. and van Ameringen, M.R., "Stress and Mental Strain in Hospital Work: Exploring the Relationship beyond Personality", *Journal of Organizational Behavior*, 12: 1991: 483–93.

5 Individual Strategies for Managing Occupational Stress

"I forget what I hear, I memorize what I see, and I learn what I do."
(Confucius)

"We can only respect others when we respect ourselves. We can only
give, when we give to ourselves. We can only love, when we love
ourselves."

(Abraham Maslow)

Introduction

It has been repeatedly demonstrated that work-related stress results in as
many painful consequences for individuals as for organizations. For this reason it is necessary for us to learn to prevent stress or, at least, to know how

to control and reduce it. There is no universal formula to fight stress. It is true that since Hans Selye introduced the term stress[1] in 1949, we now know much more about this phenomenon, its causes and consequences, but nevertheless statistics also indicate that more and more people are affected by stress-related problems.

"It is necessary for all the interested parties to recognise that occupational stress is a real risk and one that is deeply rooted in the workplace. Industrialists, workers and governments will have to step up preventive measures in this field. Good stress management practices in the workplace are required for tackling this ever-increasing problem."
(Anna Diamantopoulou, European Commissioner for Employment and Social Affairs)

Interesting to know

Several years ago Lisa Whaley, sitting in her Mercedes, set fire to her car to put an end to it all. The break-up of her marriage, having to look after her teenage daughter, an ill father and a highly-demanding job to which she was devoted like a "workaholic", led her to neglect her own health and brought her close to committing the unthinkable. Today, however, with her life back on track, Lisa Whaley documents the true dangers of burnout at work in her book *Reclaiming My Soul from the Lost and Found.*

1   Be yourself and don't try to be somebody you are not. Success does not depend so much on who we are but on what we do. As we get older, pretending to be somebody or trying to create a different personality for ourselves can take an immense amount of energy and it leads us inevitably to failure. Accept who you are, who you are not and who you will never be.

2   Set yourself realistic goals that are not in conflict with your personal values. Our goals are going to guide us in the right direction and should not get in the way of our individual standards and priorities. Each person must define their own success and not allow other people or society to determine it for them. We should make sure that our goals are our own and not those that others expect us to have.

3   Take charge and be responsible for your own professional career and your own life. Be proactive and not reactive in personal matters. Don't allow actions and external events to dictate your decisions. Measure your progress with respect to the realistic goals that you have drawn up. When changes and disagreements arise, adjust your goals accordingly, and always in line with these changes.

4   Develop abilities that are valued inside and outside your present job. Today's corporate environments demand continuous development of new skills and for employees to be ready to use them inside and outside the company.

5   Have supportive relationships in your personal and professional life and use them. Relationships are a powerful tool. Do not be afraid to ask people for help. Have at least 2 people who can support you in your personal life and 2 people in your professional life. Use them. Nobody will be able to help you if they are unaware you need their help. Sometimes we don't get what we want out of life because we don't give ourselves the time to ask for it.

6   Make time for yourself. Set it aside in your schedule and make sure that you have enough time for relaxation. Remember that you are the most important person in your own life. Whether a hobby, exercise, meditation or simply reading, take time to enjoy your own company. We cannot take care of others if we do not take care of ourselves first. If you think that you do not have time for yourself, then give something up for your own sake.

7   Enjoy life. Have fun. Nobody is guaranteed they will be here tomorrow. Do not let work take over your life. Whatever you want to do in life, do it now. Nobody has ever said at his or her funeral, "I'd like to have spent more time at work." You are replaceable at work but irreplaceable for your family and the people who love you.

Source: Whaley, L. J. *Stress Management: Top 7 Success Strategies to Avoid Burnout.* Lisa J. Whaley is President of Life Work Synergy, LLC, an organization dedicated to revitalizing and motivating individuals to be the best they can be in every dimension of their lives – physical, emotional and spiritual. http://top7business.com/?Stress-Management:-Top-7-Success-Strategies-To-Avoid-Burnout&id=727

© 1998–2006 Top7Business.com.

In the following pages we discuss some of the most effective individual strategies for tackling stress. Nevertheless, and in contrast to what has been held as fact for many years, we consider that these are not enough. Increasingly, more data are being revealed confirming the enormous relationship that stress has with organizational and work factors, for instance: organizational culture, the type of structure adopted by the company, the leadership style exerted, and how jobs are designed, amongst others. *Is it enough for workers to practice relaxation techniques and/or improve time management?* We are inclined to consider that they are necessary but insufficient, since these types of actions imply involvement only at an individual level, whilst stress also has an organizational component.

Strategies to manage stress connected with physiological and motor characteristics

What can we do when stress has already begun to show? In the first place, we might try to control it or, at least, to have the "perception of control" over it. To be stressed means to perceive that we have no control over what surrounds us and even over ourselves. When we feel relaxed and happy, we have the sensation of exerting greater control on the things around us. On the other hand, to try to have everything always under control can be a self-defense mechanism behind which is a lack of self-confidence and security in oneself.

Some people have the type of personality profile in which they like to control all the inputs that take place around them (for example, clients, boss, co-workers, children, partner, business trips, stockmarket decisions, holidays, etc.). At the same time, it is usually very difficult for them to carry out *de-stressing* daily activities, such as communicating with their partner, practicing a sport, turning off their mobile phone, and so on. However, there is another personality profile of people who can live *happily* without this excessive need for control. Who will be more stressed? In all probability, the person who most resembles the first profile.

Not everybody has the same need to control their surroundings and themselves. Rotter[2] formulated the concept of internal and external locus of control. The person with an internal locus of control tends to always want to dominate the situation that confronts him, and considers that this situation will depend on the decisions, attitudes and behavior that he adopts. In contrast, the person with an external locus will believe in luck, causality, destiny or the power of others. Let's imagine how a person with an internal locus of control would react to a stressful situation. What would he do? Most likely he would tend to over-activate and launch into several activities to deal with the situation. However, a person with a more external locus of control, may instead become inhibited and avoid the situation, given that "it is the outcome of bad luck, chance, and that nothing can be done about it". Probably, higher levels of stress would be found in the first profile as opposed to the second profile. This suggests that those who stress most are people with a certain degree of commitment to the work they do, and who are dedicated and motivated to improving themselves every day.

How many days like this one would a person be able to put up with? Tolerance to stress is related to the amount of stress that a person is able to put up with without it significantly affecting normal functioning. A person with a high level of stress tolerance will normally show symptoms of the negative consequences of stress much later than someone with a low level of tolerance. What does the tolerance level depend on? There is an individual component, related overall to personality characteristics (levels of anxiety, impulsiveness, reflection, etc.). However, it is also related to socio-cultural and organizational factors, as we shall see further on, factors on which we can also try to act.

Table 5.1 shows some of the strategies for managing stress proposed by some of the top international scholars in the field.

Table 5.1 **Strategies to confront occupational stress**

Burke (1978)[3] categorized the behaviors for tackling stressful situations into 5 groups:

1   speaking to other people,
2   working harder and longer,
3   changing to a free-time activity,
4   adopting a problem-solving approach, and
5   moving away from the stressful situation.

Dewe et al. (1998)[4] came up with 4 types of strategies:

1   targeting the source of the stress,
2   expressing feelings and looking for support,
3   doing non-work-related activities, and
4   passive attempts at hoping the situation will go away.

Parasuraman and Alutto (1984)[5] distinguished between adaptive and non-adaptative answers to tackling stress:

●   In the first category are included: planning, organizing, prioritizing tasks, and getting support from others.
●   In the second category are: working harder but making more mistakes; and making unrealistic promises and avoiding supervision.

The type of approach developed in the Organizational Stress Indicator (Cooper et al., 1988)[6] distinguishes six types of approach:

1   social support,
2   strategies referring to the task,
3   logic,
4   family and work relationships,
5   time, and
6   implication.

RELAXATION TECHNIQUES

Relaxation techniques are a very highly sought-after tool in present-day society where the stress and fast pace of modern life is a source of psychological disorders for a large part of the population. Relaxation, a classic technique in psychology, is still being widely used as an end in itself as well as a means of complementing other types of therapies. Research has demonstrated the effectiveness of relaxation techniques (including progressive muscle relaxation, meditation, hypnosis and autogen training) in the treatment of many problems related to tension, such as insomnia, essential hypertension, headaches brought on by tension, bronchial asthma and tension in general.

Relaxation techniques are used as a means to alleviate the symptoms of stress; nevertheless, they can hardly be considered to be a radical treatment in and of themselves for the causes of stress. If stress is generated by the alteration of an individual's subjective perception of his work, it is therefore necessary to work on the perception or the idea that this individual has of his work. If, on the contrary, a work-related problem does in fact exist, the individual is of little importance, and there will always be adaptation problems; in this situation it will be necessary to analyse the job, its content and its context.

There are many different types of relaxation techniques. Nevertheless, not all of them are suitable for everybody. Each person will have to choose the relaxation technique that is best-suited to his or her personality traits. And so, for example, techniques involving muscle relaxation will be appropriate for those people who have considerable muscle tension derived from stress.

Two of the most widely-known relaxation techniques are Jacobson's Progressive Relaxation technique, and Schultz' Autogenous Training.

Progressive Relaxation (Jacobson)[7]

At the beginning of the 20th century, Edmund Jacobson conceived a relaxation method that was intended to induce a state of mental calmness as a result of progressively suppressing muscular tension. This method introduces learning how to progressively relax all parts of the body. However, the amount of hours proposed by Jacobson for learning how to use the progressive relaxation technique is a serious limitation in terms of applying the technique.

> Jacobson ... discovered that by systematically tensing and relaxing several muscle groups and learning to take note of and to distinguish between the resulting sensations of tension and relaxation, a person can eliminate muscular contractions almost completely, and experience a sensation of deep relaxation. The culmination of his research was *Progressive Relaxation* (1938), a theoretical description of his theory and procedures. From 1936 to the 1960s, Jacobson continued his research at the Laboratory of Clinical Physiology in Chicago. From 1962 onwards, the basic relaxation procedure included fifteen muscle groups. Each group was treated in daily sessions that lasted from one to nine hours, before carrying on with the next group, a total of 56 sessions of systematic training.[8]

Autogenous Training (Schultz)[9]

From 1912 onwards, Schultz worked on the principles of autogenous training, based on his observations on the use of hypnosis, which he mastered perfectly. The denomination of autogenous training was etymologically based on the Greek words *autos* (oneself) and *gen* (to happen), and could be translated as: an exercise or training, developed from the individual's own "self" and which shapes this "self".

According to Schultz:

> The principle on which the method is based consists of producing a general transformation in the subject under study by means of using certain physiological and rational exercises (heaviness exercise, heat exercise, pulsation exercise, respiratory exercise, abdominal regulation) and which, in analogy with the oldest exogenous hypnotic practices, enables the subject to obtain identical results to those obtained by the real suggestive states.

YOGA, MEDITATION AND OTHER RELAXATION TECHNIQUES

Yoga is a broad term for a series of practices that were developed over several millennia to bring practitioners into a state of wholeness and completeness. The sanskrit word *yoga*, which literally means "to unite", has many branches, including *Hatha Yoga*, which consists of concentration techniques, breathing exercises, dietary guidelines, and a series of stationary or moving poses – also called *asanas*. These body movements are what we commonly refer to today when we use the word "yoga".

Yoga postures balance the different systems of the body, including the central nervous system, the endocrine (or glandular) system, and the digestive system. By slowing down the mental activity, and by gently stretching the body and massaging the internal organs, yoga creates a climate of dynamic peacefulness within. This relaxing and rejuvenating experience momentarily removes us from involvement with the stressors in our lives – our "to-do" lists, unresolved issues from the past, or worries of the future. By practicing yoga on a regular basis, we build up a natural response to stress, and bring the relaxed state more and more into our daily lives.

The health benefits of yoga are tremendous. Feeling better physically counters the effects of stress. Yoga, according to advocates of this method, claim that it produces the following physical health benefits:

- improves flexibility and muscle joint mobility
- strengthens and tones muscles
- increases stamina
- relief from back pain
- increases vitality and improves brain function
- improves digestion and elimination
- decreases cholesterol and blood sugar levels
- increases circulation
- boosts immune response

The history of meditation goes back even further than that of Hatha Yoga, with its origins beginning around 3,000 BCE. Meditation evolved as a way for the ancient spiritual seers – known in India as *Rishis* – to gain direct knowledge of the nature of Ultimate Reality. Today, meditation is recognized for its myriad health benefits, and is widely practiced as a way to counteract stress. Meditation brings together all the energies of the mind and focuses them on a chosen point: a word, a sound, a symbol, an image that evokes comfort, or one's own breathing. It is typically practiced in a quiet, clean environment in a seated posture with the eyes closed.

As with yoga, a regular practice of meditation conditions a person to bring the meditative state into daily life. Holistic-online.com reports that "hormones and other biochemical compounds in the blood indicative of stress tend to decrease during (meditation) practice. These changes also stabilize over time, so that a person is actually less stressed biochemically during daily activity."

In meditation there is both *effort* and *passive participation*. The practitive continually brings attention back to a chosen focus (effort), and simply becomes a *witness* of all that transpires (passive participation) – incorporating thoughts, sensory input, bodily sensations, and external stimulus into the meditation experience. The result of centring the mind in this way is a corresponding calming and relaxing of the body, down to the cellular level, providing stress reduction.

Herbert Benson developed a technique called **the Relaxation Response**, which makes the basic steps of meditation easy to understand and apply. In his website, the following steps are offered as a simple way to begin practicing meditation:[10]

1 Pick a focus word, short phrase, or prayer that is firmly rooted in your belief system, such as "one", "peace", "The Lord is my shepherd", "Hail Mary full of grace", or "shalom".
2 Sit quietly in a comfortable position.
3 Close your eyes.
4 Relax your muscles, progressing from your feet to your calves, thighs, abdomen, shoulders, head and neck.
5 Breathe slowly and naturally, and as you do, say your focus word, sound, phrase, or prayer silently to yourself as you exhale.
6 Assume a passive attitude. Don't worry about how well you're doing. When other thoughts come to mind, simply say to yourself, "Oh well", and gently return to your repetition.
7 Continue for 10 to 20 minutes.
8 Do not stand immediately. Continue sitting quietly for a minute or so, allowing other thoughts to return. Then open your eyes and sit for another minute before rising.
9 Practice the technique once or twice daily. Good times to do this are before breakfast and before dinner.

BIOFEEDBACK

Biofeedback (biological feedback) is a technique that, with the aid of detectors placed on various organs or different parts of the body, enables the individual to perceive signals by sight or sound. Perceiving these signals allows the individual to control a function that would normally evade his voluntary control. The objective of the training in biofeedback is to get the subject to process the biological data he receives and use them to gain control over specific processes and biological parameters.

There are three main approaches to biofeedback:

- *Skin temperature methods.* Adrenaline diverts blood from the body surface to the core of the body, in preparation for response to danger. As less warm blood is going to the surface, skin temperature drops.
- *Skin electrical activity methods.* When you are under stress you sweat more. Skin that is damp (sweating) conducts electricity more effectively than skin that is dry. These methods of biofeedback measure the amount of electricity conducted between two electrodes on the skin.
- *Muscle electrical activity.* These methods measure the electrical activity of muscles under the surface of the skin. This is useful in measuring the tension of these muscles.

These techniques have been the object of considerable criticism and occupy a certain position in the psychosomatic treatment of the consequences derived from stress. As such, in certain cases, migraines respond well to biofeedback treatment, and results in individuals under treatment reducing their arterial tension by using the same type of technique.

HUMOR AND LAUGHTER THERAPY

Is there a correlation between stress, particularly negative perceptions and emotions, and disease? The premise of humor therapy is that if negative

> **A smile is the shortest distance between two people.**
>
> **Victor Borge**

thoughts can result in illness and disease, positive thoughts should do the opposite and enhance health.

Researchers at the University of California have been studying the effects of laughter on the immune system. To date their published studies have shown that laughing lowers blood pressure, reduces stress hormones, increases muscle flexion, and boosts immune function by raising levels of infection-fighting T-cells, disease-fighting proteins called

Gamma-interferon and B-cells, which produce disease-destroying anti-bodies. Laughter also triggers the release of endorphins, the body's nat-ural painkillers, and produces a general sense of well-being.[11]

Laughing is aerobic, providing a workout for the diaphragm and increasing the body's ability to use oxygen. Experts believe that, when used as an adjunct to conventional care, laughter can reduce pain and aid the healing process. For one thing, laughter offers a powerful distraction from pain. For example, in a study published in the *Journal of Holistic Nursing*, patients were told one-liners after surgery and before painful medication was administered. Those exposed to humor perceived less pain when compared to patients who didn't get a dose of humor as part of their therapy.

Steps to initiate humor therapy may include the following elements:

- learn not to take yourself too seriously;
- find one humorous thing a day;
- work to improve your imagination and creativity;
- learn to hyperexaggerate when telling a story;
- build a humor library;
- find a host of varied humor venues;
- access your humor *network*; and
- boost your *self-esteem* daily.

Interesting to know

The value of humor has been confirmed to the point that many hospitals and ambulatory care centers now have incorporated special rooms where materials – and sometimes people – are there to help make people laugh. Materials include movies, audio and videotapes, books, games and puzzles for patients of every age. Movies and TV shows by popular comedians from Laurel and Hardy to Bob Hope and Bob Newhart, humorous songs, the joke of the day on the Internet, the one-paragraph jokes and funny stories from the *Reader's Digest*, all have value in helping patients who would otherwise have little to laugh about.

A hospital in North Carolina created a "laughmobile" that visits bedridden patients. Many hospitals throughout the USA now use volunteer groups who visit patients with carts full of humor devices, including slapstick items such as water pistols and rubber chickens. They visit patients who are fighting cancer and other serious illnesses, providing an oasis of laughter during an otherwise difficult time.

Source: http://www.phoenix5.org/humor/HumorTherapyACS.html

Does Humor really help? In the 1960s, Norman Cousins, then editor of the *Saturday Review*, an influential intellectual magazine, returned from a visit to Moscow. He became suddenly ill and was hospitalized in the US. With high fever, severe pain and increasing difficulty in moving about, his doctors couldn't figure out what was wrong.

Cousins decided to leave the hospital and try a unique approach to medical treatment. He checked into a hotel and began watching some of his favourite Marx Brothers movies and Candid Camera TV episodes. In short, he deliberately tried to use laughter as medicine. The pain eventually disappeared. Cousins wrote a book about the experience, and people around the world shared his story of using laughter to his benefit.[12]

Despite this interesting story and the relief that Cousins received from humor, there is no scientific evidence that the laughter was responsible for Cousins' cure. Scientists today believe that, even though humor cannot cure disease, it has profound physical and psychological benefits. As with so many mind–body situations, humor provides relief from worry. In so doing, it relaxes and reduces stress. Endorphins are released. The entire process is helpful, and it can enhance the quality of life.

VITAMIN C INTAKE AND BOOSTING THE IMMUNE SYSTEM

According to the Nobel Prize-winner Linus Pauling, vitamin C is one of the best remedies to fight stress as it works directly on boosting the immune system. There has been more research about the immune-boosting effects of vitamin C than perhaps any other nutrient. Pauling asserts that vitamin C (also known as ascorbic acid or sodium ascorbate or calcium ascorbate) is involved in a great number of biochemical reactions in the human body. Two of its major interactions are in potentiating the immune system and aiding the synthesis of the protein collagen, which is a very important substance that holds together the human body. Collagen strengthens the blood vessels, the skin, the muscles and the bones. You cannot make collagen without vitamin C.

Vitamin C increases the production of infection-fighting white blood cells and antibodies and increases levels of interferon, the antibody that coats cell surfaces, preventing the entry of viruses. Vitamin C reduces the risk of cardiovascular disease by raising levels of HDL (good) cholesterol while lowering blood pressure and interfering with the process by which fat is converted to plaque in the arteries. As an added perk, persons whose diets are higher in vitamin C have lower rates of colon, prostate and breast cancer. Pauling developed his vitamin C theory extrapolating from animal food consumption. Most animals, except humans, monkeys and apes, manufacture vitamin C. They don't rely on vitamin pills or on foods – they make vitamin C in their liver in amounts proportional to body weight. For an adult man the proportion turns out to be on the average about 10 or 12 grams (12,000 mg) a day. That's 200 times the recommended dietary allowance (RDA) – 200 times the amount people get in an ordinary diet! This is why Pauling suggests that we should be getting 200 times the amount of vitamin C that the Food and Nutrition Board recommends. The RDA, 60 mg, is far too small and indicates the importance of taking vitamin C supplements.

There is some controversy over Pauling's theory in general, and the quantity of vitamin intake. In the 1960s, Pauling published his theory on vitamin C and the common cold. The "Establishment" quickly branded him a "Quack" while suggesting he remain a chemist, for which he received a Nobel Prize. When he suggested that vitamin C had efficacy with cancer, the "Establishment" as well as the mainstream media considered it nonsense. They demeaned and vilified the altruistic Pauling for years afterwards.

Lipoprotein(a) "small a" or Lp(a) is a variant of the so-called "bad" LDL cholesterol. Lp(a) is a "sticky" substance in the blood that Pauling and his colleagues believe is the lipid that begins the process of forming atherosclerotic plaques in heart disease. The 1985 Nobel Prize in medicine was awarded for the discovery of the cholesterol binding sites. The so-called *Lysine binding sites*. We now know that it is Lp(a) and not ordinary cholesterol which binds to form plaque.

Briefly, Lp(a) has lysine (and proline) receptors. We can think of a chemical receptor as a simple lock and key. Only one key (e.g. lysine) will fit into the lock (receptor on the Lp(a) molecule). There may be multiple receptors on the molecule, but once they are all filled up with keys (lysine or proline) the Lp(a) molecule looses its ability to bind with any more "keys". When all the Lp(a) locks have keys, Lp(a) will no longer be able to create plaque.

Once Linus Pauling learned that Lp(a) has receptors for lysine, he knew how to counter the atherosclerosis process chemically. His invention, the "Pauling Therapy",[13] is to increase the concentration of this essential and non-toxic amino acid (and proline) in the blood serum. Lysine and proline supplements increase the concentration of free lysine and proline in the blood. The higher the concentration of the free lysine (and proline) in the blood, the more likely it is that Lp(a) molecules will bind with this lysine, rather than the lysine strands that have been exposed by cracks in blood vessels, or the other lysine that has been attracted to the Lp(a) already attached to the blood vessel wall.

According to Pauling, a high concentration of free lysine can destroy existing plaques. It is important to keep all this in perspective using the Pauling/Rath "Unified Theory". If a person is not getting enough vitamin C to produce collagen, and their blood vessels are wearing down, then the Lp(a) plaque is of great benefit to them. Simply removing plaque without restoring the vein or artery to health is like tearing a scab off a wound. You do not want to remove the scab until after the tissue underneath has started healing. The body needs sufficient vitamin C so that veins and arteries can heal.

Interesting to know

The Pauling Therapy

A "natural cure" for heart disease as described by Pauling

Daily Lp(a) binding inhibitor dosages:

Vitamin C (as ascorbic acid), natural agent 6 g to 18 g, take with or before meals, i.e., 2 to 3 times daily

Lysine 3 g to 6 g, natural agent
Matthias Rath also recommends:

Proline .5 g to 2 g, natural agent

and Owen Fonorow recommends adding:
CoQ10, 150 mg to 300 mg, natural agent

The Unified Theory blames mechanical stresses (high blood pressure, stretching and bending, etc.) on the blood vessels for exposing lysine that Lp(a) is attracted to. This explains why plaque doesn't always form. Atherosclerosis is a healing process. Like a scab, plaques form after a lesion or injury to the blood vessel wall. There is an awesome elegance that these binding inhibitors (vitamin C/lysine) are completely non-toxic. They are also the basic building blocks of collagen. The unified theory blames poor collagen production for the entire problem of heart disease. Therefore, the Pauling Therapy not only melts plaque, but it attacks the root cause by stimulating the bodies' production of collagen.

With enough collagen, arteries remain strong and plaque-free. The Pauling/Rath theory postulates that the root cause of atherosclerotic plaque deposits is a chronic vitamin C deficiency, which limits the collagen, our bodies can make. A surprising body of experimental research supports the Pauling/Rath view. Careful studies with animals that do not make their own endogenous vitamin C prove that when the dietary intake of the vitamin is low, collagen production is limited, and blood vessels tend to become thinner and weaker from wear and tear. Plaque deposits then form to compensate for this weakness. Such animals are rare. Large population studies also support the view that increased vitamin C intake results in lower incidence of cardiovascular disease and lower death rates.

Strategies to manage stress connected with cognitive, behavioral and emotional characteristics

COGNITIVE RESTRUCTURING

Cognitive restructuring is a useful tool for understanding and turning around negative thinking. It helps us put unhappy, negative thoughts "under the microscope", challenging them and in many cases changing the negative thinking that lies behind them. In doing this, it can help us approach situations in a positive frame of mind. This is obviously import-ant because not only are negative moods unpleasant for us, they also reduce the quality of our performance and undermine our working and social relationships with other people. In addition, research has now sub-stantiated the hypothesis that negative thoughts can *suppress* the immune system.

The key idea behind this tool, as with the other tools in this section, is that our moods are driven by what we tell ourselves, and this is usually based on our interpretations of our environment. Cognitive restructuring helps us evaluate how rational and valid these interpretations are. Where we find that these assumptions and interpretations are incorrect, this changes the way we think about situations and in the process changes our moods.

We must distinguish between *positive* and *negative* thoughts. Positive thoughts are those that help us to reach our objectives. Negative thoughts are those that prevent us from reaching our objectives and which, at the same time, make us feel bad. Both positive as well as nega-tive thoughts can be either *rational* or *irrational*. Irrational thoughts are those that are not based on sufficient real or objective data or may even contradict reality.

Exercise: thoughts and mood

Situation	Moods	Automatic thoughts & images	Evidence that supports hot thought	Evidence that doesn't support hot thought	Alternative/ balanced thoughts	Mood now, actions & positive thoughts

Based on the "Thought Record" worksheet from *Mind Over Mood* by Dennis Greenberger and Christine A. Padesky © 1995 The Guilford Press.

The template above can be used as a work sheet in recording events and training in cognitive restructuring. In order to do that, the following steps feelings that we need to be undertaken:

1   **Write down the situation that triggered the negative thoughts** (make a brief note of the situation in the first column of the worksheet).

2   **Identify the moods that you felt in the situation** (in the second column, enter the moods that you feel in the situation; moods here are the deep feelings that we have about the situation; they are not thoughts about it).

    Mind over Mood offers an easy trick to help tell moods from thoughts: It is usually possible to express moods in one word, while thoughts are more complex. Keep in mind, you may well feel several different moods at the same time. These reflect different aspects of the situation. For example, "he is trashing my suggestion in front of my co-workers", would be a thought, while the associated moods might be "humiliated", "frustrated", "angry" and "insecure".

3   **Write down the automatic thoughts that you experienced when you felt the mood.** In the third column, write down the thoughts that came into your mind when you felt the mood. Identify the most distressing of these. In the example above, thoughts might be:

    ● Maybe my analysis skills aren't good enough…
    ● Have I failed to consider these things?
    ● He hasn't liked me since…
    ● How rude and arrogant of him!
    ● Everyone will think badly of me
    ● But my argument is good and sound…
    ● This is undermining my future with this company

    In this case, the person in this example might consider that the most distressing thoughts (the "Hot Thoughts") are "maybe my analysis skills aren't good enough", and "everyone will think badly of me".

4 **Identify the evidence that supports these hot thoughts.** In the fourth column of the worksheet, write down the objective evidence that you can find that supports the hot thoughts. Developing this example, the evidence written down might have been:

- The meeting moved on and decisions were taken with no account being taken of my suggestion.
- He did identify a flaw in one of the arguments in my paper on the subject.

5 **Identify the evidence that does not support the hot thoughts.** In the next column, write down the objective evidence that contradicts the hot thoughts. Evidence contradicting the hot thought in the example might be:

- The flaw was minor and did not alter the conclusions.
- The analysis was objectively sound, and the suggestion was realistic and well founded.
- When I trained in the analysis method, I usually came close to the top of my class.
- My clients respect my analysis and my opinion.

6 **Now, identify fair, balanced thoughts about the situation.** By this stage, you will have looked at both sides of the situation as far as you can. This should have clarified the situation, and you may now have all the information you need to take a fair, balanced view. Alternatively, you may find that there are still substantial points of uncertainty. If this is the case, then you may need to clarify this uncertainty, perhaps by discussing the situation with other people who have a view or by testing the question in some other way. Obviously, the amount of effort you put in does depend on the importance of the situation.

Do what is needed to come to a balanced view and write the balanced thoughts down in the sixth column of the worksheet. The balanced thoughts in this example might now be:

- I am good at this sort of analysis. Other people respect my abilities.
- My analysis was reasonable, but not perfect.
- There was an error, however it did not affect the validity of the conclusions.
- The way he handled the situation was not correct.
- People were surprised and a little shocked by the way he handled my suggestion (this comment would have followed a conversation with other people at the meeting).

7 **Finally, observe your mood now and think about what you are going to do.** You should now have a clearer view of the situation. Look at your mood now. You will probably find that it has changed and (hopefully!) improved. Write this in the final column. The next step is to think about what you could do about the situation. You may conclude that no action is appropriate. By looking at the situation in a balanced way, it may cease to be important.

Alternatively, you may choose to do something about the situation. If you do, you may find that some of the techniques explained elsewhere are useful. The Assertiveness tool is most likely to be particularly useful in dealing with problems with other people!

Make a note of these actions in the final column, but also put them on your To Do List so that you act on them. Finally, think through positive affirmations that you can use to counter any future negative thoughts of this type, and see if you can spot any opportunities coming out of the situation.

Mood. Compared with the moods felt at the start of the example, the mood experienced by the person completing the worksheet will have changed. Instead of feeling humiliation, frustration, anger and insecurity, this person is most likely to feel only anger.

- **Actions.** A first action will be to use relaxation techniques to calm the anger. Having done this, the person may take away two actions: first, to check his or her work more thoroughly, and second to arrange a meeting to discuss the situation in an assertive manner.
- **Positive thoughts.** This person could also create, and use, the following positive thought in a similar situation: "My opinions are sound and are respected by fair-minded colleagues and clients. I will rise above rudeness."

Examples in cognitive restructuring in organizational settings

The manager of a company asks one of his foremen to pass on a message to two workers. He wants to talk to them personally in his office. He summons one at 5 pm and the other at 6 pm. The foreman passes the message on to both workers without giving them an explanation as to the reason for the meeting.

Let's see what both workers think about this situation:

Worker 1: What will the manager want now? I'll probably have done something wrong [negative-irrational thought] I haven't even realised. I just know I'm in for a right good ticking off [negative-irrational thought]. I might even get fired [negative-irrational thought]. What a disaster! I'll get really nervous when I talk to him [negative-irrational thought/catastrophist].

Worker 2: Strange the manager should want to talk to me. What will he have to say? Perhaps he wants me to collaborate on one of the company's new projects. In any case, it's not worth giving it too much thought beforehand. I'll find out soon enough when the time comes [positive-more rational thought].

POSITIVE THOUGHT

Why do some people tend to see the glass half full while others see it half empty? As we commented in the previous section, thoughts can be of two types: positive and negative. The first type includes those that push us on and give us the energy to achieve personal objectives. However, the second type drains our energy levels and, in addition, makes us feel bad on an emotional level.

Negative Messages	Converted into Affirmations
"Don't say anything"	"I have important things to say"
"I can't do anything!"	"I'm a success when I want to be."
"Don't expect much."	"I'll make my dreams come true."
"I'm not good enough."	"I'm great!"

What we feel depends on what we think and vice versa. For this reason, thinking positive can help us to overcome situations that may be stressful and difficult for us. The following are some of the distorted negative thoughts that we can develop in a stressful situation:

- *Polarized thought*: thinking that things can only be black or white, without considering that there is a whole span of greys in between. This consists of always considering the two most extreme options, making it very difficult to come to a halfway agreement with other people.
- *Filtered thought*: this is a type of negative thought in which we tend to interpret the things that happen based on a series of "filters" or fixed and preconceived ideas, quite often biased, and which make us deform reality.
- *Catastrophist thought*: this consists of thinking that misfortune and negative events always have to happen to us.

Thinking positive can help us confront stressful situations with a greater guarantee of being able to control the situation:

- *Minimization*: this allows us to relativize the importance of the consequences resulting from the problem or situation that is generating stress: "I've decided I don't need it as much as I thought."
- *Spacing or emotional cooling down*: protecting ourselves against the impact of the problem.
- *Selective attention*: this consists in focusing attention on the positive aspects of the problem.
- *Positive comparisons*: this is a mechanism to induce satisfaction based on contrasting differences.
- *Drawing positive values from negative events*: putting this into practice makes it easier for negative situations to be perceived more positively.

SEEKING SOCIAL SUPPORT

Many people when stressed tend to set aside those things that normally satisfy them, including their closest circle of family and friends. There is an escalating and "unreal" feeling that they don't need anybody, that they will be able to solve their problems on their own. Nevertheless, we see how this is not how it works: quite the opposite in fact. The more stressed we are, the more we will need to get support from others, although in many cases it might be that we do not ask for it and may even refuse the help offered by others.

People are social creatures by nature, which implies that we need to feel a part of a social structure that we are satisfied with, at work as well as in our personal and home lives. Social support refers to the perception that we have concerning quality interpersonal relations for dealing with difficult situations. It acts as a shock absorber for stress. Research in various disciplines from medicine, to psychology and management show that social support has an impact on reducing stress. Studies show that social support decreases the stress response hormones in our bodies. People who have close relationships and a strong sense of connection and community enjoy better health and live longer than those who live in isolation or alienation.[14] People, who suffer alone, suffer more.

Benefits of social support include:

1   *Emotional support and encouragement*: a shoulder to lean on and an ear to listen. Talking about feelings (ventilation) reduces stress and helps us to work through problems and feel better about ourselves.
2   *Logistical support*: at times of overload, illness or injury, people can take care of our children, help with tasks or errands or drive us to medical appointments.
3   *Mentoring and coaching*: after a job loss or relationship break-up, it helps to talk to people who have been through a similar experience and can share the lessons they've learned. They can also show us how to use a computer, build a deck, write a resume or prepare for an interview.
4   *Networking*: people in our support system can tell us about a job opportunity, a good car mechanic or a new book club.

How to develop and use a support system

- Find people whom you trust and who care about you. You don't need a gallery of folks – a few close friends or relatives will suffice.
- The best time to develop a support system is before you need it. Don't wait till you're halfway up the twist and then run out to some passer-by on the street and say: "I have to tell you about my day!"

- The best way to develop a support system is to give support to others. This establishes a relationship and builds trust and goodwill. When you know someone is upset, ask if they'd like to talk about it. Then listen patiently and empathically. Call or visit someone who's sick or going through a rough time. Then, when you need a listening and caring ear, you'll have built a connection that can be reciprocated comfortably. As my father put it: "Just keep giving and the taking will look after itself."
- Confide only what's comfortable for you. You don't have to divulge your entire life story. Venting feelings is more important than sharing details. A couple went through a very tough time when their child was hospitalized after a serious injury. "We called on our support system and told them what we needed. We knew we couldn't get through it alone."
- Turn to people with whom you feel comfortable (relatives, friends, neighbours, colleagues at work, family doctors, clergymen, or even specific professionals such as therapists – what a colleague of mine calls "renting a friend").
- Don't judge yourself as weak or "less than" when you seek support. We all feel stressed, angry, frustrated or scared at times. It's a mistake to keep those feelings in. Having problems doesn't mean you're weak. It only means you're human. And there's a saying that "A problem shared is a problem halved."

ASSERTIVENESS

"One half of words belongs to the one who utters them and the other half to the one who hears them."

(Montaigne)

Human beings are social by nature. As a result, we use communication as a vehicle for interaction with others. Some of us speak more than others. But we don't always succeed in establishing effective interpersonal contact. This is something that is very complex, and it is not only a matter of making and listening to comments. Many factors influence the messages that are sent. For this reason, what we say is often not as "logical" and "quite so clear" as we might think. In addition, our communication is conditioned by our prejudices, attitudes, ideals, interests, feelings, defenses, anxieties and fears. On the other hand, we select what we hear according to our motivations. When it comes down to it, we hear what we want to hear. In addition, the same words can have a different connotation for different people, depending on previous experiences and cultural differences.

We can distinguish three different styles of communication: *aggressive*, *passive* and *assertive* (Table 5.2). The aggressive style is characterized by a lack of respect towards the speaker where people try to impose their point of view and/or opinion, without listening to others. Behavioral signs of this type of communication are shouting and insulting the other person, a lack of argument or point and excessive gesticulating and/or movement of the upper extremities. It is normally accompanied by rage, emotional outbursts and scorn directed at others; it usually appears as a result of rage or anger and the inability to use self-control.

> ### Assertiveness techniques
>
> - **First step II: Engage in active listening**
> - **Second step II: Spell out your thoughts and express your opinions.**
> - **Third step III: I: Say what you expect to happen.**

At the opposite extreme we could include the passive style. This is used to describe the passive person who does not know how to express his feelings and does not know how to defend his rights. This leads, in general, to the individual not feeling satisfied, since he is unable to say what he thinks or feels and does not get his point across to others. It usually produces insecurity, a feeling of being poorly accepted and of not being taken into account by others. All of this leads to a deterioration of personal self-esteem.

Between the aggressive and the passive style, we can position assertiveness. This is defined as a personal ability that allows us to express feelings, opinions and thoughts, at the appropriate time, in a suitable manner and without denying or failing to consider others people's rights. In order to give an assertive answer, the first step is actively to listen to others and give them signs that we understand what they are thinking or feeling (Step 1). Next, we express what we think or give an opinion (Step 2). And, finally, we communicate to the person what we want to happen (Step 3). Traditionally, assertiveness has had little recognition in our society in terms of its importance in human communication. Thus, for example, success has been associated more with verbal and nonverbal behaviors more commonly associated to an aggressive style. Nevertheless, this stereotype is changing.

In the middle of the last century the image of a leader was associated with an image of a person who was sure of himself, with clear ideas, who knew how to impose his criteria and opinions on others, without caring if he was being more or less threatening and/or contemptuous of his collaborators. Luckily this situation is changing. At the moment and, more so in the years ahead, the person who wants to be successful in business will have to be skilled not only in finances, marketing and strategic planning, but also in communication and interpersonal skills. In this sense, they will need to develop their emotional intelligence more than their technical intelligence. *Why should we use assertiveness when we feel stressed at work?* We have seen that many of the factors leading to stressful situations have a lot to do with the interpersonal relationships established in the workplace (relationships with people on the same hierarchical level, relationships with people from outside the organization, relationships with superiors and with those under our command. Also, as we have commented previously, people can use different styles of communication (aggressive, passive and/or assertive), although due to tradition, we have grown especially accustomed to using the first two of these styles. In terms of our work, this can lead to us being exposed to situations that represent sources of stress. The use of assertiveness at work has numerous advantages for the person who puts it into practice:

- It allows them to express positive and negative feelings and desires effectively, without denying or disregarding the rights of others and without creating or feeling shame.
- It allows them to defend themselves, without aggression or passivity, from the uncooperative, inappropriate or unreasonable behavior of others.

This way, it will help to reduce stress levels since it increases the perception of control over the situation, self-confidence and with it the feeling of personal self-esteem. The advantage of learning and practicing assertive behaviors is that these get through to other people, the messages themselves expressing opinions, showing that they have been taken into consideration. They obtain feelings of security and social recognition. Without a doubt, assertive behavior helps to maintain high self-esteem (Table 5.2).

Table 5.2 **Styles of behavior**

Behaviors	Aggressive	Assertive	Passive
Posture	Leaning forward	Firm posture	Cowering
Head	Head held high	Head held firm	Head lowered
Eyes	Fixed stare, penetrating	Looking directly at people, normal eye contact	Poor eye contact, avoids looking directly at people
Face	No facial expression	Expression matching words	Smiling even when displeased
Voice	Raised voice	Voice modulated, in accordance with what is being said	Hesitant, low voice. Faltering words and sentences
Arms/hands	Arms controlled, gestures pronounced and marked, pointing fingers	Arms and hands relaxed, moving with ease	Arms held still

(Continued)

Table 5.2 Continued

Behaviors	Aggressive	Assertive	Passive
Movements/ manner of walking	Slow and labored movements	Movements in accordance with the situation	Brusque movements, rapid or slow
Speech patterns	Rigid	Structured	Disordered
Listening	Unidirectional, does not listen	Active, asks for confirmation, clarifications, asks questions when something has not been understood	Passive, does not ask questions
Attention	Gets the attention of others when speaking. Uses repetitive resources	Gets the attention of others when speaking. Uses creative resources	Does not get the attention of others when speaking
Problem solving	Does not give in, tends to get own way	Looks for consensus	Accepts others' ideas
Empathy	Does not put him in the place of others	Is capable of putting him in the place of others	Shows understanding
How disagreement is expressed	Says no emphatically	Knows how to say no without upsetting others	Has difficulty expressing disagreement

Exercise: self-assessment of assertiveness

The purpose of this quiz is to help you understand better if you are more "Assertive" or "Non-assertive" in your communication style.

1	2	3	4	5
not really	more or less	quite a bit	a lot	a great deal

1 Are you openly critical of others' ideas, opinions, and behavior? ▢

2 Do you speak out in protest when someone takes your place in line? ▢

3 Do you often avoid people or situations for fear of embarrassment? ▢

4 Do you usually have confidence in your own judgement? ▢

5 Do you insist that your spouse or roommate take on a fair share of household chores? ▢

6	Do you find it hard to say "NO" to salespeople?	☐
7	Are you reluctant to speak up in a discussion or debate?	☐
8	Are you disturbed when someone watches you?	☐
9	Do you find it difficult to maintain eye contact when talking with another person?	☐
10	Do you return faulty merchandise?	☐
11	Are you able to openly express love and affection?	☐
12	Are you able to accept unreasonable requests from friends?	☐

Score and interpretation

(A) Total up your scores for questions: 1, 3, 4, 5, 10, 11 (the range is between 6–36). The higher the score, the more assertive you are. And, vice versa, the lower the score the more non-assertive you are in your communication style.

(B) Total up your scores for questions: 3, 6, ,7, 8, 9, 12 (the range should be between 6–36). The higher the score, the more non-assertive you are in your communication skills. And, vice versa, the lower the score the more assertive you are.

Remember, this quiz is valid if you get a high score on dimension A and low score on dimension B, or if you obtain a lower score on dimension A, you also obtained a high score on dimension B. If both your scores are close to each other, it means that you are in between assertiveness and non-assertiveness.

DELEGATING EFFECTIVELY

We often wish that there were more than 24 hours in a day because, if there were, we would have enough time to do all the activities and tasks that we have to do. Is this good time management? The answer is more likely than not going to be no. Effective time management for individuals requires good delegation. To delegate means to yield the authority and the means for carrying out a task without renouncing responsibility over the final result. The difficulties that we face in delegating are due to several factors, both individual as well as organizational. The following is a detailed list of some of the most frequent factors:

- Excessive desire for perfection, lack of time, fear of being outshone by the person who is being delegated to do the task. Behind this attitude, the person is usually someone who is excessively controlling, who has a lack of self-confidence and who is insecure, in other words, who has a lack of personal self-esteem.
- Difficulties in finding a person in whom to delegate through a lack of professional competencies.

Table 5.3 **Tasks to delegate**

What can I delegate?	What shouldn't I delegate?
• Routine work • Subjects that call for specialized knowledge • Details	• Setting objectives • Controlling results • Motivating personnel • Important subjects • Critical or urgent tasks, in which there is no time for explanations and control

• Lack of a delegation "culture" (there is no tradition of this in the company). The person who delegates is described as one "who tends to slope off from doing the work themselves", and "who does not get involved and take responsibility for their work".

Table 5.3 summarizes the tasks that are normally delegated and those that are normally not recommended to be delegated. Delegating will dictate whether or not you manage to control your sources of stress. Are you one of those people who think that "if you want something done well, do it yourself"? Do you think that, in the time it takes to tell someone what he or she has to do, you could have done it yourself?

Advantages of Delegating

• It frees up more time for managing and supervising tasks.
• It alleviates tension. A frequent error lies in *wanting to do things* instead of *supervising*.
• It improves know-how amongst personnel.
• It provides a climate that facilitates motivation.
• It provides standards for evaluating performance.
• It improves results.
• It perfects company organization.
• It increases team participation.

TIME MANAGEMENT

Expressions such as "I don't have time" or "I need time", form part of every-day language. In the work environment, these expressions are associated in many cases to a situation of professional and personal success in life in general. Nevertheless, behind this superficial image is a heartrending reality, and one, which in many cases masks a situation of stress and tension at the personal and family level.

There is a certain paradox in our present society. On the one hand, employees are expected to learn to manage the time they dedicate to their work in order to optimize the resources that are destined to it. This in turn is supposed to entail a qualitative improvement in working conditions (for example, better ways of combining professional and personal life, offloading certain tasks and more routine activities). In many cases, companies provide their employees with training on how to optimize their working time. Nevertheless, those who claim "to have free time" and are proud of it may be described as being "work-shy" or "irresponsible".

When a person suffers stress, their "internal clock" becomes altered. Being able to manage their professional and personal time well will help them to recover this internal rhythm.

> **Draw up a list every morning of the tasks to be done throughout the day. Then, score out the bottom half of the list!**

Knowing how to manage work time does not mean working more, it means working better. When a person feels stressed, they have more likelihood of being robbed of their time. Time thieves are situations, behavioral patterns, others' attitudes (external thieves) and our own personal attitudes (internal thieves) that make effective management of working time difficult. In Table 5.4, we summarize the more common time thieves.

Once the main time thieves have been identified, it is important to differentiate between what is urgent and what is important. Stressed people tend to confuse both. According to the economist, Pareto, 20 per cent of our activities at work should provide approximately 80 per cent of our output results. If this is not the case, we will have to analyse whether or not we are leaving aside important activities in order to do those that are urgent but which do not contribute toward obtaining the results we have set ourselves.

Table 5.4 Principal internal and external time thieves

External time thieves	Internal time thieves
● Television	● Lack of prioritization
● Unexpected telephone calls	● Absence of a daily work plan
● Telephone calls from work during free time	● An "open doors" policy and a feeling of having to be permanently available
● Unexpected visits	● Excessive perfectionism
● Bureaucratic proceedings	● Inability to say no (lack of assertiveness)
● A disorganized mind	● Being disorganized

If your work implies rotating shifts:	Our internal clock tends to adjust to our daily routine.To do so, it needs an adaptation period of 2 to 3 weeks. In the event of frequently changing shifts, our internal clock will not have enough time to adapt and it will always be "out of synch", generating a constant sensation of fatigue and a general lack of well-being in the individual.
If your work requires changes long-haul journeys:	In general, journeys that involve time zone break the internal routine more easily. If these journeys are unavoidable, remember that it is easier to adapt to the new schedule if you stay awake rather than going to sleep in the old time schedule.

In short, *does managing time effectively reduce stress?* This will depend on the sources causing the stress. If the cause resides in a lack of planning and/or an unexpected increase in the volume of work, then it can be an ally. Nevertheless, if the stress factors are related more to the nature of the work in itself, independently of the volume of activity that there might be, learning to manage personal time will be of little help in reducing stress levels.

Exercise: self-test of time management

The following list contains questions on how you organize your time. Please, circle YES or NO to indicate your response.

1	Do you tackle the most difficult tasks first thing in the morning?	YES/NO
2	Do you write a list of "things I have to do today"?	YES/NO
3	Do you sometimes say "NO" when asked to do something?	YES/NO
4	Do you ever ask "WHY?" when you are invited to attend a meeting?	YES/NO
5	Do you think that your bosses waste less time than you do?	YES/NO
6	Do you give more priority to the urgent matters than to the important ones?	YES/NO
7	Do you arrange tasks by priorities and carry them out following that order?	YES/NO
8	Do you undertake a single task, finish it and then move on to the next one?	YES/NO
9	Do you try to have a minimum of paperwork and notes at meetings?	YES/NO
10	Do you accept all unexpected interruptions?	YES/NO
11	Do you regularly take work home at night or at the weekends?	YES/NO

12	Do you prefer doing things yourself rather than getting other members of your staff to do them?	YES/NO
13	Do you meet deadlines on time?	YES/NO
14	Do you talk to your boss about daily work events?	YES/NO
15	Do you mention your work to colleagues?	YES/NO
16	Do you ask other people how you should organize your time?	YES/NO
17	Do you leave the factory to work somewhere else if you have something important to do?	YES/NO
18	Do you hire your staff personally?	YES/NO
19	Do you try to avoid problems before they arise, instead of having to solve them after they have cropped up?	YES/NO
20	Do you set aside a little time every day during which you can work in peace, without interruptions?	YES/NO
21	Do your employees cooperate enthusiastically in the tasks that are assigned to them?	YES/NO
22	Do you delegate well?	YES/NO
23	Do you do something every day that takes you nearer to your long-term goals?	YES/NO
24	Can others take on most of your responsibilities if you are absent from work?	YES/NO

Source: Garrat (1998) *Organice su tiempo* (Barcelona: Gestion 2000): 13–14; translated and adapted. Used with the publisher's permission.

EFFECTIVE CHANGE MANAGEMENT

We live immersed in constant situations of change: at work and in our personal life. Nevertheless, this does not imply that we know how to adapt to these constant changes. Generally, any situation of change is associated with a certain amount of stress. Depending on our capabilities to manage this stress, we will be able to adapt better or worse to the new situation. To do so, we can act on our own and/or seek the help of others. In the next chapter, we will see some of the resources that can be used by organizations to help their employees successfully confront situations of organizational change.

Interesting to know

To change means KNOWING HOW TO ADAPT to a new situation. ADAPTATION capacity is measured based on different factors:

● Intelligence (a series of different registers that we are able to use according to our surroundings).

- Personality: personal self-control.
- Attitude: open, flexible, relativist, non-ethnocentric.
- Skills: communication, leadership, negotiation.
- Accumulated experience in different surroundings.

What happens to people during change?

Changing and making changes is no easy task. If I want to introduce a change in the way my team works

> **"Fear of the unknown is normal."**

and in how we communicate, I have to be aware that any change will produce in people – those who are affected by this change – a series of reactions, including *stress*.

The most common error is to think that people will change just because they have been told to do so. Change begins when people perceive that the change is necessary and that it is possible. It is important to understand that the people in whom change causes a feeling of loss are not weak or old-fashioned. It is healthier to recognize and to express loss when it takes place, so that the participants can cope with the transition process more quickly. When the loss is not recognized, it is common for this to be translated into resistance and disorganization in the future.

During change, people look back on the past and deny the change. Then, they go through a period of worrying, during which they ask themselves where they fit into the new scheme of things and how the change will affect them. This is normally when resistance arises and stress occurs.

Boosting our self-esteem

Self-esteem lies at the innermost core of our lives. The level of well-being that we are capable of experiencing, the success that we can achieve,

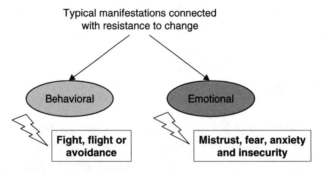

Figure 5.1 **What can happen to us?**

the creativity that we allow ourselves to express, the achievements that we are able to enjoy, amongst others, are intrinsically linked to our self-esteem.

In this chapter we have presented some individual strategies that can help a person who feels stressed to reduce their levels of tension. Without a doubt, this will help people to increase their personal and professional self-esteem. One of the consequences of stress is the appearance of a feeling of personal uselessness (state of defenselessness), lack of confidence in their own personal possibilities, all of which reduce personal self-esteem. The question is, however, does it also reduce organizational self-esteem? I will explore this in the next two chapters. Discovering our level of self-esteem is fundamental in establishing our personal situation and in deciding what we want to do. We can help ourselves find out our level of self-esteem by trying to recognize in ourselves some of the resources we have mentioned in the previous pages. Self-esteem is essential for our ability to interact functionally and harmoniously in our daily lives. Our level of self-esteem is responsible for everything that happens in our lives. Our self-esteem develops as we form our own image of ourselves, and we do this through our experiences with other people and our activities. Among these are those experiences that have to do with work.

Our level of self-esteem can be high or low, and consequently either of these levels will affect our quality of life. For want of a solid base of self-esteem, it is difficult for us to take risks and make the necessary decisions that will allow us to live a productive and rewarding life. A low level of self-esteem adversely affects our family relationships, friendships and relationship with our partner or spouse, our personal and professional performance, and, most importantly, our inner feeling of well-being. Individuals can benefit from any of the strategies (physical, cognitive, emotional or behavioral) that we have commented on, helping them to feel good about themselves. Many of them do not look for the approval or the well-being of others, although indirectly they end up attaining it. If a person feels good about himself, it is most likely that they will also behave in a more tolerant, friendly and understanding way towards others, which will help them to feel good emotionally. *A high level of self-esteem* results in a high level of confidence in our abilities to resolve situations, and the assertiveness required to allow us to be all we can be. A high level of self-esteem allows us to have more functional, healthier and more meaningful relationships, most importantly with ourselves. However, people who have *a low level of self-esteem* depend on the present results to establish how they should feel towards themselves. They need positive external experiences to resist the negative feelings that they harbour towards themselves.

Interesting to know

A PERSON WITH LOW SELF-ESTEEM CAN BEHAVE IN DIFFERENT WAYS

The Impostor: although this person seems happy and successful, in fact he is terrified of failure and lives with the constant fear of "being found out". He needs constant external triumphs in order to keep up his charade of high self-esteem, which could lead to him having problems with perfectionism, competitiveness or being over-demanding.

The Rebel: this person acts as if the opinions or good intentions of others, especially important or powerful people, do not matter. He lives with constant rage as a result of not feeling "good enough". He continually needs to prove that the judgments and the criticism of others do not hurt him, which could create problems when blaming others excessively for their slip-ups, breaking the rules and/or laws, or defying and fighting with authority figures.

The Loser: this person gives the appearance of being defenseless and incapable of fending for himself, and hopes that somebody will come and rescue him. He uses self-pity or indifference as a barrier against the fear of assuming responsibility for his actions. He always looks for the guidance of others, which could lead to a lack of assertiveness, lack of own achievement, and an excessive dependency on the other people in his relationships.

In summary, a positive level of self-esteem is based on our ability to evaluate ourselves objectively, really to know ourselves, and to be able to accept ourselves and to value ourselves unconditionally, in other words, to be able realistically to recognize our strengths and limitations, and at the same time to accept ourselves as being valuable without conditions or reservations. However, it is important not to confuse a high level of self-esteem with egotism or a feeling of superiority, which are in fact attempts to hide negative feelings about oneself. Positive self-esteem allows us to realize our dreams. The more we accept and appreciate ourselves, the more we behave in a way that allows us to be accepted and appreciated by others. The more we think that we are capable of reaching our goals, the better our chances of turning our aspirations into reality.

So, how to go about boosting self-esteem? While there are many, many ways to boost self-esteem, here is a simple strategy tips that can prove instrumental:[15]

- **Tip 1**: think back to when you did something new for the first time – learning something new is often accompanied by feelings of nervousness, lack of self-belief and high *stress* levels, all of which are necessary parts of the learning process. The next time you feel under-confident, remembering this will remind you that it's perfectly normal – you're just learning!

- **Tip 2**: Do something you have been putting off – like writing or calling a friend, fixing the car, organizing the bills, making a tasty and healthy meal – anything that involves you making a decision, then follow through!

- **Tip 3**: do something you are good at – examples? how about swimming, running, dancing, cooking, gardening, climbing, painting, writing. If possible, it should be something that holds your attention and requires enough focus to get you into that state of "flow" where you forget about everything else. You will feel more competent, accomplished and capable afterwards, great antidotes to low self-esteem! And while you're at it, seriously consider doing something like this at least once a week. People who experience "flow" regularly seem to be happier and healthier.

- **Tip 4**: stop thinking about yourself! This may sounds strange, but low self-esteem is often accompanied by too much focus on the self. Doing something that absorbs you and holds your attention can quickly make you feel better.

- **Tip 5**: get seriously relaxed. If you are feeling low, anxious or lacking in confidence, the first thing to do is to stop thinking and relax properly. Some people do this by exercising, others by involving themselves in something that occupies their mind. However, being able to relax yourself when you want is a fantastic life skill and so practicing self-hypnosis, meditation, or a physically based relaxation technique such as Tai Chi can be incredibly useful. When you are properly relaxed, your brain is less emotional and your memory for good events works better. A great "rescue remedy"!

- **Tip 6**: remember all the things you have achieved – this can be difficult at first, but after a while, you'll develop a handy mental list of self-esteem boosting memories. And if you're thinking "But I've never achieved anything", I'm not talking about climbing Everest here. Things like passing your driving test (despite being nervous), passing exams (despite doubting that you would), playing team sports, getting fit (even if you let it slip later), saving money for something, trying to help someone (even if it didn't work) and so on.

- **Tip 7**: remember that you could be wrong! – If you are feeling bad about yourself, remember that the way you feel affects your thoughts, memory and behavior. So when you feel bad, you will only remember the bad times, and will tend to be pessimistic about yourself. This is where the tip "Get Seriously Relaxed" comes in!

Chapter postscript

Increasingly in organizations, we are observing that workers as well as human resource managers worry about the need for a preventive approach to the problems that they come across every day. Nevertheless, experience demonstrates that until now, the majority of measures have only been directed towards the first stage, but in very few cases, have these been transferred from the individual sphere to the organizational sphere.

The elaboration of preventive intervention strategies from the individual point of view also comes, to a large extent, from the traditional school of medicine. Nevertheless, the psychosomatic aspect of work-related stress entails and needs a therapeutic team with a multidisciplinary approach. This team, in addition to being made up of a doctor and a psychologist, should also have a human resources manager, and, evidently, the worker or his representative. This is not, therefore, a scene for confrontation, but rather a scene for agreement, that is to say, one for sharing resources and techniques from each of the disciplines, as well as the worker's.

Decalogue of good practices to avoid feeling stressed

- Clarify goals and values in life and try to be coherent
- Be flexible
- Take life with a sense of humor
- Laugh at yourself
- Take more time over tasks and enjoy all your daily activities
- Accept your own limitations and recognize your qualities and possibilities
- Regularly learn and practise some relaxation or meditation techniques
- Remember your achievements (work-related or otherwise), both on a quantitative as well as on a qualitative level
- Get into shape, by doing moderate physical exercise
- Let your family know that you have a right to spend time by yourself
- Decide to think positive
- Eat healthily
- Others: ....

The strategies presented in this chapter address the problem of dealing with stress from the individual perspective. Nevertheless, in terms of work-related stress, numerous authors have highlighted the need to look at various levels of analysis: individual, group and organizational. Unlike other areas of life, the strategies considered for dealing with stress in a work environment are not effective in reducing the relationships between stressors and their consequences. As the effectiveness of the above-mentioned coping strategies depends on the possibility of controlling the stressor, in work situations these strategies are ineffective since the control of stressors is rarely in the hands of the individual. Most of the work-related stressors are characterized by being unsuitable for individual solutions. Dealing with stressors, instead, requires cooperative, organized efforts that go beyond the individual level, not depending on the ability of the person to handle their individual resources in order to find a solution to the source of the stress. As such, it is necessary to identify the group and organizational strategies to cope with stress as the stressful situations frequently come from those levels.

The European Agency for Health and Safety at Work recently pointed out that the following actions, amongst others, are necessary in order to combat occupational stress: better to define work roles and to improve the individual's self-control and communication inside and outside of work. This would improve job satisfaction and would bring with it greater job quality. Stress appears following continued exposure to a situation for which the person has not found adaptative answers. It seems logical that intervening only at an individual level (learning relaxation techniques, cognitive reconstruction) will not be enough to solve the problem.

Until now few organizations have been concerned about the well-being and the occupational health of their workers. They have been concerned with improving product quality, increasing the effectiveness of the personnel selection processes, training high performance work teams, and training executives. How many companies would we be able to find that have adopted strategies to avoid "falling ill" among themselves and/or their workers? This indicates that having individual strategies to fight against stress can be of help, although this is not enough to eliminate and/or prevent its consequences on a physical and mental health level.

Exercise: a practical technique for reducing your level of family, social and/or work stress

This technique was elaborated by the famous psychologist, Albert Ellis, in the 1950s. It is based on a cognitive reconstruction strategy, and its effectiveness, if you follow his advice, is immediate and has almost no cost.

The strategy is based on the following hypotheses:

1 Each person is responsible for his own emotions and actions.
2 Harmful emotions and dysfunctional behaviors are the product of irrational thought.

3   It is possible to learn to have more realistic thoughts and approaches and with practice make them a part of each person.

4   Developing realistic thoughts, each person will experience greater acceptance and greater satisfaction in life.

This technique clearly distinguishes two types of difficulties: the practical problems and the emotional problems. Flawed behavior, unfair treatment from others and undesirable situations represent practical problems. Unfortunately, the tendency is for humans to be affected by these problems, and we unnecessarily generate in this way a second type of problem: emotional problems.

The proposed strategy is detailed in the following points:

1   To take responsibility for our anxieties. The first lesson in healthy emotions was given by the Roman philosopher, Epictetus, more than 2000 years ago: you should only feel bad about events in themselves, regardless of how undesirable the event may be, and never feel bad about yourself.

Recognise that neither a person nor an adverse circumstance can upset you, only you yourself can do that. Nobody can enter into our innermost self and shake us up. Some people will be able to cause us physical harm – striking us on the head with a baseball bat for example, but each of us generate our own emotional suffering or self-destructive behavior upon which others act or speak.

2   Identify the three "I MUSTs". Once we have admitted that we ourselves distort our own emotions and actions, we can accurately determine that the culprit usually lies in one of the three I MUSTs.

● "I must" #1 (a demand made of oneself): "I must do things well and be accepted, otherwise I am worthless." This demand causes anxiety, depression and a lack of assertiveness.

● "I must" #2 (a demand made of others): "You must treat me reasonably, considerately, and affectionately, otherwise you are not a good person." This "I Must", leads to resentment, hostility and violence.

● "I must" #3 (a demand made of situations): "Life must be fair, straightforward and problem-free, otherwise it would be a wretched life." These thoughts are associated with desperation, addiction and abandonment.

Establish the demands you make on yourself, on the people around you and those made of your life's circumstances. Once you discover your own "I MUSTs", you will be able to reduce your anxiety effectively.

3   Challenge your "I MUSTs". The only way that you will be worried about adversity is if you persist in accepting some of the three "I MUSTs". Once you have discovered them, face up to them and question your demands implacably.

Begin by asking yourself, What is the evidence for this "I MUST"? Why it is a truth? Where is it carved in stone? And soon, respond by saying that "There is no evidence", that "My I MUST is entirely false", "Nothing is carved in stone". Once you succeed in producing thoughts that are free of "I MUSTs", then emotions will heal.

4 Reinforce your preferences, conclude therefore:

- Preference # 1: "I'd PREFER to do things well, to be accepted and, if I fail, I will accept myself completely."
- Preference # 2: "I'd PREFER you to treat me reasonably, considerately and affectionately. Nevertheless, since I do not control the universe, and since it is part of human nature to make mistakes, neither can I control you."
- Preference # 3: "I'd PREFER life to be fair, straightforward and problem-free and it is frustrating that it is not like this, but I can put up with this frustration and enjoy life all the same."

Assuming that you take the recommendations and suggestions to heart, you may reduce your anxiety, hostility, depression and addictions to a great extent. You will see that this strategy will be useful in quickly and enjoyably taking control of your own life, instead of being at the mercy of a therapist for many years. Being equipped with the tools that manage to identify and overcome the true sources of your difficulties, you will be well on your way to preparing yourself to become your own therapist. Additionally, you will be helping to reinforce your realistic thoughts, those that will enable you to get rid of your present emotional problems and to avoid similar problems in the future.

REFERENCES

1 Selye, H. (1936). "A Syndrome Produced by Diverse Nocuous Agents", London, *Nature*, 138: 32.; Selye, H. (1952). *The Story of the Adaptation Syndrome* (Montreal: Acta Inc. Med. Pub.); Selye, H. (1958). *The Stress of Life* (New York: McGraw Hill); Selye, H. (1955). "Stress and Disease", *Science*, 122: 625; Selye, H. (1975). *Tensión sin angustia* (Madrid: Ed. Guadarrama).

2 Rotter, J.B. (1966). "Generalized Expectancies for Internal versus External Control of Reinforcement", *Psycological Monographs: General and Applied*, 80.

3 Burke, W.W. (1978). "Improving Stress Management", in W.W. Burke (ed.), *The Cutting Edge* (San Diego, CA: University Associates).

4 Dewe, Bruce and Dewe, Joan (1998). *Controlar el estrés fácilmente* (Barcelona: Índigo).

5 Parasuraman, S., and Alutto, J. (1984). "Sources and outcomes of stress in organizational settings: Toward the development of a structural model." *Academy of Management Journal* 27: 330–350.

6 Cooper, C. and Payne, R. (1988). *Causes, Coping and Consequences of Stress at Work* (New York: John Wiley).

7 Jacobson, E. (1978). *Progressive Relaxation* (Chicago: University of Chicago Press).

8 Bernstein, D.A. and Brokovec, T.D. (1983). *Enternamiento en relajación progresiva* (Bibau: Descté de Brouwer).

 9 Schultz, J.H. (1972). *El Entrenamiento Autógeno*. 12th edn (Barcelona: Ed. Cientifico-Médica).
10 Benson, H. (1987). *Minding the Body, Mending the Mind* (Reading, Mass.: Addison-Wesley).
11 Source: http://www.pbs.org/bodyandsoul/218/meditation.htm
12 Wooten, P. (1997). "Psychoneuroimmunology of Laughter: An Interview with Lee Berk, Dr. P.H.", *Journal of Nursing Jocularity*, Fall 7(3), pp 46–47.
13 Cousins, N. (1979) *Anatomy of an Illness as Perceived by the Patient: Reflections on Healing and Regeneration* (New York: Bantam).
14 Source: http://www.paulingtherapy.com
15 Omish, D. (1998). *Love and Survival* (New York: Harper Perennial).

6 Organizational Strategies for Managing Occupational Stress

Human Evolution: Man continues his struggle in life – always stressed – in and out of the office.

General framework and perspective within the European Union

The International Labor Organization (ILO) has carried out research in this area and recommends the following general strategies for the management of work-related stress:

- Discover the sources and actual stress levels.
- Develop a preventative plan to reduce or avoid stressors which may be causing the environmental demands.
- Set up stress prevention and intervention programs in those areas or groups at greatest risk.
- Evaluate these programs to determine their efficacy and make changes if necessary.

Within the European Union, the evaluation and supervision of work design and management is becoming a priority given that, currently, new work models are developing which may imply additional or little known risks for workers and organizations. Some of these new models include: an increase in teleworking, smaller companies, an increase in workers' ages, and so on. We will come back to these strategies from a Human Resources perspective later in the chapter. In the EU, it is recommended that occupational stress be placed within the context of other, interrelated problems, such as social and sexual inequality, physical handicap and age or ethnic discrimination. This is essential in order to have a more complete perspective regarding the management and control of occupational stress.

In the collective management of stress-causing factors, the predominant objective is to minimize the situations that create tension within the company or organization. Specific actions to do this are aimed at the organizational structure, communication styles, the decision-making process, corporate culture, work functions, and hiring and training methods.

Within the work environment, it is important to take into account physical improvements, including ergonomic factors, safety and hygiene. These are particularly relevant concerns for workers. For the company, they represent a latent effort with the aim of improving employees' well-being.

As a general rule, organizational changes are aimed at the restructuring of processes and tasks, which allow workers to develop their skills and increase their responsibilities while improving communication. This is achieved by means of assistance programs for workers, quality circles, assessment groups, support groups, active participation, teamwork, solidarity, professional development, promotion of creativity, and continued improvement methods. Dolan et al. (2004)[1] suggest that change should be supported via the gradual incorporation of workers into the organization. Different strategies should be used, such as the development of a "healthier" culture, adapting leadership styles, the redistribution of power and authority, and responsible and active participation in decision-making, developing both formal and informal internal communications, improving the general work atmosphere and creating a favourable environment for the sustained, healthy and complete development of workers' productive life in the company.

However, the first stage in managing stress at the company level is to understand its causes and to know which specific measures must be introduced from a wide-ranging list of options. The recent European Commission Communication *How to Adapt to Changes in Society and the Workplace: A new European strategy* (2002–06), defines different ways to combat occupational stress, including the following:

- To begin with, the communiqué stresses that "real well-being – physical, moral and social – has to be promoted in the workplace; it should not be measured solely by the absence of work-related accidents or illnesses." Within this new, global focus, one of the objectives is defined as follows: "To prevent social risks: stress, harassment, depression, anxiety, and the risks associated with dependence on alcohol, drugs or other medicines."
- It highlights that the preventative services within the company should in fact be multidisciplinary and that they should consider social and psychological risks.
- Lastly, it states how important it is for this social dialogue to include new risks, "stress in particular, whose diverse and multiform character – especially due to the wide variety of pathologies manifested – completely justifies a proposal of this type, with the implication of the social representatives."

Interesting to know

An official WHO document states that occupational stress can be reduced in many ways, including the following:

Primary prevention: stress reduction by:
- Ergonomics;
- Defining job roles and environmental design;
- Fine-tuning organization and management.

Secondary prevention:
- Educating and training employees.

Tertiary prevention:
- Developing more sensitive management systems with a greater response capacity and improving occupational health services.

Source: WHO, Series on the *Protection of Workers' Health*, # 3, 2004.

Main obstacles to stress intervention in the company

When a problem such as stress occurs within a company, those in charge of occupational health are faced with various obstacles that must be overcome. Although it is subject to debate whether the organization of a human group should be based on technical limitations or in terms of jobs, generally the company's technology and job organization go hand in hand. In many cases, human resources and the possible ways to organize employees have already been determined.

However, new management trends favor the reevaluation of the "company's human capital", incorporating a new vision of the business reality in which greater relevance is increasingly being given to employees, applying a range of knowledge, methods and techniques from the field of behavioral sciences. Studies, carried out by various scholars (Herzberg, McClelland, Likert, Argyris, etc.) in social sciences, are being successfully put into practice in many companies. It is recommended that those in charge of occupational health be allowed to carry out these types of tasks while, at the same time, the company charter or bylaws enable them to do so.

Intervention in these types of problems is difficult, generally due to:

- a greater knowledge among managers of the "technical" or "economic" functioning of the company, rather than the "human" functioning;
- a non-specific presentation of the problem to managers;
- a lack of conviction regarding the scale of the associated costs of problems or the lack of trust that these costs can be controlled by planning, organization and management;

Interesting to know

Why the CEO would reject a study on work-related stress in his organization?

The director of a large hospital in Catalonia declared (literally) to researchers offering to carry out research on stress among hospital staff:

"You know our personnel are very stressed. We have more and more work to do, with patients and more aggressive families, and with fewer and fewer resources (human, technological and financial). My staff is stressed now, but if we have a formal diagnosis of this, they'll be even more stressed. I'm afraid to open a Pandora's Box, so we're not going to carry out a formal study; I accept the status quo."

- the non-existing relationship between preventative goals and management's goals; and
- the fear of many managers that running a formal diagnosis would open a "Pandora's Box".

To overcome these obstacles, adequate tools need to be used, which enable quantification of the problem. The use of these tools by those responsible for occupational health cannot be limited solely to developing a good diagnosis. They must be able to provide clear, unequivocal and comprehensible data, which will allow for the different groups within the organization to become aware of the problem.

Very frequently, economic profit is the main reference used in terms of whether a given measure is convenient or inconvenient. For this reason, those responsible for occupational health must provide data which demonstrates that the measures to be taken in terms of employee organization are in fact profitable. By the same token, proposals for change must be carefully planned, adapting them to frameworks in terms of utility, profitability and practicality and taking into account costs, partial objectives, goals, processes, and so on, and controlling the entire process of change while searching for a convergence between management's goals and those related to prevention within the company.

Stages and methodologies for occupational stress management

The program for this epidemiological control can be structured in six stages as shown in Figure 6.1.[2]

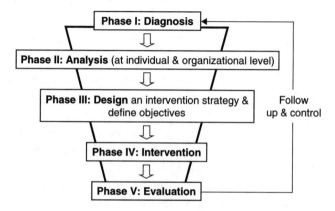

Figure 6.1 **The main stages in occupational stress management**

Stage I

Diagnosis. As described above, identification of the psycho-social risk factors requires the use of different strategies, including: personal interviews, direct observation and a tool designed to measure the answers provided by the workers and their perceptions regarding the presence and frequency of the different psycho-social risk factors and where they stem from.

1   The individual
    – personal, psychological appraisal;
    – use of psycho-technical tests;
    – clinical psychological history.

2   The internal working conditions
    – measurement tool;
    – direct observation.

3   The conditions outside of work
    – report in personal interview.

Stage II

Analysis of results.

1   Special cases of individual therapy are identified.
2   Group weaknesses by job title are identified.
3   Along with the results from the tool, more complete and accurate information should be provided in terms of every category measured. This analysis will determine not only the most frequent psycho-social risks, but also to what degree these have affected the organization's employees and executives leading to occupational stress.

Stage III

Design of the intervention strategy. Once the most representative risks effecting workers have been identified, the most appropriate methodology to minimize the risk factors, both at their source and in terms of their effects on the workers, should be studied and determined. By the same token, an intervention schedule is needed in which those responsible for each activity are specified, along with the corresponding time limits and objectives. In order to evaluate the program's impact, management indexes must be determined to verify the increase or decrease in the risk factor incidence.

Stage IV
Intervention. At this stage, all the established measures in the intervention plan are implemented to control the risk factor. The objective is to:

1   Minimize the risk agent (source): the methodologies to eliminate these risk factors are implemented and the administrators are incorporated so that they commit themselves to the change and help achieve the success of the program's goals in managing the psycho-social risks.
2   Control the risk factors present in the work environment: upon identifying the risk factors present in the workplace, the ideal methodology to improve the organizational atmosphere is determined, generating greater commitment as a result, the sense of belonging, and a better atmosphere and environment in the workplace.
3   Develop skills (individual) so that employees can more easily adapt to their environment and cope with the various daily problems. They should have the applicative and practical tools necessary and develop their skills to modify their behavior and environment, encouraging a better quality of work life.

Stage V
Evaluation of the results. Once the intervention stage has been completed, the tool for measuring results should be implemented to measure and quantify the psycho-social risks, their incidence or absence, determining the change in the risk factor and the efficacy of the program for this epidemiological control.

Stage VI
Follow-up and control. The development of this stage is divided into two time segments: one consists of periodic controls to determine the prevalence and/or reduction of the risk factor; the other comes at the end of the control program to determine whether it has met its objectives by means of control measures.

When referring to the aspects which commonly lead to occupational stress, we should not only refer to certain conditions that the individual has to cope with. In their specific area of work, employees undergo an adaptative effort. This effort will be greater when the characteristics or conditions of the job put their abilities to the test and/or less significant when the conditions are less than their expectations or needs. Given

> **"There is a difference between the buzz people get from doing a busy and challenging job and an unreasonable pressure which can harm health."**
>
> **(Bill Callaghan, UK Health and Safety Commission)**

that stress factors are accumulative, the greater the number of aspects requiring an intense, frequent or long-lasting adaptive effort, the greater the possibility that workers' adaptation abilities will be overwhelmed. As such, the greater the number of stressors, the greater the sense of threat and the higher the level of stress produced.

To alleviate the effects of the different stressors, different measures can be applied at different levels; some are focused on the reorganization of the work tasks, others on the organization of the branch or headquarters; some are focused on the reorganization of resources and means, and others on personal intervention.

In general, and depending on their flexibility, the alternative systems proposed allow for a better adaptation to workers' abilities, needs and expectations. All these types of measures could be described as an increase in the attention and trust shown to workers. The fact that these types of measures imply a different orientation for the company focused on process, technology and production does not, however, imply a rejection of aspects such as productivity or profitability. Simply put, however, workers' health is not subordinated to these objectives.

At the same time, the implementation of these measures in the organization implies intervention at the personal level, and trains workers in order to obtain the best possible results from these measures. However, when intervening at the organizational level, and in order to avoid causing stress, four important elements responsible for generating stress have to be remembered: the presence of stressful demands or work conditions; the perception of these conditions as threats; the difficulty in coping with these demands; and the corresponding, inadequate physiological and emotional responses they provoke.

First, these objectively stressful work demands and conditions have to be reduced or minimized. Generally, certain work demands have to be determined depending on the workers' abilities (not only taking into account the service or production needs) while an increase in demands should only occur when there is a correlative increase in the workers' abilities.

Working conditions should not only be determined by the criteria set by the market, the productive process, technology, and so on, but also by certain needs (safety, affiliation, a sense of belonging, status, etc.), expectations and the legitimate aspirations of employees. However, this, in and of itself, would not be completely effective if the workers continued to perceive that some conditions and demands were stressful. The fact that an individual perceives a certain demand as threatening is also a result of the individual's ability to cope with this situation. For this reason, it is important to provide the individual with the behavioral abilities and skills to cope with these situations. The company should provide clear and unequivocal information about the worker's responsibilities and functions, the objectives (product quantity and quality), the methods and means of work, deadlines, and so on.

IMPLEMENTATION PLANS

Some conditions that need to be taken into account when implementing any measure within the company include:

> **Working conditions should not only be determined by the criteria set by the market, the productive process, technology, etc., but also by certain needs (safety, affiliation, a sense of belonging, status, etc.), expectations and the legitimate aspirations of the workers.**

- The workers' and their representatives' active participation should be counted on regarding the changes to be made, not only so that these are accepted by the workers, but also because it is helpful to contrast opinions in order to adopt the most appropriate decisions.
- Conflictive company–worker situations or general crises are contraindications for carrying out changes as they may interfere both in the adequate implementation of the measures or in their functioning. It is extremely important to choose the right moment to implement any change in order to avoid the risk of failure.
- It is advisable that changes be made progressively, by means of pilot programs. This will allow the comparison between two systems at the same time, to try out different models without high costs (in case of failure) and, in reduced groups, experimentally control the different variables that arise in the new work systems, changes in information channels, etc. At the same time, the advantages of the new system will be perceived by workers who have not been included in the study group and will have a motivating effect on them.
- The advantages and disadvantages regarding who is promoting the change (whether it is someone within the organization or an external consultant) have to be taken into account. It is possible that people within the organization will have greater knowledge of the organization's idiosyncrasies, but, on the other hand, may express greater resistance to change.
- The experiences prior to the implementation of the measure have to be controlled in all their extremes, attempting to periodically track all the circumstances and comparing the results with the original hypotheses.
- For best results, it should be remembered that a certain period for the workers to adapt to the new situation is necessary and that the implemented measures may require a certain amount of fine-tuning.

Intervention within the company: focus on classic origins

| **Organizational change** | **Stress management** | **A healthy workplace** |

Reduced stress disorders
Satisfied and productive
workers
Profitable and competitive
organizations

Figure 6.2 **Preventing stress at work: a comprehensive approach**
Source: *http://www.cdc.gov/niosh/stresswk.html*

For good stress management within the organization, the specific character-istics that may be sources of stress, as described in the previous section, have to be identified. It must be remembered that these problems arise progres-sively. In other words, we will find them in different stages of development from their initial appearance onwards, both at the individual and collective levels. As such, it is worth detecting the symptoms that indicate stressful situ-ations within the organization, and what provokes them, quickly.

Various studies have identified some classic causes of this problem:

- excessive work demands;
- an imposed work pace;
- role ambiguity and conflict;
- bad personal relationships;
- inadequate management and supervision styles;
- lack of adaptation to the job;
- important responsibilities;
- instability at work; and/or
- carrying out dangerous tasks (by the nature of the tasks themselves or the conditions in which they are carried out).

IMPROVING EMPLOYEES' SENSE OF CONTROL

With reference to the possibility that a situation is perceived as threaten-ing (or otherwise), the final determination will be based on the individual's ability successfully to control and cope with the situation. At the same

Interesting to know

British companies are required to protect their employees from work-related stress or assume the legal consequences.

The Head of the UK Health and Safety Executive, Bill Callaghan, has defined six stress indicators that companies are required to measure. Companies have to support their employees and ensure that they do not feel stressed at work. Companies will be evaluated on these indicators to make sure that they are complying with the acceptable stress levels as defined by the following scale:

The Six Stress Indicators

1 Demands: 85% of employees should be able to meet the demands of their jobs.
2 Control: 5% of employees should have an adequate opinion of their jobs.
3 Support: 85% of employees should have the necessary support to meet their obligations.
4 Relationships: 65% of employees should not have to cope with unacceptable behavior.
5 Role: 65% of employees should have a clear idea of and understand their roles and responsibilities.
6 Change: 65% of employees should be involved in the company's organizational changes.

Source: http://news.bbc.co.uk/1/hi/health/2993116.stm

time, controlling the situation depends on the effective possibility the worker has of working directly on the situation and whether he or she has the necessary strategies available to cope with it.

To this end, one of the measures that must be taken is increasing workers' degree of control over their jobs, this is a necessary condition and ensures workers' health and boost their job satisfaction level. Studies have shown that this type of measure is particularly effective in situations involving heavy workloads with few possibilities for the person to control the variables affecting task performance.[3]

When referring to workers' control over their own jobs, we refer to the control over the following aspects:

- What the worker is expected to do (functions, competencies, responsibilities, quantity and quality of the results of their job).
- The way or method of carrying out their job.

- Time schedule and breaks (temporal autonomy), work pace, choice of shifts, flexi-time, etc.
- Participation in decision-making concerning those aspects related to their jobs.

With an increase in workers' discretionary control, there must also be adequate and precise training provided for the workers' specific job and general training successfully to carry out these types of measures (time management, decision making, etc.). It is important not to forget that giving employees freedom with respect to their job, without being adequately prepared for this freedom, may be a great source of stress in itself.

IMPROVING INFORMATION AND COMMUNICATION SYSTEMS

Given the significant problems which can arise from poor information and communication, in order to correct this situation, effective information and communication systems (including top-down, bottom-up or horizontal) need to be developed, not only directed at achieving productive efficacy, but also to respond to workers' needs and to help them adjust to the new work organization.

A given work demand involves the person concerned carrying out a specific task. Situations where what is expected of the worker is not clearly defined, when their role is ambiguous or there is a lack of free-flowing communication, are among the most important stressors in the workplace. Not knowing exactly what to do, how to do it and what the specific job responsibilities are, create a sense of doubt and threat. It is no longer a question of responding to a demand, but, rather, the worker not knowing what the demand actually is. That, and how it is presented to him, can lead to questions of the following type: Can he ask for clarification? Will it be provided? Are these tasks contradictory? Are different things assigned to him at the same time? Is advice provided? Can he disagree with what has to be done? Is it easy? and so on. The problems that can arise from this poor communication and lack of information and the ambiguity or conflict in roles that may develop as a result are two of the most potent stressors. In addition, they are factors which most affect the company's efficiency.

For these reasons, it is extremely important to revise the company's information system, paying special attention to the following variables:

- precision of information;
- coherence between information provided;

- congruency of the decisions made based on the information provided (both with the same objective);
- use of appropriate language for the specific recipient;
- frequency of communication adequate to the needs; and
- adequate procedures to collect, process and transmit information.

A good information system will allow everyone to understand exactly what is expected of them (tasks or objectives to be met) and access the results of the work already carried out.

We can differentiate between horizontal communication (among people at the same hierarchical level) and vertical communication (among people at different hierarchical levels). Within vertical communication there is top-down communication from a higher level to a lower level and bottom-up communication from lower to higher levels.

Top-down Communication

The objective of this type of communication is to:

- Coordinate the members of an organization in order to achieve their objectives.
- Inform people so that they contribute to meeting the objectives and have a better understanding of their tasks and the organization, thereby boosting their motivation. Knowledge and understanding the job and organization can have motivational effects.

It is worthwhile to bear in mind a couple of points, as described by various researchers. In terms of message content, precision must be sought to provide good information. Content simplicity and clarity facilitate message assimilation.[4] In terms of messages transmitted through a hierarchy, it must be remembered that the following problems may arise:

- If the same message is delivered to all the recipients (irrespective of their hierarchical level), its meaning may require it be interpreted differently at each level.
- If the message is adapted for different levels, distortions may arise with respect to the meaning of the original message.

Also worth noting is that the recipients' interest in the message content may be a more determinant factor than the degree of information contained. Good information is characterized not by its scope or frequency, but by its ability to respond to employee's expectations.

Bottom-up Communication

Although management generally tends to view bottom-up communication less positively than other types of communication, bottom-up communication is particularly useful because it fosters the working of the organization, as well as having a positive role in personal relationships:

- It allows for points of view to be expressed and channels workers' initiatives regarding different working aspects of the company.
- It encourages feedback regarding top-down communication and the degree to which workers have taken on the organization's objectives.
- It constitutes a basic condition for facilitating worker participation.

In reality, this type of communication is generally problematic in two respects. On the one hand, some companies restrict this type of communication when dealing with certain issues; on the other hand, in some contexts workers are reluctant to use this type of communication. When the upper hierarchical levels are the recipients of this information and the source of retribution or reward, employees may have reservations about the content of their messages and will tend to modify the possibly negative aspects, filtering that information which may provoke negative reactions or undesired consequences for the sender.

Another problem in terms of communication originating from the lower ranks occurs when the hierarchical pyramid is extremely narrow at the top; in other words, when the information has to travel up through various levels before reaching the final recipient.

Horizontal Communication

Horizontal communication refers to the exchange of messages between members of the same hierarchical level within the organization. This type of communication enables activity coordination and conflict resolution (although in highly bureaucratic organizations these coordination and conflict resolution functions may be reserved for upper levels).

Generally, it is a means of facilitating emotional support among employees and, at the same time, a source of satisfaction.

TACKLING METHODS FOR CONFLICT MANAGEMENT

In any company there are generally people or groups of people whose objectives and interests are different and, at times, conflicting. The emergence of conflict can be considered normal and foreseeable and this is why it is necessary to create the means to resolve these conflicts. These measures must be designed to foster:

- reduction in the appearance of conflicts;
- creation of arbitration and mediation procedures; and
- training for workers in non-traumatic conflict resolution.

One of the greatest sources of conflict in any company is related to problems arising from the non-definition of employees' roles. To avoid this role ambiguity and conflicts between individuals and instructions that may be the source of these conflicts, a clear and unequivocal definition of each person's tasks and their role within the organization must be sought, as well as the means and contents of their interactions with others. In addition, adequate coordination of all their activities and a sustained coherence in terms of the instructions they are given are necessary. In this respect, the establishment of adequate information channels is especially important.

Nevertheless, given that companies are prone to change, it is necessary to design systems to regulate conflict and to develop structural procedures for the mediation and arbitration of possible conflicts. In addition, employees should be given training in how to interact with others.

IMPROVING OR INITIATING SOCIALIZATION PROCESSES

Interpersonal relationships are one of the most important aspects when we refer to the problem of stress within organizations. This is due to the fact that they are in themselves a source of stress and dissatisfaction as relationships are one of the aspects most appreciated by workers in terms of their job satisfaction. As such, it is now considered common practice to pay special attention to the socialization process and training in interpersonal relationships as a way to avoid inadequate relationships becoming possible sources of stress and dissatisfaction.

Interesting to know

Stress prevention programs lead to better results at work

St. Paul Fire & Marine Insurance Company in the United States has carried out various studies on the effects of stress prevention programs in hospitals. These programs included the following activities: (1) training sessions in occupational stress for employees and managers; (2) redefinition of policies and procedures to reduce the effects of stress; and (3) definition of employee assistance programs.

In one of the studies, the results indicated that errors related to the dispensing of medication were reduced by 50% after these preventative programs were put into practice in a 700-bed hospital. In another study, there was a 70% decrease in mal-practice lawsuits in 22 hospitals that implemented stress prevention programs.

By the same token, social support must be considered a resource in dealing with a stressful situation: it has been demonstrated that a positive social atmosphere in the workplace eases the emotional impact of stressful situations and the development of physical and psychological consequences.

In terms of a worker adapting to a specific job, it is worth noting that it is necessary clearly to explain the job to the candidate as well as provide necessary training prior to beginning the job or when the job changes.

Many of the measures proposed so far need to be complemented by employee training programs (both managers and workers) regarding how they must act within the redesigned organization. When faced by change, individual intervention is necessary and complementary. It entails providing the individual with the strategies to adapt to some aspects, which are difficult to cope with by means of organizational measures.

Intervention within the company: focus on human resource practices and policies

From a human resource management perspective, prevention has to be initiated from the outset, intervening during the design phase and bearing in mind all the elements regarding the new job, the physical and social environment and the possible repercussions on health. To this end, intervention is required on aspects related to controlling tasks and the organization of work:

- excessive work demands;
- imposed work pace;
- work schedule;
- organization of one's own task;
- complexity of the administrative processes;
- role ambiguity and conflict;
- employment instability;
- high degree of responsibility;
- systems for promotion;

- performance evaluation; and
- interpersonal conflicts.

Some of these are a part of good human resource management practices and policies, which are briefly described below.

IMPROVE THE EMPLOYEE SELECTION AND PROMOTION PROCESSES

The employee selection and promotion processes should broaden the criteria normally used with the aim of encompassing the descriptive elements of the psycho-social dimension of the demands of the job. The physical health risks that individuals will be exposed to should be assessed at the beginning, and the expectations and personal needs of each candidate should be mapped out. In addition, and with the aim of avoiding candidates fostering unreal expectations regarding their future job, they should be informed about the general requirements expected of them within the organization and the philosophy behind human resource management.

IMPROVE TASK DESCRIPTIONS

In the area of human resource management, the aim is to offer the optimal degree of challenge and complexity. No matter how compassionate human resource managers' intentions are when redefining tasks as part of an enrichment or development program, the observed results are disappointing when those new descriptions are implanted without any sort of discrimination in the organization as a whole. This type of enrichment program offers an excellent means for reducing stress among workers who want to take on more responsibilities and want more autonomy regarding their own management. However, for other workers, the consequences may be harmful in terms of their health and job performance. Ever more frequently, it is admitted that, even among those wanting more responsibility and autonomy, a lack of training or self-control can lead to the risk of producing dire consequences. Other factors causing stress have to be taken into account when redefining tasks, for example, role clarification, the inherent workload and the skills level required. Without a doubt, in these three cases, the existence of role ambiguity and conflicts, work overload, or underuse, are actual sources of stress.

DEVELOP MORE INNOVATIVE PROFESSIONAL CAREER PLANS

When developing career plans, it is essential to outline the criteria used for promotion as clearly as possible. Organizations have been rightly criticized for neglecting to define career plans. None, however, would dare forget to develop the company's financial or production plan. In an organization, stress is drastically reduced when workers perceive less ambiguity in terms of their professional career. If the promotion criteria are clearly established and if each individual knows what they have to do to advance within the organization, there will be less risk of suffering from stress. In human resource management, efforts must be made to offer different options in terms of professional careers, which take into account both horizontal readjustments as well as vertical promotion.

PERSONNEL TRAINING: KEEPING SKILLS UPDATED

In this aspect, employees' skills should be maintained. This practice is justified by the fact that the individual tends to mistrust his ability to carry out his job correctly. This is even more important when the worker is highly specialized and works in an area where knowledge tends to become obsolete very quickly. Also included in this area are the different programs and techniques aimed at reducing the symptoms of stress described above.

IMPROVE PERFORMANCE EVALUATION SYSTEMS AND THE TECHNIQUES TO RECOGNIZE EFFORT

The current trend is to involve subordinates in evaluating their own performance. All bilateral appraisal techniques, such as management by objectives, are especially aimed at stimulating individual motivation by allowing the individual to take part in the evaluation process, diminishing the perception of unilateral judgements and at the same time reducing feelings of doubt or injustice.

DEVELOP MORE EQUITABLE REMUNERATION SYSTEMS

The current trend to increasingly individualize salary programs based on the needs of each worker must be further accentuated. Many advantages could be obtained through the use of recently acquired knowledge regarding theories of compensation, theories of equity and the theory of expectations. In terms of expectations, human resource managers argue that a solid salary plan would clearly establish the relationship between effort, performance and relationships. They should ensure that these relationships are as clear and explicit as possible so as to avoid generating tension.

In terms of equity, the company's pay policy should be public. This supposes that the changes made to the policy as well as the criteria used are communicated to the workers and are not kept under lock and key. Without a doubt, the aim is to reduce the tensions that may arise from remuneration in a context where salaries tend to be personalized.

OFFER FLEXIBLE WORK SCHEDULES

There is increasingly more talk about flexitime, flexible work schedules. This approach is also becoming popular among human resource managers. For an organization, this type of schedule resolves a good part of the problems related to late-coming since it allows workers to choose the start and finish times that most suit them. This concept could also be extended to include weeks with a variable number of hours.

ESTABLISH WELL-BEING PROGRAMS

Corporations are focusing more often on maintaining their workers' health instead of helping them recuperate from illness. They are therefore investing in well-being programs, which seem to help employee morale and performance, while at the same time reducing absenteeism and health costs.

Cases and examples of occupational stress prevention programs[5]

EXAMPLE 1: A SMALL SERVICE ORGANIZATION

The head of a department in a small public service organization noticed an increase in tension and low morale among her staff. General unhappiness with work and symptoms of bad health, such as headaches, also seemed to be on the rise. Suspecting that there was a problem with stress, she decided to meet with the different groups within her department to find out more. These meetings could be described as brainstorming sessions where each employee freely expressed their opinion about stress and its sources within their groups and the measures that could be applied to alleviate the problem.

With the information obtained from these meetings and other meetings held with middle managers, she concluded that there was a serious problem and that something needed to be done. Since she wasn't familiar with the

field of stress in the workplace, she decided to enlist the help of a consultant (a faculty member at a local university) who lectured on occupational stress and organizational behavior.

After reviewing the information collected in the brainstorming sessions, they decided that it would be useful for the consultant to give informal classes on how to increase awareness of stress at work – its causes,
effects, and prevention – to all the workers and department managers. At
the same time, they decided that a study would be useful to get an idea of
the problematic work conditions and health complaints related to stress
in the department. The consultant used the information from the meetings with workers and managers to design the study. He was also involved
in the distribution and collection of anonymous studies so that workers
would feel free to answer frankly and openly on the problems. He then
helped the departmental manager analyse and interpret the data.

The data analysis from the study suggested that there were three types
of work conditions linked to the workers' complaints regarding stress:

- unrealistic deadlines;
- low levels of support from supervisors; and
- scant worker participation in decision-making.

Having identified these problems, the department manager developed
and prioritized a list of corrective measures to be implemented. Examples
of these actions included: (1) greater employee participation in planning
their work so as to reduce unrealistic deadlines, and (2) more frequent
meetings between workers and managers to stay abreast of unresolved
problems.

EXAMPLE 2: A LARGE MANUFACTURING COMPANY

Although there were no obvious signs, the medical director of a large
manufacturing company thought it would be useful to set up a stress-
prevention program as a practical measure. As a first step, he discussed the
idea with upper management and union representatives. Together they
decided to organize a work and management team to develop the program. This team was made up of worker representatives, representatives of the medical/employee assistance department, the human resources
department and an external human resources consultancy firm. The latter
provided technical advice on program design, implementation and
evaluation. Team funding came from upper management who indicated
their clear support for the team's activities. The team designed a two-part
program, the first part focused on management practices which could

lead to stress and the second part focused on individual worker health and well-being.

The team began with the first part of the program. A survey on employees' opinions of the company had already been carried out. The team and the consultancy firm added some questions on stress to the existing survey. They used the data gathered from the survey to identify the stressful conditions at work to suggest changes at the worker level and/or at the organizational level. The second part of the program consisted of 12 weekly training sessions during which the workers and managers learned about the common sources and effects of work-related stress, about strategies to protect themselves from these as well as relaxation techniques and improved behavior to promote better health. These training sessions were offered during and after work hours.

The team followed up on the program with quarterly studies on the work conditions and symptoms of stress to monitor the program's efficacy, and the results were very satisfactory.

EXAMPLE 3: COMBINE OR BALANCE WORK AND FAMILY[6]

Companies are beginning to adapt their human resource policies to the family and personal needs of their employees as a way of keeping talent within the company.

At 6.15 am, the alarm rings. Leonor Pablos, head of Human Resources at Bull España has just one hour to read the paper and have coffee with her husband before leaving to work. After a half hour's journey by car to the Juan Carlos I Trade Fair (where her office is located), she decides to plan the day's agenda with her secretary, check her email and prepare the meetings with her team. These are the first few minutes at work for a 35-year-old woman with a Law degree and mother of two children. Her day is full of meetings, a business lunch and a long afternoon of work, finishing at 8.00 pm. This is when her duties as mother begin.

Luckily for her, the family chores are shared. While her husband gets the children ready for their bath, she is busy in the kitchen, defrosting the night's meal so they can sit down and have dinner together. Afterwards, several loads of laundry have to be done, the following day's clothes need to be ironed, the mail read and then she can spend a few minutes' talking to her husband. During the week, it is the only time of the day when she can disconnect from work and enjoy being with her family. A few hours later at 11.30 pm, she goes to bed and the next day, starts all over again.

Leonor Pablos is one of the company's 877 employees who benefit from the company's family-responsible policy. She admits that when she joined the company as head of Labor Relations, there were a lot of time gaps which have been resolved, making life easier for employees. Besides, being a working mother has helped her understand the added difficulties of the 262 women who work for the company and have decided to combine work and family.

This company, in the technological sector, has an equal opportunities policy for men and women. Career plans take into account the difficulties employees may have as a result of being parents. Training and promotion are designed in terms of meeting objectives, not physical presence, avoiding the development of a culture of workaholics. Middle managers understand and support employees when they have to deal with family-related issues.

EXAMPLES OF COMPANIES DEVELOPING HUMAN RESOURCE POLICIES

- **Airtel (SPAIN)**, with a high proportion of young professionals, has adopted a Professional and Personal Life Harmonization Plan. It consists of a flexible work schedule, freedom to choose holiday time, special leave to take care of children, two weeks' paid pre-natal leave, addition time off to breastfeed or five days paternity leave.
- **IBM** has a Mobility Plan, which provides the company with the tools and technology necessary to work from anywhere and with a flexible schedule.
- **Deloitte & Touche** and **HP** have also developed a Professional and Personal Life Harmonization Plan, allowing for flexible schedules, part-time contracts, purchasing free time and year-long sabbaticals.
- **The Boston Consulting Group** offers its executives a paid sabbatical of two months every five years.
- **General Electric** holds the job for someone who leaves the company on personal grounds but who intends to return.
- **Guinness UDV** allows its employees to purchase up to five additional holiday days per year, while **Microsoft** offers a total of 28 holidays per year; five more than the sector average.
- **Unilever**, **Cisco** and **Amadeus** allow for part-time work, which many other multinationals in the same sector are now considering.

Chapter postscript

When you think about it, the organization's commitment to reduce stress begins with the planning of a series of organizational changes. The first is the content of the change and the second is the process of the change. In common-sense terms, the content of change is what you want to do and the process is how you are going to do it.

In practical terms, the primary goal of any change process needs to reflect that overarching goal. Healthy organizational change includes employee health and satisfaction as an explicit and independent outcome measure. These outcomes should be the key goals of the change effort. So, in order to reduce employee stress, a healthy organizational diagnosis should be carried out, benchmarks should be carefully analysed and corresponding changes addressed. As an example, think about the following causes and remedies:

- If stress is caused by lack of autonomy and control[7] – changes should be addressed to increase employees' autonomy and control.
- If stress is caused by obsolescence of employees' knowledge and skills – changes should be addressed to increase the skill levels of employees.
- If stress is caused by lack of sustained social support systems[8] – changes should be addressed to increase levels of social support (both supervisory support and co-worker support).
- If stress is caused by poor physical working conditions – changes should be addressed to improve physical working conditions.
- If stress is caused by improper use or implementation of new technology[9] – changes should be addressed to make a healthy use and implementation of technology.
- If stress is caused by unreasonable amount of job demands – changes should be addressed to provide a reasonable level of job demands.
- If stress is caused by lack of career plans and threat to employability – changes should be made to address job security and career development.
- If stress is caused by unhealthy work schedules – changes should be made to provide for healthy work schedules.

Obviously, we need to translate these broad objectives into concrete steps and programs, but it is sometimes useful to first see the forest and then the trees. Broadly speaking, reducing unhealthy job stressors involves a workplace in which employees have a sense of control, connectedness, where they are working at a reasonable pace, where they are challenged and motivated, and where they have a sense of support and security.

It is relatively easy to initiate an organizational intervention strategy that results in a deterioration of the quality of working life. One common problem is spending considerable effort in identifying stressors on the job, and then not addressing them in a serious way. Or designing an intervention of insufficient intensity or duration.[10] Or making changes that have the net effect of making employees feel more overwhelmed and confused than before. Change for the sake of change is not a goal of stress reduction programs. One effective way to avoid these negative outcomes is to design an assessment mechanism (for example, a survey, or medical record review) that will accurately measure key aspects of the work environment and stress symptoms before, during and after an intervention.

Interesting to know

How a simple change in promotion policies contributed to better health of employees, or **a career promotion can actually kill you**!

A consulting firm working for a medium-size Pulp and Paper production plant in Montreal (about 350 employees) discovered among other things, during an annual companywide "stress Audit", that of the 17 first-line supervisors, 11 had severe or mild problems connected with their digestive system. After discounting causes of poor nutrition and other traditional potential causes, a hypothesis was made connecting these illnesses with the stress of promotion. Like most companies, some of the best line employees were offered the possibilities to become first-line supervisors. Most people accept promotions as it not only improves their autonomy but also improves their economic well-being. However, people are not born to become supervisors (and especially not first-line supervisors. . .). Sometimes referred to as the sandwich people: senior managers view them as glorified employees, and employees, on the other hand, really do not view them as "real" managers. The job of a supervisor is extremely difficult and if the only reason to accept the promotion is the money that comes with it . . . then stress is also introduced. Most supervisors in this plant were not trained to become supervisors and were not given real offices to be able to do their job properly. In an interview it was found that many did not care or did not want to have the promotion. The only reason for the acceptance, once again, was the money. The consultants reached the conclusion that having such a high incidence of peptic ulcers and other digestive problems for the first-line supervisors was not normal.

Thus, a new promotion policy was suggested and implemented. This included the following elements: (1) if a worker is doing a job extremely well, his or her economic well-being can be improved via financial incentive plans which do not require an actual promotion to a supervisory position. This was the case for the employees that were not interested in such promotions. (2) And for the employees that were interested in promotion, a mandatory training in the art of supervising as well as new tools (offices, computers, etc.) was supplied.

In this company, numerous supervisors have chosen to go back to their old positions, and other employees have been trained to become supervisors along with the existing supervisors. The end result: a follow up study conducted two years later showed that only 3 of the 17 supervisors still had digestive-related problems. Most were content and satisfied with the new policies that were introduced.

Source: Data supplied by Gestion MDS Management Inc., a consulting group based in Montreal, Canada.

In sum, organizational changes that improve employee health by reducing the sources of stress are difficult. While changing individual behavior is tough enough, changing organizations is even more difficult. However, it is also important to remember that the costs of stress can be extremely high both to individuals and to the organization and thus the cost of not intervening is by far greater than the costs and difficulties of doing something.

Stress diagnosis inventory (SDI)

Managing stress has become a daily battle for many corporations. Knowing what causes stress at the individual and organizational level is the first step to overcoming it – a process made easier with the SDI (Stress Diagnosis Inventory)®, a new online tool being introduced by Octrium BV and Gestion MDS Inc (see: www.hrmsuite.com) SDI®, now offered to employers by Octrium and MDS, provides both workers and their employers detailed information on the origins of their stress as well as instant ideas of steps they can take to combat it. For employees, the tool provides an individualized stress management plan, including a way to measure stress and understand the symptoms and sources of stress. It also helps employees understand their own personal susceptibility to becoming overly stressed under various circumstances.

For employers, the program provides collective data about the origins of stress for their employee body so that they can make workplace changes to help reduce their employees' stress levels and improve health and productivity. Octrium and MDS is offering the SDI® through a collaboration with Spirit Consulting group (www.spiritcg.com), a company specializing in change management and stress management.

"Successful stress management requires both individual and organizational behavior change. Individuals must learn to identify their own stressors and develop skills to better control their stress," said Keith Dixon, Ph.D., President and Chief Executive Officer of CBH. "At the same time, employers need better to understand what makes their employees stressed, and develop clear plans to address workplace-related causes. By attacking stress from both sides, we can help workers be healthier as well as more focused and productive at work."

Using the SDI®, employees complete a 30-minute online stress assessment test to determine their individual stress level and areas of concern. Questions cover a variety of topics. At the end of the test, participants receive an instant customized report with information on risk profile and ideas on how to reduce them. Each person's individual plan also includes actions to help alleviate causes of stress, enabling employees to take charge of their own health, reduce stress, and enhance on-the-job performance.

At the same time, the SDI generates benchmarks and an organizational stress diagnosis. In this report, the principal causes of organizational stress are identified, the risk for certain groups or locations is revealed and solutions to correct or modify factors that cause on-the-job organizational stress is provided. The SDI® can impact the bottom line by saving the company significant amount of money connected with health benefits, disability, turnover, absenteeism and many more.

As a reader of this book you have a free access to the personal diagnosis portion of SDI, which is completely confidential. For more information, click on: www.hrmsuite.com

---

REFERENCES

1   Dolan, S.L., Martín I. and Soto, E. (2004). *Los diez mandamientos para la dirección de personas* (Barcelona: Gestión).

2   *Source*: Dolan, S.L. and Arsenault, A. (1980). *Stress, Santé et Rendement au Travail* (prologue by Hans Selye) (Montreal: Université de Montreal Press).

3   For example: Karasek, R. (1979). "Job Demands, Job Decision Latitude, and Mental Strain: Implications for job redesign", *Administrative Science Quarterly*, 24: 285–306; Karasek, R.A. (1989). "Control in the Workplace and its Health-Related Aspects" in Sauter, S.L., Hurrell, J.J. and Cooper, C.L. (eds) *Job Control and Worker Health* (New York: Wiley); 129–59.

4   Dolan *et al.*, *op. cit.* (2004). Chapter 2 ("Segundo mandamiento – comunicaras tus ideas e influirás").

5   *Source*: NIOSH (U.S.) http://www.cdc.gov/spanish/niosh/docs/99-101sp.html

6   *Actualidad Económica*, 25 September 2001.

7   See for example: Dolan, S.L., van Ameringen, M.R., Corbin, S. and Arsenault, A. (1992). "Lack of Professional Latitude and Role Problems as Correlates of Propensity to Quit amongst Nursing Staff", *Advanced Nursing*, 17: 1455–9.

8   See for example: Dolan, S.L., van Ameringen, M.R. and Arsenault, A. (1992). "The Role of Personality and Social Support in the Etiology of Workers' Stress and Psychological Strain", *Industrial Relations* (Canada), 47(1).

9   See for example: Dolan, S.L. and Tziner, A. (1988). "Implementing Computer-based Automation in the Office: A comparative study of experienced stress", *Journal of Organizational Behavior*, 9: 183–7.

10 See for example: Dolan, S.L. (1994). "Stress Intervention and Assessment: An account of two experiences", in Korman, A. (ed.), *Human Dilemmas in Work Organizations* (SIOP: The Professional Practice Series) (New York: The Guilford Press): 37–57.

7 Corporate Self-Esteem, Leadership, Stress and Organizations of the Future*

Chapter outline

"The companies most able to face the future do not believe in themselves for what they are, but in their capacity to stop being what they are. They do not feel strong through their culture and their structures, but through their capacity to take on others when necessary."

(Ernesto Gore)

"Well, you should know that the more brilliant someone is, the more willing they will be to share their knowledge and help those who are just starting out; this is because, confident of their own worth, they are not afraid of being eclipsed by anybody else, which, by the same token, they don't even take into account because the genius does not cast a side-ways

---

* Some sections have been borrowed from Dolan, S.L., García, S. and Richley, B. (2006) *Managing by Values: A corporate guide to living, being alive and making a living in the 21st century* (Basingstoke: Palgrave Macmillan).

glance, but lives engrossed in his studies and accomplishments, all too fascinated and overwhelmed by the pleasure of creation to need the banal and bastard recompense of recognition or opinion. After all, who could be their equal? Very few, and the one continues as engrossed as the other in the search for truth and the creation of beauty. We are only concerned with what Hermes and Prometheus may think of us."

(*La Sonrisa de la Gioconda*, Luis Racionero, Edicion Planeta Barcelona 1999)

Introduction

Organizational self-esteem is a new concept that brings together the self-esteem of the members of the organization as a whole. In this sense, organizational self-esteem represents the dominant culture of the company and its values. Of course, the self-esteem of an organization depends on the self-esteem of its people. Economic, social and emotional values, amongst others, are a part of corporate self-esteem. But, from the systemic point of view, the self-esteem of a society depends on the self-esteem of the organizations that make it up and of the organization's members (Figure 7.1).

After decades of intense efforts to ensure the effectiveness of our organizations, we have reached the point where we must admit that it is not easy. But before conceding that previous efforts have been futile, we should examine the paradigms and tools that have been used in order to understand organizations. One conclusion emerging from this examination is that if we maintain current management theories, we must accept that no significant advances have been made toward a comprehensive understanding of which organizations will succeed and why. But if we change our mind-set and view organizational reality through a new prism, we may find the answers.

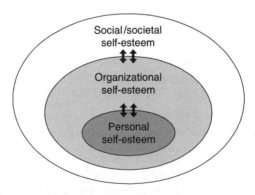

Figure 7.1 **A systemic vision of self-esteem**

Traditional visions of organizations (and of the world in general) have always searched for the easiest way to explain and predict natural phenomena. In this search, we have attempted to understand the universe by examining and explaining its separate parts. But partial analyses, as opposed to global ones, yield partial solutions.[1] The importance of holistic perception is embodied in the folk-tale of four sightless people encountering an elephant for the first time. Each described the animal in terms of the part they happened to touch, yielding four disconnected theories about the nature of the beast. The same partial and distorted view of global reality applies to organizational theories of the past. Unfortunately, reality is not as simple as we would like. It has complex rules that can't always be understood through their individual parts.

Many articles published in scientific and popular journals have argued that the emerging global economy of the 21st century is forcing most organizations to operate in turbulent environments. In physics, turbulences are high-intensity movements seen in fluids, whose flow shows random variations in time and space. This metaphor fits the turbulent economical, political and social-cultural environments where organizations have to grow and prosper.

In the current world, turbulences are identified through the existence of unexpected changes, uncertainty, lack of control, inhibition anxiety, complex decisions, group interdependency, high performance demand, confusion, disintegration, de-humanization, and neurotic organizations. Organizations are such living systems. Making an anthropomorphic analogy, we can argue that organizations, whether public, private or NGOs, have a greater or lesser self-esteem or appraisal of themselves, just like living systems.

A healthy organization succeeding in these turbulent environments, has to have good self-esteem, without becoming arrogant and overconfident. The maximum conceit an organization can commit lies in believing that it is superior to its people, suggesting high levels of deep-rooted insecurity. It is also frequent for them to believe that they are superior to their clients or suppliers, which only results in distancing themselves from their stockholders.

On the other hand, people with greater self-esteem aim to work with organizations that are leaders in their sector, sure of themselves, that stand out from the others not only through their products but through their leadership and their culture and how they do things.

> Humility is a highly recommended virtue to be upheld by organizations that seek to learn and work in an amiable and trusting atmosphere, not only with their employees, but also their clients, their suppliers and society in general.

Organizational self-esteem is developed based on different variables:

1 The existence of strong leadership, capable of harmonizing people's ideals with the pragmatic realism of the search for productivity and effectiveness.

2 A synergetic balance between the organization's economic, ethical and emotional achievements.

3 The establishment of realistic, participative objectives of moderate-high intensity.

4 A creative celebration of collective, group and individual goals.

5 The construction of authentic bonds of mutual confidence from the outset, between its proprietors and all their agents, from upper management to the suppliers and clients, including other employees.

6 Integrity or coherence between the values that it declares to have and what is done on a day-to-day basis.

7 The establishment of a mission or "reason for being" which, of course, includes economic profit and efficiency, but which understands that these are not the only final values to be achieved at whatever the cost, but rather as a means for the organization's own survival and development. Also the understanding that in an organization you need to satisfy all the stakeholders and not just the shareholders.

8 External reputation: inclusion in rankings of excellence, avoiding scandals or news concerning bad practices of any type.

9 Commitment to and respect for cultural and environmental surroundings.

10 Respect for its people, empowering them and enabling them to release all of their potential and let them simultaneously, enjoy the greatest possible balance between work and other aspects in their private life.

> **An organization that does not take care of its self-esteem runs the risk of becoming stressed, depressed and, possibly, inflicting harm on itself before ultimately disappearing.**

An organization that does not take care of its self-esteem runs the risk of becoming stressed, depressed and, possibly, inflicting harm on itself before ultimately disappearing.

Sometimes, autolysis can be expressed in the form of excessive growth. One of the most important and difficult strategic decisions to be taken, in that case, is that of not growing in excess in order to maintain essential levels of quality, friendliness, identity and self-esteem.

> **One of the most important and difficult strategic decisions to be taken is that of not growing in excess in order to maintain essential levels of quality, friendliness, identity and self-esteem.**

Interesting to know

Success usually leads to arrogance and arrogance usually leads to failure. When a company achieves success it may become arrogant and, in the process, become unsuccessful.

Examples:

- **Telefónica (Spain).** When Telefónica (the largest company in Spain) was the only telephone company operating in Spain, it was obvious that a person interested in acquiring a telecommunication service (land line, mobile phone, pager, Internet, etc.,) had to turn to this company, where the client was obliged to fulfil certain requirements (guarantor, credit card, etc.,) in order to be able to *buy* the service. But, in addition, the client had to wait a certain length of time for his request to be processed and approved. Years later other telecommunication companies joined the market (UNI2, ONA, etc.,), and these companies abandoned certain requisites. By being more flexible, they seized control of a market that had been mismanaged and subordinated by the arrogance of Telefónica. And although Telefónica did not go under, after the arrival of its competitors it did have to withstand the consequences of not only the "law of success" but also the law of supply and demand.

- **UnumProvident (US).** This largest disability insurance company has been cleansed of the "arrogance" brought about by market dominance, said Tom Watjen, president and CEO. Watjen stepped in 2004 to replaced ousted president and CEO J. Harold Chandler. "It was very much a top-down, don't really care what the employees think attitude'", he said. UnumProvident's financial problems came about in part because the company became "a little too enamoured of growth", and focused on increasing the number of clients rather than on whether the policies themselves were making money, Watjen said.

- **Fall of the arrogant (US).** Enron's demise has discredited a vicious market ideology and given a boost to the anti-corporate cause. Enron provides a textbook case of how corporate power subverts the political process in whatever country it operates (the US, the UK or India) through donations to political parties combined with intensive lobbying. It's mucky stuff, and heads will roll, but it's also a very familiar theme. What makes Enron such an extraordinary story is that it spells the end not just to some nasty pork-barrel politics but also to an ideologically driven, vicious corporate model, which was rippling from its Houston base across the globe.

The role of leadership in increasing or reducing corporate self-esteem

Executives with deep-rooted low self-esteem, who are isolated, stressed and stressful to be around, who lack time for thinking or living, with insufficient

> **Becoming tired as well as tiring. execu-
> tives with deep-rooted low self-esteem,
> stressed and stressful to be around, who
> lack time for thinking or living, with insuf-
> ficient social support, who are isolated
> and have little in the way of psycho-
> logical or philosophical education, tend
> to be excessively controlling, emotion-
> ally thwarted, with little social solidarity.**

social support, are becoming tired as well as tiring. They have little in the way of psychological or philosophical education, they tend to be excessively controlling, emotionally thwarted, with little social solidarity.

In this sense, Peter Senge, a well-known author and corporate consultant, advanced a concept labelled "Experiments in Silence":[2]

It is tragic to think that the people to whom we hand over enormous responsibilities regarding our societies and our social welfare, rarely get the chance to have real conversations in which they can speak honestly about their hopes, their fears, their concerns, their personal dilemmas; the type of conversations on which we are all based, looking for a feeling that we connect when we are faced with difficult challenges. The result of this is the existence of people very isolated as human beings but who we look up to from below, and who I am sure must suffer tremendously. We are not accustomed to thinking of them as suffering, since we see them as powerful. Nevertheless, when we are around them, we immediately feel the constrictions of the burden that is placed upon their shoulders.

People with needs for power and influence tend to neglect their own needs in terms of establishing meaningful trusting relationships with others, or – equally to – their need to love and be loved. These people tend to be relatively sensitive to their superiors' loss of trust in them, and have difficulties in trusting their own subordinates or in getting their subordinates fully to trust in them.

The current economic downturn, over the last few years, is not much fun, but there is a silver lining: arrogance is now viewed as among the greatest sins in corporate life. Executives with massive egos are now held in disrepute, and the hubris that pervaded so many companies during the economic boom of the 1990s is blamed for provoking and prolonging our current economic troubles. The beliefs about the dangers of swaggering corporate superstars are bolstered by Jim Collins in his essay: "Good to Great".[3]

Having identified the companies that made the leap from Good to Great, Collins and his team set out to examine the transition point. What characteristics did the Good to Great companies have that their industry counterparts did not? What didn't the Good to Great companies have? Collins maps out three stages, each with two key concepts at the heart of their success:

- Level-5 leadership
- First, Who… then, What
- Confront the brutal facts
- The hedgehog concept
- A culture of discipline
- Technology accelerators

> The old Chinese proverb, "Arrogance invites ruin; humility receives benefits", is appealing but is a half-truth. It holds for CEOs of big companies and many other executives, including some CIOs, but not for everyone.

Collins characterizes the level-5 leader as "a paradoxical blend of personal humility and professional will". The level-5 leader is not the "corporate saviour" or "turnaround expert"; most of the CEOs of the Good to Great companies as they made the transition were company insiders. They were more concerned about what they could "build, create and contribute" than what they could "get – fame, fortune, adulation, power, whatever". No Ken Lay of Enron or Al Dunlap of Scott Paper, the larger-than-life CEO, led Good to Great companies. This kind of executive is "concerned more with their own reputation for personal greatness" than they are with "setting the company up for success in the next generation".

True, arrogant executives tend to overestimate how smart they are, so they often do a bad job of weighing competing demands and frequently take unreasonable risks. They also tend to be ill-suited for keeping diverse constituencies happy. Inflated self-assessments mean they assume that everyone admires them and that their detractors can be easily defeated or persuaded to join their side. And they do not realize how much their pompous attitudes annoy everyone and generate stress within the organization. Yet this same stubborn pride makes arrogant people well-suited for turning new ideas into reality, especially risky and unpopular ones.

Beyond the classical self-esteem needs defined by Abraham Maslow, David McClelland[4] formulated a model of three basic human needs: achievement, search for power and influence, and affiliation (need to love and be loved). Determined to demonstrate that citizens in the third world could develop entrepreneurial patterns of behavior given the right training, he put a specific program to the United Nations on the matter: UNCTAD – EMPRETEC Program.[5] Nevertheless, it is curious to discover that the aim of this program is to stimulate the need for achievement, the need for power and – as a substitute for the need for affiliation – the need for "planning" (!).

What are needed are entrepreneurs and leaders "with values" who not only have a high need for material achievement, but who harmonize this

Table 7.1 **Needs of a leader who generates positive self-esteem**

- Need for an ethical meaning to life and to feel socially committed, useful and important through their entrepreneurial projects
- Need to be creative and to show their worth to others
- Need to attain power and influence
- Need for material prosperity
- Need to give and to receive love, pleasure and affection
- Need for freedom and control of their own life
- Need for time to enjoy life without blaming themselves
- Need for aesthetic development of their surroundings

Table 7.2 **Evolutionary competencies of the mature person with good deep-rooted self-esteem, able to formulate challenging but attainable objectives in their own life**

- They feel comfortable with themselves
- They do not collapse under their own emotions, fear, wrath, love or envy
- They are able to bear the disappointments in their life
- They are tolerant because they are able to laugh at themselves
- They try to be even-tempered and balanced in their words and deeds
- They accept their defects and limitations and for that reason they respect themselves
- They enjoy the simple pleasures of life
- They think well of others because they are able to love and to respect the interests of their community
- They have lasting and rewarding personal relationships
- They respect the intercultural differences that they find in other people
- They have a sense of responsibility and solidarity with respect to their neighbors, colleagues and friends
- They are able to confront the demands their lives make of them
- They exert influence on their surroundings whenever possible and they adapt to it whenever necessary
- They plan their activities and they are not afraid of their future because they set themselves challenging but realistic objectives for themselves
- They have the capacity to make their own decisions and seek the opinions of their colleagues
- They put their knowledge and effort into attaining their objectives and results
- They know how to and can say "NO" with solid and coherent arguments

with a high need for ethical and emotional achievement, thereby producing a broad concept of self-esteem and "success in life" (Tables 7.1 and 7.2).

Whereas adaptive changes look for optimization or reduction, transforming changes look for reinvention, recreation, essential renovation of the system by means of new beliefs and legitimizing values of new possibilities for action. Adaptative changes need managers who can handle numbers well; transforming changes need leaders who can legitimize and initiate the construction of new values, of course starting with themselves.

In most firms today we can find relatively good executives managing the status quo, capable of increasing efficiency levels within the system. But what we need more of are leaders who are able to ask themselves, "At what cost?" We also have a share of executives who even act as "dys-utopian" leaders, belittling people and generating a feeling of being in a situation with "no way out" and a loss of self-esteem, potentially detrimental to their health at as yet unknown levels.[6]

Without ignoring the existence of economic, biological or cultural circumstances, we should consider the need to counteract the "tyranny" of so much intimidating talk (called "realistic" by many) on the importance of surroundings, the global market, the system, deplorable human nature, fear and mere inertia.

In his important work in the early 1960s (*The Human Side of the Enterprise*[7]), Douglas McGregor had already defined humanist executives as professionals who, with the purpose of managing people and obtaining business results, applied knowledge derived from human sciences, such as social psychology, anthropology, political science and philosophy. Economics is clearly not enough when it comes to knowing how to manage people and projects.

> From a position of a somewhat consciously adopted "eutopian" naïveté, we need more leaders who are capable of combining the "eutopian" values of the humanist dream of the person with a capacity for "realistic" management of pragmatic thought: "increasingly with less costs" (although without asking for this at the expense of other results and of values).
>
> *Eu* in ancient Greek means suitable, good, happy. And *topos*, means place. Eutopian leadership is at the service of the creation of good places to work and invest in spaces offering a creative flow between eutopia and reality through which life can be expressed.
>
> *Source*: Salvador García, Internal memo for the Eutopia Forum, 2005 (translated from the original text in Spanish). Used with permission of Salvador García.

Engineering and humanities are mutually necessary. *We can neither fly in paper airplanes nor can airplanes be used to make sense of our flight through life.*

Unfortunately, and sadly enough, there are very few humanist leaders at the helm of companies and organizations. Most organizations are run by mediocre managers for whom the values that really matter are those of short-term efficiency and the non-creation of problems (a don't-rock-the-boat attitude).

Interesting to know

- **Do not expect arrogant leaders to change their ways. The famous architect Frank Lloyd Wright bragged, "Early in life I had to choose between honest arrogance and hypocritical humility. I chose honest arrogance and have seen no occasion to change."**
- **Do not expect arrogant leaders to heed their critics.**
- **Know that the "overbearing pride" seen in many teams and companies can lead them to persist when more modest ones would admit defeat.**

So, how to reduce the emotional wreckage caused by arrogant leaders?

- **First, it is probably best to isolate arrogant leaders. Otherwise, they will undermine teamwork, spark anger and stoke dysfunctional competition.**
- **Second, do not let arrogant people do the diplomatic work needed to win crucial support for their innovations.**

Source: excerpt from "When Arrogance Is Bliss", Ziff Davis, CIO Insight, February 2003, as found in http://www.findarticles.com/p/articles/mi_zdcis/is_200302/ai_ziff36970

THE NEW BREED OF LEADERS CONSTRUCTS CONFIDENCE AND OVERCOMES STRESS AND FEAR

> The higher the leader moves up through the hierarchic levels of the company, the less time he has to read, to understand what he is reading, to care for his partner and his children, to have relaxing friends, to think, to reflect or simply to enjoy life or take time out to do nothing in particular. This stress or adaptative failure has important negative emotional, commercial and social consequences.

Habitually, the higher the leader moves up through the hierarchic levels of the company, the less time he has to read, to understand what he is reading, to care for his partner and his children, to have relaxing friends, to think, to reflect or simply to enjoy life or simply take time out to do nothing in particular. This stress or adaptative failure has important negative emotional, commercial and social consequences.

The many conventional leaders (clichéd) work very hard, almost always too much, administering hierarchies, resources and numbers. They also treat "human resources" as just another resource. By contrast, the few but new breed of leaders have the special value of being able to think differently, to decide to develop themselves as people, to release the creative energies of their colleagues, to contribute to the creation of a more solidarity-oriented society and to create conversational spaces for the true construction of shared values. The management of their own fears and the fears of others is their main value.

Horace said: *Qui metuens vivet, to liber mihi non erit unquam* (He who lives in fear, I can never consider to be free). In this context we propose: *Qui metuens vivet, lider mihi non erit unquam* (He who lives in fear, I can never consider a leader). The truth of the matter is that we need this new breed of business leaders, capable of facilitating creative flowing between realism and ideals. But in order to assume such role, executives and managers have to have the courage to overcome their fear of dreaming, of expressing what they really think about their colleagues and their company; they have to overcome their fear of change, of sharing, of living, of enjoying and of being.[8]

In essence, what is expected of the new leaders is the capacity for building confidence and overcoming fear. Confidence is the belief in something or somebody, starting with oneself. Fear is feeling vulnerable when confronted by a lack of control or stress. Stress is uncontrollability, fear, mistrust, hostility, inhibition, avoidance, displeasure, submission and illness.

The word "confidence" is *empistosini* in ancient Greek[9] and means "to believe in". The need for confidence arises when we decide to take a risk and this make us vulnerable to the consequences of our own conduct or that of others. Confidence is the keystone to all lasting, fluid, happy and effective human organization. Without it, the entire structure crumbles, having then to be shorn up with support structures that come with a high emotional and economic cost. At an individual level, a lack of confidence in oneself as we have seen in Chapter 3, inhibits the will to risk undertaking new projects, to confront changes or, "simply", unlearn and evolve. Confidence is the antidote to fear and is the main characteristic of the leader who believes in himself, in his colleagues and in the meaning of his actions.

Generating confidence and not misusing the confidence that others place in us are a variable of conduct with a clear ethical content. Ethics may be interpreted as the art of confidence.

People have more fear at the workplace than, at first, would seem. They are scared to express what they think about their bosses, to question the system, they fear being dismissed, reprimanded or unfairly treated at any time. They are scared to be

> **Business leaders are needed who can serve as "tranquilizers", emancipators and transformers, who can help to overcome the pressures of threatening and limiting surroundings.**

themselves, to decide to have time to take care of themselves and their friends and interests or, "simply" to give full meaning to their life through their work, on which they spend according to some estimates between

70,000 and 75,000 hours in the course of their lifetime, representing about a third of their lives.

It is necessary to start thinking seriously about new "sensitive" work contracts rather than flexible contracts, in which the employability of the professional and the evaluation of their performance in terms of results determine their freedom of schedules, thereby avoiding the increasingly common absenteeism due to psychological and life-style dissatisfaction. New labor contracts based to a lesser extent on control and to a greater extent on the trust, freedom and creative initiative of people are required.

Business leaders are needed who can serve as "tranquilizers", emancipators and transformers, who can help to overcome the pressures of threatening and limiting surroundings abusively run by business tycoons all too often with scant ethical and poetic inclinations and excessively managed by bosses or foremen who are emotionally challenged, who aspire solely to manage the system *status quo*.

THE EVOLUTION OF INDUSTRIAL LEADERS: A MORAL-CONSCIENCE PERSPECTIVE

Writing about "neurotic organizations", Kets de Vries and Miller[10] have proposed that the neurotic defense mechanisms that leaders use to confront their own personal anxiety (such as negation, projection, compulsively working or paranoiac-type reactions resulting from distrust) have a cascading impact on the organization that they manage as a whole. Kets de Vries and Millar have identified five neurotic organizational styles connected with the kind of cultures that leaders set and support: Paranoid Style; Compulsive Style; Dramatic Style; Depressive Style; and Schizoid Style. All these styles breed stress. The organizational style may greatly affect the degree to which leaders can influence the organization, and it also may give strong indications as to what kinds of responses leaders may expect from the organization, and will certainly influence a host of other issues.

By the same token, the level of evolution of the leaders' moral conscience can have a significant impact on the axiological capital of the organizational system that they manage. The evolutionary psychologist, Lorenz Kohlberg,[11] has proposed the existence of three sequential levels for the development of a mature moral conscience in the individual, from childhood to adulthood.

1   *Pre- moral conscience*: the person judges what is or what is not correct from the perspective of his own immediate interests, of what suits or does not suit him in an egoistical and unsupportive manner. The right

thing to do is seen as the option that does not lead to punishment, which follows the norms that have been laid down by authority figures and whatever brings immediate benefit. According to Kohlberg, this is the moral reasoning of young children, although, he affirms, "a good number of adolescents and adults still persist in using this way of thinking". Would anybody imagine that a child wants to go to school claiming that it "is essential for my psycho-evolutionary development"?

2   *Moral conscience*: when integrating into the educational system within the family and school – Business Schools included – people look at the moral questions according to the rules, expectations and interests of the established social order, giving greater importance to being accepted by the reference group and believing that adapting to whatever their society considers as good to be *good* in fact.

The clichéd manager with a conventional conscience is overwhelmed by his excessive daily commitments, and habitually thinks and acts conservatively, fearfully and authoritatively, adapting to the dominant line of thought within his circles of reference and social influence. In fact, he is not a leader exercising his own initiative properly speaking, but a resource and values manager or administrator of the *status quo* that surrounds him. He is more of an "order-taking leader" than an "enterprising leader" or a visionary, transformer and creative leader. Instead of improving his surroundings, he only dares to do what will merit general approval, instead of changing and transforming everything that reeks of corruption and endogamy, he directs his efforts to doing more of the same so that nothing actually changes.

In fact, many of the new and interesting *management buzz words* these days (Codes of Ethics, ISO Standards, Integral Balance Scorecards, lean management, etc.) are, in essence, no more than mere "neo-Taylorisms". Perhaps for that reason they are never able to transform the essence of the system, although they do go about perfecting it little by little, though so little, that we may be correct in thinking that, deep down and on the surface, they have never really been interested in changing.

3   *Post-moral conscience*: starting from their basic cultural and educational map, though going further, individuals can use their own criteria to distinguish between the norms of their surroundings and those ethical principles that may be considered universal and defensible, such as freedom, cooperation or happiness. Kohlberg affirms that this is less frequent, going on to mention examples, such as Socrates, Gandhi or Martin Luther King. This is also the level of conscience associated with the most evolved democratic societies.

Interesting to know

Some examples of how outstanding (out of the box) business leaders think:

"It is necessary to think about a new type of company with a new type of sensitive man in mind and about responsible freedom, that is to say, with maximum creative potential, because there is no creativity without freedom. And through his sensitivity, this type of man may feel the need to promote and firmly encourage moral, cultural, ethical and aesthetic values at a personal and social level, so that these values converge and do not diverge as has been the case until now, with the admirable material development of our time." (Pere Duran Farell, President of Natural Gas – Spain)

"When people give their very best to the company, the very least one can do is to be able to take care of them." (Justo Soria, founder and director of ASM)

"To be realistic and pragmatic does not mean giving up on your ideals, which should not be confused with wishful thinking and pipe dreams, but accepted as objectives to be put into practice... Existence – in terms of human existence – cannot be silent, nor be nourished on false promises, but on true words on which men lean and transform the world. People are ends in themselves, not resources." (Jose Maria Arrizmendiarrieta, founder of the Mondragón cooperative experience)

"If people have fences built around them, they will act like sheep." (William McKnight, CEO of 3 M)

"My work consists of making it easier to communicate ideas freely and assure a work atmosphere in which creativity and initiative are recognised and rewarded." (Minoru Makira, President of Mitsubishi)

"In ten years' time, we want specialist magazines to be saying that GE is a place where people have the freedom to be creative, a place which promotes the best of everyone, a welcoming and fair place where people have the sensation that what they do matters, and where this sense of fulfilment has its reward in their pockets as well as in their souls." (Jack Welsh, President of General Electric)

"The hierarchical systems have failed. In order to advance we need to give people confidence and freedom. Money is not everything. The main thing is to serve people. I am an entrepreneur." (Reinhard Mohn, President of Bertelsmann Group)

"We must make our company a place where people can feel the freedom of innovation. In an atmosphere that makes it possible to bring out the best in each person, stimulating an exchange of ideas and sharing successes. And where achievements are rewarded in people's pockets and in their hearts. It should serve as a platform for the development of different business units with a common denominator: solutions in identification and traceability of products." (Jordi Piñot, General Director of MACSA)

"When there is unity and agreement ('oneness'), there is success, and along with success comes cooperation. It is with cooperation that we will create a better world together." (Dadi Janki, Adjunct Director of the Brahma Kumaris World Spiritual University)

Table 7.3 shows an evolutionary matrix of leadership styles. While the autocratic style can be discarded for being outdated, the resources management style is clichéd but meritorious and basically necessary, especially if it does not try to govern the system as a whole solely through this approach. The difficult thing, however, is that it is not easy for excellent managers and leaders to know how to work in a team, or even want to or be able to do so.

This new breed of leaders corresponds to the profiles described by many recent scholars who are also interested in pointing out the incoherence between organizational models and new organizational possibilities. For example, Gary Hamel when he radically talks of "revolutionary activists",[12] or Charles Handy, when describing social revolutionaries as

Table 7.3 **Evolutionary matrix of leadership styles and other social and organizational dimensions**

Organizational Dimensions or Parameters	AUTOCRATIC. IMPOSER	CLICHÉD RESOURCE MANAGER. CONTROLLER	NEW AUTHENTIC BREED OF A CONFIDENCE BUILDER
Type of world surrounding him	Scared	Regulated	Confident
Promoted capitalism	Savage	Sustainable	Sensitive
Moral conscience	Pre-conventional	Conventional	Post-conventional
Company management system	Management by Instructions (MBI)	Management by objectives (MBO)	Management by values (MBV)
Type of organizational control	External control	External-internal control	Internal control
Organizational structure	Top-down (military); the manager assigning missions and tasks	Flat	Organic, molecular, alive
Essential values	Respect for hierarchy, obedience	Optimization, simplification	Creative, professional latitude, happiness, confidence, sensitivity

"new alchemists",[13] who he compares to agile fleas in collaboration with the large elephants that represent multinational companies, or Richard Boyatzis and Annie Mckee who write about the need for leaders to connect with others through mindfulness, hope, and compassion.[14]

Gary Hamel introduces us to the concept of "revolutionary activist" business leaders with the following attributes:

- informative democracy;
- popular capitalism where everybody can be a shareholder;
- continuous improvement and non-linear innovation; and
- visionaries, activists for creating wealth.

We have to consider why in these few years of information democracy we have seen so many episodes of endogamy and corruption. It is not that similar situations did not exist in the past. We just did not have the possibility of finding out about them quite as fast as we do now.

Let us also examine the essential question about having to work lit erally – like the downtrodden and "poor" Chinese, who went from feudalism to communist dictatorship and from communist dictatorship directly to the tyranny of capitalism, with neither ethical nor poetic reflection, advocated in a multitude of academic, political, commercial and journalistic forums devoted to the "realistic" religion. Its most oft-repeated litany is "this is all there is" and its base philosophy is "increasingly more results at increasingly less cost", without stopping to question the expense of these results and values.

> **The capacity for utopian leadership comes through choosing to let life unfold through them.**

The real leaders are those who serve life, acting as sources of inspiration and "legitimators" of conversations to build confidence, sensitivity and freedom; as suggested by Greenleaf's beautiful expression,[15] "their leadership capacity comes through choosing to let life unfold through them". Some of them, those of greater worth, have even paid the price of this with their own intense life. Many others have lived and continue living happily.

The rise of the management by values philosophy[16]

WHAT ARE VALUES?

A certain amount of confusion arises when "values" and "ethics" are put forward as synonyms. Value is what something is worth, what it weighs, something that guides action. Valor is synonymous with courage. Value and valour are not synonymous with ethics, but they include it as a central theme. Value is everything and at the same time it is nothing, according to how it is defined. Our definition, then, will have to be a little more precise.

Human beings are afraid and defenseless; we lack valor – and values – to become more fully human in these times of escalating fear, complexity and economic, moral, political, emotional, aesthetic and social uncertainty. Evaluative capacity is the capacity to choose strategically, to regard-disregard, to evaluate, to choose, to ponder, to weigh, to guide actions and to give meaning to existence.

In spite of its popularity, there is a lack of consensus as to the nature of values. Among other things, values have been considered as ethical principles, needs, objectives, attitudes, personality types, interests, habits or competencies. According to Rockeach,[17] a value is a lasting belief that a specific form of behavior or purpose in life is personally or socially preferable to another form of behavior or purpose for existing. For other authors,[18] a value is an idea, explicit or implicit, unique to an individual or characteristic of a group, concerning what is desirable, something that influences the selection of the accessible forms, means and purposes of our actions. Or, also, as desirable trans-situational aims or goals, which vary in importance and which serve as guiding principles in people's lives.[19]

When we speak of company "values", both at a popular level as much as on an academic level, we normally restrict the term to ethical or moral values, such as integrity, sincerity, honesty, justice, dignity or respect. Of course, these ethical values are essential for the survival and evolution of the human species, and correspond to the social and environmental dimension of the present discourse on sustainability and Corporate Social Responsibility. Nevertheless, in a broader sense, a value is something worthy of esteem, which opens up the field of values, for example, to creativity, happiness or even efficiency.

VALUE AS WORTH, AS VALOR AND AS STRATEGIC CHOICE

The word value in itself contains a great hermeneutic or interpretative richness. It is polysemic, laden with multiple layers of meaning and usage. The word "value" basically has three meanings in Romance languages: economic, emotional and ethical.

Value as Economic Worth

Value as the inherent worth of a person, a product, an object, a service or a result in relation to its merit, shortage, practical utility, associated status symbols, price or interest, making it attractive to possess or to use. Such worth is always subjective and is culturally defined. The need to demonstrate worth to others explains a good part of the professional efforts we make.

In business terms, much is said about theories of added value, the chain of value analysis, the stockmarket, the Securities and Exchange Board, and so on. In fact, stock exchange values are those that define the greatest number of strategic decisions in the companies listed on the stockmarket, which is one of the main sources of dehumanization in many large companies and in the capitalist system itself.

In many contexts of social reality, the chrematistic (money = *jrima* in Greek) is the only thing that matters, the only thing that holds any value. Of course, economic values are important; they are not trivial. In ancient Greece, the value of money was in relation to its weight, which is where the word *pound* comes from in English or *peseta* or *peso* in Spanish currencies. There is no doubt that the competencies or worth of a good professional, a good leader or a good consultant are something useful, scarce and important, which is why they fetch a high market price in the business world.

Value as Valor

> Stress is pure fear of not being recognized as valuable, of not being worthy enough. From here stems the incessant eagerness of obviously stressed people to demonstrate their worth, people who are deeply insecure and – deep down – who have little self-esteem.

Significantly, the dictionary also defines valour as the *moral quality that moves great companies to act without fear.* Valor is, then, courage and self-confidence. When have we ever seen a cowardly entrepreneur or business leader? And when have we seen a leader who does not trust – who does not believe – in himself and in his team? Of course, he would be not much of a leader and he would build little confidence around himself.

Stress is pure fear of not being recognized as valuable, of not to being worthy enough. From here, as we have already mentioned, stems the incessant eagerness of obviously stressed people to demonstrate their worth, people who are deeply insecure and – deep down – who have little self-esteem.

The word "good" (*agathos*) has interesting semantic nuances in Greek. It means the brave one, the hero, the one able to guide, the one who is useful, the one who is at the service of others. However, for value in the sense of valour, ancient Greek had reserved the discriminating term of *andros*, male. It is also interesting to note how the ancient Greeks were so afraid of valiant women that it was impossible to express this effectively in their language.

Value as a Strategic Ethical Choice

A value is an internalized belief as to how we should act, on which the rules of engagement are based. Human freedom allows us to choose values, which is something that animals are unable to do. In the same way it raises the issue of ethics, Man is made human through his capacity to choose between good and evil. Values are strategic choices between one way of acting and its contrary action in order to achieve our aims, so that things turn out well for us based on suitable principles.

As a result, in order to reach our goals, quality may be preferable to shoddy work, loyalty preferable to treason, imagination preferable to imitation, solidarity preferable to egotism or happiness to bitterness. Values are key words for organizational and personal self-esteem.

What does it mean to be successful and to live well? Enjoying the present moment can be supreme when it excludes all fears concerning the future. In the same way, a past full of resentments, grudges or unsettled scores clouds our present happiness. What immediate assets should we forsake in order to obtain better ones in the future? What risks should we undertake? All these choices are strategic ethical questions.[20]

> **Values are strategic choices between one way of acting and its contrary action in order to achieve our aims, so that things turn out well for us based on suitable principles.**

Interesting to know

Some famous values quotes that can trigger serious philosophical reflexions by both political and industrial leaders

- "Treating people with respect will gain one wide acceptance and improve the business." (Tao Zhu Gong 500 BC, Assistant to the Emperor of Yue, 2nd Business Principle)
- "We do not act rightly because we have virtue or excellence, but we rather have those because we have acted rightly." (Aristotle 384–322 BC)
- "Although gold dust is precious, when it gets in your eyes it obstructs your vision." (Hsi-Tang Chih Tsang 735–814 AD, renowned Zen master)
- "Many men have imagined republics and principalities that never really existed at all. Yet the way men live is so far removed from the way they ought to live that anyone who abandons what is for what should be pursues his downfall rather than his preservation; for a man who strives after goodness in all his acts is sure to come to ruin, since there are so many men who are not good." (Niccolò Machiavelli 1469–1529, in Il Principe (The Prince), chapter 15, p. 56 (1513))

- "The value of life is not in the length of days, but in the use we make of them; a man may live long yet very little." (Michel de Montaigne 1533–92, French writer and philosopher)
- "You cannot teach a man anything; you can only help him to discover it in himself." (Galileo Galilei 1564–1642)
- "Grief can take care of itself, but to get the full value of joy you must have somebody to share it with." (Mark Twain 1835–1910)
- "Nowadays people know the price of everything and the value of nothing." (Oscar Wilde 1854–1900, Anglo-Irish dramatist and poet)
- "How much truth can a spirit bear, how much truth can a spirit dare? ... That became for me more and more the real measure of value." (Friedrich Nietzsche 1844–1900, German classical scholar, philosopher and critic)
- "People exaggerate the value of things they haven't got: everybody worships truth and unselfishness because they have no experience with them." (G.B. Shaw 1856–1950)
- "Earth provides enough to satisfy every man's need, but not every man's greed." (Mahatma Gandhi 1869–1948)
- "Try not to become a man of success but rather try to become a man of value." (Albert Einstein 1879–1955)
- "The first step in the evolution of ethics is a sense of solidarity with other human beings." (Albert Schweitzer 1875–1965)
- "Price is what you pay. Value is what you get." (Warren Buffett 1930-, American Investment Entrepreneur)
- "Management is doing things right; leadership is doing the right things." (Peter F. Drucker, American Management Guru)
- "Personal leadership is the process of keeping your vision and values before you and aligning your life to be congruent with them." (Stephen Covey, American leadership consultant and writer, 1990)
- "Out of 5.8 billion people in the world, the majority of them are certainly not believers in Buddhism. We can't argue with them, tell them they should be believers. No! Impossible! And, realistically speaking, if the majority of humanity remains non-believers, it doesn't matter. No problem! The problem is that the majority have lost, or ignore, the deeper human values – compassion, a sense of responsibility. That is our big concern." (The Dalai Lama in *Time*, December 1997)

VALUES AND CORPORATE CULTURE

Values constitute the essential component of organizational culture and are often recognized as factors for commercial differentiation and success. Both values as much as their antecedents and beliefs, constitute the heart or essential core of the so-called "culture" or "personality" of a company.

What people really think is one thing; what they do is something else. And what people admit to thinking and seem to be is something quite different altogether. Regrettably, there are still companies that confuse "modernizing" their values with comparing computers or, worse still, with changing their logos.

Values are intangible mental structures, which – metaphorically speaking – cannot or must not be handled, even more so if the hands that touch them are soiled. The risk of encephalitis or cerebral infection would be enormous, and the death of the system is practically assured.

But beliefs and values, no matter how intangible they may be, are intelligible, which means that not only can they be clearly understood, but that they are understood as pure knowledge, with no need to resort to the senses nor to statistical packages.

Beliefs and Values, Structures and Results

What is perceived is what we have been taught to perceive. Our world vision, our vision of the universe, or the self-explanatory internal dialogue of the present and wished for reality of things is made up of a "hard core" of essential beliefs developed through what we learn in life. This core organizes values by way of a centre of gravity, and projects habits and specific objectives regarding coherence of action to corroborate our beliefs, to satisfy our needs and, in short, to convert our values into reality, taking them beyond mere words.

A change in beliefs and values precedes that of structures and processes of interaction. It is more significant and can extend the concept of results itself, going beyond the economic dimension and including the individual and ethical-social dimension. As shown in the following outline, a fundamental question is that, independently of the meaning of ethical-social results in themselves, it is highly likely that caring for the internal humanization of the company and its social responsibility contributes to increasing its economic results.

In the present language, values are elements that are much "softer" than structures and processes. Nevertheless, the supposedly "softest" or most irrelevant can often turn out to be the "hardest" or most significant.

Common beliefs with respect to human nature and work

Luckily, the following beliefs are already beginning to be outdated in many organizations with greater self-esteem):

- What cannot be measured does not exist (and, in any case, it does not have too much commercial importance, which means there is no need to promote it).

- Workers do not go to work to have fun.
- Knowledge (even regarding values) is at the top.
- It is inevitable that "the large" companies dehumanize employees in order to be able to work efficiently.
- Work-related stress is a personal question for each individual, and basically depends on his or her lack of stamina and which – as a result – is neither the responsibility nor any reason for formal concern on the company's part.
- The negative impact of work on employees' personal lives is something normal and inevitable, and it even constitutes a sign of status and social triumph.

Emerging beliefs with respect to human nature and work

These, hopefully, are beginning to emerge in humanly advanced companies with greater self-esteem):

- The more important a value is, the more useless it is to have to be measuring it all the time to know that it exists, and especially to promote it (e.g. friendship). However, it may be advisable to evaluate its subjective perception from time to time and to even define some indicators to stimulate learning.
- Creative work is often confused with playing though it is a legitimate aspiration of human dignity. An excess of control structures stifles initiative, creativity and happiness and, therefore, it is a clear obstacle to efficiency.
- How frequently data are reproduced is not the same as how important they are.
- The world is comprehensible for normal and ordinary people, and their knowledge of it must and can be organized collectively and meaningfully.
- People wish for and can create their own future. Doing this is characteristic and distinctive of the human race.
- People work more and better when they perceive that they are treated as such and that they are taking part in something new and special.
- People seek opportunities to get involved at work, using their brains and hearts as much as their hands.
- Once their material needs have been reasonably satisfied, the possibility of showing their worth to others is the main mechanism for motivation or attribution of meaning behind high performance.
- It is necessary to balance the energy spent on work, one's family and oneself.

- A good leader is a facilitator of his employees' success, which is why he is more concerned with developing them than simply controlling them.
- If the opportunity presents itself, people are much more inclined to cooperate than to cause trouble. The leader's task is one of structuring opportunities to engage in dialogue, to cooperate and to learn.
- It is not the same to have an opportunistic business as a true company. A lot of "large companies" have small values.
- Training in values is as important as training in knowledge or skills and competencies.

FINAL AND INSTRUMENTAL VALUES

There are two essential types of values: final values and instrumental values. Final values respond to the questions: What do you want to become in life? What do you want for the world? What does your company dream of becoming and why?

According to Aristotelian eudaemonic ethics, the final value, par excellence, is happiness or the search for a suitable destiny, and examples of instrumental values for reaching this destiny are generosity or happiness. When a lot of importance is given to an instrumental value, it ends up becoming an end value: this is the case of money or good physical shape, for example.

In the business context, final values correspond to the formulations of vision and mission, whereas instrumental values have to be used to achieve the vision and to fulfil the mission.

PRAXIC AND POIETIC COMPETENCE VALUES

Milton Rockeach clearly differentiates between two large groups of instrumental values and potential regulators of behavioral choices used to reach end values: ethical values and those related to competence (Figure 7.2).

Ethical values, such as solidarity, honesty, dignity, generosity, humility, sincerity or respect

> *Praxic* values are oriented towards controlling the system and people, and are systematically inculcated and reinforced, like a new religion, from the political, economic, academic, efficientist communicational and neo-liberal powers dominating the planet.

for others or the environment are a sub-group of instrumental values, the most important in terms of the survival and happiness of the human species. Further on we will take a more detailed look at ethics.

Figure 7.2 **Taxonomy of corporate values**

Competence values are those required to compete socially: flexibility, personal impact, resistance to stress, creativity and so on. "Management by competence" makes explicit reference to these types of values. Developing the ideas put forward by Rockeach, competence values can be differentiated along two different axes that should be harmonized: (1) the axis of economic values (*praxic* values) or control values, and (2) the axis of emotional-creative values (*poietic* values) or development values.

Praxis means to work, to act, and also to transact, to negotiate, and from this Greek root come the terms "prose" and "pragmatism". Values along this axis include, for example, size, technology, prestige, work effort, obedience, efficiency, and, of course, money. Due to these values, human beings have obtained achievements as appreciable as the telephone, the washing machine, air conditioning and Internet, although these benefits are still not available to all.

Praxic values are oriented towards controlling the system and people, and are systematically inculcated and reinforced, like a new religion, from the political, economic, academic, efficientist[21] communication and neo-liberal[22] powers dominating the planet. These can also be called materialistic values and they correspond to the models of economic and political values put forth by Allport.[23]

An excessive focus on control is usually based on mistrust, insecurity and fear of uncertainty and freedom. Taken to an extreme, it implies an aversion to risk, resistance to change and the inhibition of one's own creativity as well as that of others. The obsession for control arises from the inability to recognise and to appreciate the value of spontaneity and happiness. This would explain why managers with a conventional education, impregnated by the rationalist-economic paradigm, see the machine and the army as the best concepts and imperative for human/employee organization.

By way of counterpoint, we have *poiesis* and the *poietic* imperative. The term comes from *poieo*, an interesting verb which in Greek means to do, to make, to construct, but also to engender and to give birth to. From the conjunction of the verb, *poieo* can also mean to create or to innovate. The word *poiema* is derived from *poiéo* and it can mean anything from the creation of the spirit to poetry. Aristotle and Plato spoke of "poetry" as creative activity in general. The main *poietic* competence values are imagination, freedom, tenderness, confidence, adventure, aesthetics, warmth, creativity, happiness, harmony, family, passion and mental openness. "Autopoiesis" (Maturana, 1981) is the self-generating capacity of living systems. Hematopoiesis is the generative capacity of blood cells to manufacture themselves and multiply.

The generative or creative *poietic* states are associated to a special positive emotional disposition. Is it possible to have a new idea without expressing happiness? Can new ideas arise that positively transform things from depressive states? Can there be creativity in states of work-related, family or personal anxiety? Of course, artistic creation can be associated with emotionally tense states, and even melancholic ones, but we are concerned here with the relationship between positive emotional values (serenity, optimism, fantasy, etc.) and creativity in order to transform the things that surround us for the better.

Poietic values are aimed at generating or developing and expressing more than controlling and measuring. They can also be called generative values. They refer to the health or "emotional sustainability" of the company and, together with ethical values, correspond to a category of values of tremendous transformational potential. However, although these values are intelligible and achievable, they are normally discarded as idealistic, "eutopian" or scarcely tangible in the business world. They are the equivalent to Inglehart's so-called post-materialistic values and to Allport's aesthetic model, centred on life harmony.[24] The successful introduction into the business world of "emotional intelligence" (Goleman, 1995)[25] has facilitated the logic behind the legitimization of emotional values.

The creation of companies – and of wealth – depends as much or more on development values than on control values. The birth and revitalization of every business project depend on *poietic* values to generate new possibilities for action, such as imagination, freedom and enthusiasm. Nevertheless, control values are essential for the effective and innovative application of new ideas, for the maintenance of the *status quo* and, in short, for the management of the wealth that is enterprisingly created through *poietic* values. An obsession about development, by contrast, can easily turn into a poetic innocence that neglects the need to control and manage the resources within the system.

ETHICAL VALUES

Ethical values are essential for the physical survival of the human species and for a healthy emotional life. As affirmed by the Spanish philosopher Fernando Savater "there are many ways of living life, but some ways do not let you live". At the company level, a breach of ethical values seriously endangers the survival of the company in the medium to long term. Cases such as Enron and Arthur Andersen have been sadly instructive in this respect.

Ethical values arise from life or, better still, from the need to confront life with human dignity. You do not first construct an ethical theory and then live in accordance with it. The formulation of ethics arises from what we learn from life to bring human meaning to social interaction.

> Ethics consist of the free, strategic choice of values and how time is used to give full, human meaning to our existence and, by doing so, to try to attain happiness.

Ethical "pre-tension" is concerned with the vital and fortunate combination of values such as dignity, efficiency, equality, joy, freedom, justice, solidarity, evidence, doubt, respect, beauty and happiness.

Praxic ethics are deontological, normative, perceptive, or action orientating, ethics focused on fulfilment, limits and control. They are the negative ethics or limiting ethics found in the first Corporate Ethical Codes and in the present norms of Corporate Social Responsibility. The concept of generosity, for example, never appears in these, although the concept of not stealing does. Passion does not appear either, just simple commitment.

> Happiness is not only based on one's divine or demonic fate, but rather, it is constructed with great effort and virtuously, or at least, in an artisan manner.

Poietic ethics are a generator of action in search of happiness as the end value, ethics to stimulate humanization and confidence, ethics for liberation, termed by Aristotle as eudaemonic ethics. *Eudaemonia* means an appropriate fate. Happiness is not only based on one's divine or demonic fate, but rather, it is constructed with great effort and virtuously, or at least, in an artisan manner.

For Aristotle, happiness was the concretion of good, perfect virtue throughout a complete life; happiness was the sum of the previous in addition to material well-being. Wisdom is the most important intellectual virtue, consisting of the contemplation of fundamental truths.

The business world requires both types of ethics. It needs controls that limit abuse, but also positive stimuli to develop generosity.

The triaxial model of praxic, ethical and poietic values

A typical error found in many companies' lists of corporate values is to name too many values, and, especially, to not classify them in a consistently theoretical manner (García and Dolan, 1997 and 2003). Other authors dedicated to "Management by Values", such as Blanchard and O'Connor (1997), do not mention this error nor do they propose a specific categorization of values.

We propose incorporating these values along three axes, the "triaxial model", to try and simply, completely and significantly systematize the different values: the *praxic, poietic* and *ethical* axes.

THE TRIPLE UTILITARIAN, INTRINSIC AND TRANSCENDENT MEANING OF WORK

The greater the value (or meaning) given by the person to the work they perform, the greater their commitment to giving the best of themselves, or, by the same token, the more enthusiastically they will work. According to some authors, there are three possible levels of value or satisfaction regarding specific actions:

1 *Utilitarian or extrinsic value*: satisfaction for the person carrying out the action implies a reaction from the environment which offers, for example, money or prestige.
2 *Intrinsic value*: satisfaction for the person carrying out the action (independently of the external effects of said action) includes characteristics such as learning, stimulus, fun, or the possibility to show one's worth.
3 *Transcendent value*: satisfaction is produced in other people rather than in the person carrying out the action, and, as such, is perceived as useful to others.

According to this concept, the completely motivating job has a triple meaning: utilitarian, intrinsic and transcendent. Being well paid for what one does, enjoying this work and feeling useful to others are a great satisfaction in life. Unfortunately, this satisfaction is seldom fully realised, though we should strive to attain it, both in terms of designing specific jobs as well as within our own mindset regarding what we want to achieve with our lives through our professional activities.

THE TRIAD OF PRAXIC, ETHICAL, AND POIETIC VALUES

As has been more or less explicitly explained throughout this chapter and as we shall see further on when discussing Management by Values, we must overcome polarities or even antagonistic relationships between the

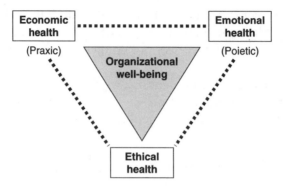

Figure 7.3 **The triaxial model: a new perspective of organizational well-being**

different types of values. According to Dolan *et al.* (2006),[26] what we have termed a triaxial model (represented by three axes and being an axiological model referring to values), ethical values are the central axis of an inverted triangle, with two other important groups of values revolving on either side: praxic and poietic values (Figure 7.3).

However, we recognize that the world does not revolve around the ethical imperative or creative or poietic emotionality, but rather around the pragmatic imperative of money, power and technology to achieve efficiency. In any case, the business world is essentially practical and prosaic and is governed by values oriented towards operability and control (for example, completion and optimization). However, its legitimization and development depend on the incorporation and development of ethical, aesthetic and poetic values, thereby achieving a socio-technical balance made to suit humanity.

> In practice, the values associated with knowing how to work tend abusively to outnumber the values associated with knowing how to live and, even more so, to those associated with knowing how to share.

As illustrated in Figure 7.3, in most companies the ethical and poietic axes are generally atrophied in comparison to the praxic axis. An entirely different matter is what the majority of its members would like in terms of their own personal values, or, at least, what they say they would like. In practice, the values associated with knowing how to work tend to abusively outnumber the values associated with knowing how to live and, even more so, to those associated with knowing how to share.

Our experience in collecting data from many companies (in Spain, Brazil, Argentina, Canada, Holland, and more) shows that in most companies

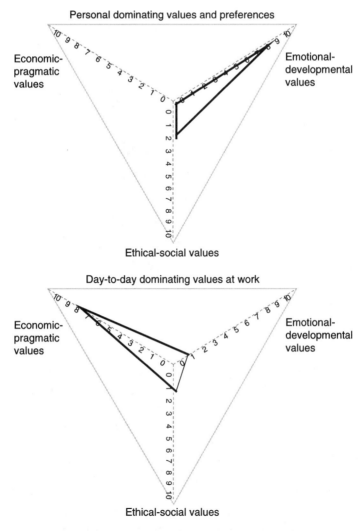

Figure 7.4 **A gap between personal and corporate values shown amongst senior executives in a large telecommunications company**

the ethical and poietic axes are generally atrophied in comparison to the praxic axis. An entirely different matter is what the majority of its members would like in terms of their own personal values or at least, what they say they would like. In practice, the values associated with knowing how to work tend abusively to outnumber the values associated with knowing how to live and even more so, to those associated with knowing how to share.

Figure 7.4 shows the typical difference found between the preferred personal values and the dominating work (day-to-day) values of a large telecommunication organization. The sample for this study includes over 800 senior executives.

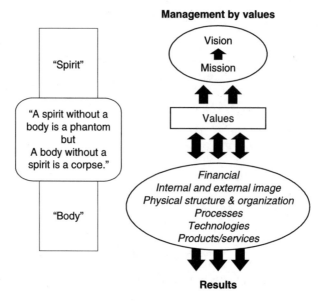

Figure 7.5 **Aligning values with the corporate mission and vision**

> **When will engineers make friends with poets? And when will poets make friends with engineers?**

The three groups of values are necessary, and a balance between them must be found in order to enhance the system's results, both in terms of organizational and individual self-esteem. The values should be aligned with the organization's mission and vision, which is developed in a participative manner (see Figure 7.5.).

Overcoming fantasies about a lack of control, daring to recognize and manage a living (and, as such, unstable) balance between the realistic imperative of praxic values and the eutopic or idealistic imperative of ethical and poietic values are necessary. Economics and humanism should not be so separate. When will engineers make friends with poets? And when will poets make friends with engineers?[27]

From a systemic perspective,[28] the balance between the three economic, ethical and emotional values has personal development at its core, the latter based on self-esteem and confidence which in turn leads to greater social development. Organizational development[29,30,31] is the intermediate subsystem between them, and it is maintained, to a great extent, more through trust than control.

Confidence or Trust is the main meta-value of the triaxial model:

(a) Confidence predicts the economic evolution of a company and its social system. Building confidence is a critical factor in increasing efficiency, though it is often not perceived as such or is underutilized. It is a simplifying and anti-bureaucratic value.

Confidence attracts clients, investors, suppliers and future employees. It creates group and organizational cohesion. It is, then, a critical variable in successfully developing high performance teams, in instilling commitment to the company project and in reinforcing leadership credibility.

(b) From the poietic point of view, confidence is an essential value for emotional well-being. As we shall see when delving further into the topic below, being able to make oneself vulnerable without feeling intimidated is an essential element of emotional health. In an organization with an excess of defensiveness, life is much more disagreeable and uncomfortable.

Management by values: a framework for combining employees' well-being and corporate success

It would be rather rash and inconsistent to propose Management by Values as an alternative "management fad". Every organization throughout history has been

> **Every organization throughout history has been governed by values, every single one at every moment of their evolution.**

governed by values, every single one at every moment of their evolution. The Mafia is run by values. China is run by values, as are the Church and the army. General Electric is run by values. The President of the United States of America states that he runs the country by values. Even Al Qaeda is run by values. Father Vicente Ferrer's NGO is run by values, although with a very different morality than the previously mentioned examples.

All human projects and, therefore, every company is governed or directed on the basis of certain values, which, from within the organization, tend to be considered as orientative, cohesive and legitimizing agents of its action. Ethics or internal adjustment of these values comes, in that case, from the conversations that arise on the matter within each organization.

> **When speaking of "Management by Values" we refer to the realization of a humanizing project consciously promoted by the owners and management of the company to make explicit the final and instrumental values to be constructed by the organization as a whole. This is followed up by equally explicit coherent actions to put into practice, to evaluate and to improve the organizational effectiveness of this new participative cultural construction.**

Although from the perspective of an external observer many of these can be – and are – more than questionable.

Sometimes, these values are stated explicitly. At times, and in the majority of the cases, they seem to float round the atmosphere or, academically speaking, are parts of the "organizational climate". In any case, there is not always a strict coherence between the declared values and those that are actually observed and put into practice in organizations, constituting their own axiological capital or assets of accumulated values over time.

In the 1960s, almost half a century ago, the executive and organizational theoretician, Chester Barnard, concluded that the fundamental role of a business leader was to channel all of his social forces into shaping and guiding values. His idea of the senior director as a value shaper, concerned with dealing with the informal social aspects of the organization was clearly pioneering. His double role as director of an American telephone company and as a theoretician of company management confers a legitimizing and special merit to his post-conventional audacity to think differently.

Subsequent popularizing contributions on the importance of shared values among "excellent companies" (Tom Peters[32]) as core elements of "company culture" (Edgar Schein[33]) have consolidated corporate values management as an essential part of the managerial function. The term "Management by Values" (MBV) applied to company management was coined at the end of the last century, in 1997, by Salvador García and Simon Dolan, the same year in which *Managing by Values*,[34] the fictionalized work of their North American colleagues, Ken Blanchard and Michael O'Connor, was published. Other authors who have proposed the same concept are Hall and Tonna (2001)[35] and Fernandez Aguado (2001), although the latter gives it a "partial" character and proposes that it be replaced by the "Management by Habits" model (MBH), which is, in his opinion, more evolved than the previous concept.[36]

Blanchard and O'Connor entertainingly put forward Management by Values as a three-phase process: (1) to clarify the objective and the values of the company, (2) to communicate these objectives and values, and (3) to align them with practices. García and Dolan suggest in a rather more academic text, though equally intended for professionals, a similar participative process, made up of four phases:

1 Authentic legitimization of the process on the part of the company owners and the management team.
2 Participative formulation of end values and, mainly, instruments.
3 Values in action. Specific project teams. Communication of values. Selection by values, specific training in the values of the future and recognition of the fulfilment of shared values.
4 An audit to check the coherence of their values.

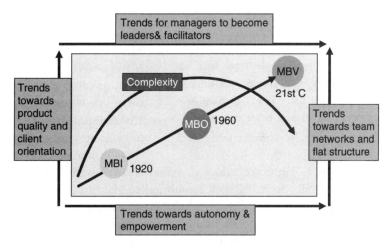

Figure 7.6 **Evolution of management philosophies**

DEFINITION AND CONCEPTUAL BASES OF MANAGEMENT BY VALUES

When speaking of "Management by Values" we refer to the realization of a humanizing project consciously promoted by company owners and management to explicitly outline the final and instrumental values to be constructed by the organization as a whole. This is followed up by equally explicit coherent actions to put into practice, to evaluate and to improve the organizational effectiveness of this new participative cultural construction. The core value of MBV is confidence. The antidote preventing it from degenerating into a coercive sectarian system is freedom while integrity or consistency is the basis for turning it into a reality.

On proposing "Management by Values" or "MBV", García and Dolan[37] make a clear distinction between vision and mission and suggest the need for a synergic harmony between ethical values, competence control values and development values, which they later term as "praxic" values and "poietic" values, respectively, integrated within a triaxial model along with ethical values.[38] As mentioned, its essence lies in building confidence as a central metavalue. And they give this a more evolved and integrating role than prior models known as "Management by Objectives" and " Management by Instructions" (Figure 7.6).

Management by Values (MBV) is a new generating proposal of ethical and creative organizational action, beyond the proposals put forward by Management by Objectives (MBO) from the 1970s and Management by Instructions (MBI) from the early twentieth century. MBV proposes moving in an efficient, ethical and emotionally positive form in the present contexts of high complexity and uncertainty which demand high performance levels, confidence, commitment and creativity from individuals.

MBV AS AN INTEGRATING IDEOLOGICAL FRAMEWORK

> **MBV does not replace MBO nor MBI, but rather it gives greater meaning to them, provided that they are not put forward in a hegemonic and disproportionate manner.**

MBV does not replace MBO or MBI, but rather it gives greater meaning to them, provided that they are not put forward in a hegemonic and disproportionate manner. For example, if agility is a corporate value, it would seem coherent to define a specific annual objective to be increasingly agile. And there should also be detailed instructions in routine or, contrarily, in emergency contexts: for example, agilely to evacuate the company premises in the event of fire. The problem is that many company owners and directors believe in staying doggedly in a dangerous situation which, logically, has to be fought at all cost.

> **The currently predominant techno-structural paradigm is excessively prosaic and normative, being very limited in terms of granting full emotional and ethical meaning to high-performance organizational measures that are nowadays essential in competitive surroundings with a highly adaptative complexity.**

It is evident that values, especially end values, must be materialized through the definition of strategic objectives. The currently predominant techno-structural paradigm is excessively prosaic and normative, being very limited in terms of granting full emotional and ethical meaning to high-performance organizational measures that are nowadays essential in competitive surroundings with a highly adaptative complexity.

MBV may be considered a new leadership and company management tool based on the participative construction of a good balance between three classes of values in order to reach its vision and to fulfil its mission (triaxial model):

1 Economic, control or habitually predominant "praxic" vales which are never sufficiently developed (e.g. efficiency or quality).
2 Emotional, development, "poietic",[39] creative or generative values (e.g. imagination or warmth), abusive and erroneously denied or despised on many occasions from the efficientist pragmatic perspective.
3 Ethical values (e.g. generosity or honesty), integrating them with complete normality with economic and emotional values, without enmeshing them in separate codes and without considering them a category as such, removed from the core of productive

business. Even considering them as the central axis around which both the conducts of control as well as those of development should revolve.

MBV essentially endeavours to construct a balance between the company's economic, emotional and ethical health, thereby generating greater internal satisfaction, a greater competitive advantage in the marketplace and a greater contribution to a better world.

A strategic declaration – and more so if it is to be shared – is a matter of company culture as much as, or more than, a question of market analysis. And, as we have already mentioned, the new company culture cannot be indoctrinated or imposed; it is built by dialogue and a willingness to learn between all of the members making up the system, beginning with the owners and senior management.

KEYS TO SUCCESS FOR MANAGEMENT BY VALUES

Successful Management by Values is when:

1   Shared end values and instrumental values govern and are expressed coherently in structures and specific spaces, new work processes and consistent personnel selection policies, training, incentives, promotion and leaving/dismissal of personnel.
2   The coherence of shared end-values and instrumental values generates synergies in terms of the organization's greater economic, ethical and emotional health.

Based on the knowledge and experience gained from various experiences in setting up and maintaining Management by (more or less satisfactory) Values over a period of time, we can point out three principles or keys of success to be incorporated by all the members of the organization, but especially by their eutopic leaders (who have to exist prior to this) and by the firm's owners and representatives:

- **Ethical audacity**. Honest and transforming ethical reflection has to be able to generate unrest and self-confidence to become thoroughly involved, with courage and prudence, in the project of defining and applying the end values and instrumental values shared by all.
- **Dialogue of imagination**. The release of creative talent in a context of participation, optimism and dialogue has to be able to formulate, to interpret and to look for ways to apply the end values and instrumental values shared by all.
- **Consistent integrity**. The solidity of declaratory coherence between what people say they are going to do and what they actually do at all

levels, has to be able to send, maintain and periodically evaluate the project of defining and applying the end values and instrumental values shared by all.

Corporate self-esteem and empowerment

"A State which dwarfs its men in order that they may be more docile instruments in its hands even for beneficial purposes will find that with small men no great thing can really be accomplished; and that the perfection of machinery to which it has sacrificed everything will in the end avail it nothing, for want of the vital power which, in order that the machine might work more smoothly, it has preferred to banish."

(John Stuart Mill, 1855)

Organizations that put into practice policies to *empower* their people obtain greater levels of organizational and individual self-esteem.[40] The MBV framework, as suggested before, is clearly doing that, but other models can apply as well.

Empowered people with responsible freedom can easily fall into the trap of becoming more involved in their work and putting in excessive hours, which is clearly detrimental to their vital balance and their personal health. For this reason, it is especially important to also take into consideration along with this *empowerment* the development of programs to balance work and private life commitments.

ORIGIN AND DEFINITION

"Empowerment" is a powerful word that arises from the tradition of thought known as "Organizational Development" (OD), introduced in the 1970s by authors from the field of academic-humanist consultancy such as Argyris, McGregor, Beckhard, Schein, Bennis, and others, attempting "to apply social sciences to increase organizational health".

Organizational Development may be defined as the application of social psychology and other behavioral sciences to increase company performance by releasing the creative, ethical and practical energy of their workforce. An essential change of beliefs and values from the bottom up is a revolution. A change of beliefs and values from the top down is OD.

We have come across at least three meanings for the English word *empowerment*, of which we would propose the translation as "strengthening", "release of talent" or "responsible freedom".

(1) *As a citizen*, I want *empowerment* to be able to decide more and better. I want to decide, for example, the medical treatment that I will receive from among the different options available. I want to be dealt with as a client in my relationship with companies or organizations of any type. I want service companies to consider me a person, not mere merchandise. I even want to take part in strategic decisions through NGOs or in future referendums via Internet. All this is *empowerment*.

(2) As a worker, I want to increase my decision-making autonomy and develop my skills to the maximum. I want to be responsible in the sense of giving answers, to give them assuming the cost and the benefit of this extension of tasks. It is not the same to feel like a "human resource to optimize" as it is to feel empowered as a person. At this level *empowerment* is defined as: "the transference of authority and responsibility related to the job from the managerial levels to the workers".[41]

(3) Finally, and this is the most profound use of the term, *as an individual* I want to expand my own generative intellectual and creative capacities of self-esteem. I want to reduce the external and internal limiting agents of these capacities, and, as a result, I want to gain in terms of *locus of control* and the feeling of self-efficiency: I am my own main factor of change and personal progress.

Empowerment refers to having the courage to choose values, to give oneself power, to tolerate ambiguity, to be able to continue working in the midst of complexity. It implies we trust in our own responsible freedom and that of others.

> *Empowerment* refers to having the courage to choose values, to give oneself power, to tolerate ambiguity, to be able to continue working in the midst of complexity. It implies that we trust in our own responsible freedom and that of others.

A more complete definition of empowerment would be the following: a participative process in which managers-leaders while not giving up their final responsibility trust in the capacity of responsible freedom of other employees, delegating effectively to them a greater degree of authority and resources for decision making, thus releasing their employees' intellectual, ethical and emotional-creative talent and conferring a sense of emotional ownership over their work, heightening self-esteem and greater enthusiasm for producing quality work in a "great" company.

In summary, what does empowerment mean in an organization?

1   Reframing the role of senior management which should change from managing and thinking to inspiring and legitimizing the release of creative energy so that ideas flow freely, ethically and efficiently.

2   Reframing the role of middle management which should change from being bosses to becoming facilitators of their collaborators' success, self-esteem and performance.
3   Reframing the role of workers: "vertical enrichment and horizontal broadening of jobs". Evolving from "human resources to be optimized" to become "people to empower".
4   Legitimization, training and organizational design to work through project teams.
5   Reframing of the selection policy, training, promotion and recognition of personnel. Selection by values. Specific training at all levels. Moral and economic recognition for increases in responsibility and tolerance of the ambiguity characteristically produced by *empowerment*.
6   Investment in developing managerial skills in communication and effective delegation.

Practical keys of empowerment and reinforcing self-esteem in the workplace by management

- Let others show their worth without attributing the merit to you.
- Prepare your collaborators well in advance.
- Be quick to praise, slow to criticize and, at all costs, show interest in finding out the results.
- Celebrate the achievements attained collectively.

In short, the company with a progressive leadership, led by means of a balance between economic, ethical and emotional values, trusts in the responsible freedom of all of its members, releasing all their potential and taking care of their self-esteem and health.

Chapter postscript: stress, corporate self-esteem, health and productivity

In a most interesting article published in the *European Business Forum*, Sheth and Sisodia (2005)[42] attribute the increasing number of organizations who disappear, and even those who have had a history of success and then fail, to two principal causes: their leadership's incapacity to change, or their *unwillingness* to do so. Leaders who develop a myopia, or who do not have the courage to engage in changing their organizations and adapting to an ever increasing environment, are doomed to create the most stressful situations for their stakeholders: extinction.

In this chapter we have suggested that neither low self-esteem nor high self-esteem of the corporate leadership is a healthy situation. While low

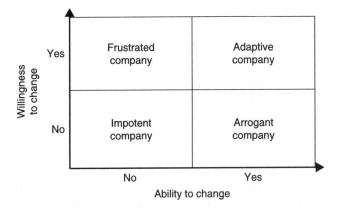

Figure 7.7 **Leadership willingness and ability to change and impact on organizations**

corporate self-esteem may lead to low morale in the corporation and to and increased amount of stress, an extremely high self-esteem may lead to myopia and high resistance to change. Figure 7.7 presents the leadership options and the organizational state resulting from their respective attitudes.

As Figure 7.7 suggests, corporate leaders can be classified as:

- *Frustrated companies* (and their respective employees) occur when their leadership is willing to change but does not have the ability to do so. Normally, these leaders do not have the skills and competencies in managing large-scale changes, they do not know how to forge alliances, and how to overcome resistance to change.
- *Arrogant companies* have the leadership ability to change, but are unwilling to do so because of myopia, certain orthodoxies based on their past success and the belief that they, and only they know what is best for the company. When executives or organizations succeed by accident, they often become very rigid about their belief system, much more than before they became successful. In a way, they become super-stitious. They end up believing what they will succeed forever, and then they become resistant to change. Employees in these types of cor-porations are highly stressed. Leaders falling into this category must continually identify and battle their own orthodoxies, which are often disguised as strengths but are, in fact, vulnerabilities.
- *Impotent companies* are such that their leaders are neither willing nor able to change, and are therefore doomed to obsolescence.
- *Adaptive companies* are those which their leaders are willing and able to change as needed. These are the companies that will survive and thrive in the long run. These are the type of leaders that may understand the benefits of constantly evaluating their mission, vision and respective culture and assure an alliance amongst them.

But, how do you become an adaptive transformational leader? Charles Handy describes living with organizational paradox like riding a seesaw, and perhaps more of a child-like appreciation of the mechanics is better preparation for what lies ahead. If you know how the process works and if the person on the other end of the seesaw also knows – the ride can be fun. If, on the other hand, the person on the other end doesn't know how the seesaw works or deliberately upsets the process the results can be an uncomfortable shock.[43]

Some leaders still hold the view that stressful working conditions are a necessary evil and that companies should increase pressure on workers and get rid of concerns about their health to continue being productive and lucrative in today's economy. But the conclusions of our and others' research question this opinion. Studies suggest that stressful working conditions are created by men, and that corporate self-esteem depends much on the vision and courage of those who manage the companies. A leadership that is not courageous enough to create a culture of shared values, integrating ethical and emotional values beyond economic values, will fail in the long-term. Putting pressure on workers, developing an arrogant culture with non-realistic levels of corporate self-esteem based only on economic values, will end up having a negative impact on the economic health of the company and the personal health of its employees. The stress that arises through non-realistic self-esteem (very high and reduced, respectively, or very low and lacking vision) is associated with absenteeism, tardiness, and a higher number of resignations – all of which have a negative effect on the company's essential performance. Moreover, a clear signal that a company is heading towards decline is the recognition that it has lost an emotional connection with its stakeholders; it is no longer emotionally bonded with them.

Recent studies on what are termed "healthy" organizations suggest that the policies that benefit workers' health also benefit the company. A healthy organization is also defined as one that has low rates of personnel with illnesses, injuries, and disabilities and that is competitive in the market. Some organizational characteristics associated with healthy, low-stress working conditions, with suitable levels of corporate self-esteem, and high levels of productivity include the following:

- leadership that generates confidence;
- recognition of employees for good work performance;
- opportunities for individual growth (professional promotion or other forms of development);
- an organizational culture that values individual workers; and
- a clear management culture that agrees with the shared organizational values (management by values style).

On the micro level, the following principles should and can be adapted by leaders who wish to join the wise club of effective organizational transformer who breed and create a culture where stress is reduced to a minimum:

- the wise leader allows the process to unfold on its own;
- the wise leader teaches by example rather than lecture on the 'shoulds';
- the wise leader listens more than talks;
- the wise leader understands that by being 'selfless' he/she enhances his or her self;
- the wise leader understands that leadership is really service;
- the wise leader understands that small changes have large impacts (leverage); and
- the wise leader understands that silence creates focus;

True leadership of a progressive 21st century company must operate through values. Indeed, the idea of managing change in turbulent environments refers to the deployment of resources in the construction of a strategic architecture, bridging the gap between the vision of the future and the current reality. Values are the framework of this structure; they are the glue that holds an organization together when confronted with chaos and the need for change.

This chapter has proposed that leadership with corporate self-esteem, links to the health of such companies. Few companies recognize this and that's a big mistake. Often companies fail to link these critical components that help to create environments where people and businesses simultaneously flourish. The concept of "psychosocial hazards" is ignored by many companies, and remains a mystery to most. In this chapter, an attempt has been made to demystify these connections. At this point you, the reader, may understand that ensuring a healthy psychosocial environment requires looking long and hard at the leadership style and management practices of your organization.

Many of the stress factors in the firm are under the control of supervisors or managers, and may vary widely within any one organization depending on the skills, abilities and values of the individual managers. Research in general shows that, while demand/control and effort/reward are powerful influences on the health of employees, the effect of these influences is multiplied when workplace conditions are perceived as unfair or indicative of the employer's lack of respect for employees. Feelings associated with a sense of unfairness are anger, depression, demoralization and anxiety. Feelings associated with fairness include satisfaction, calmness, enthusiasm and happiness. The strong negative feelings translate chemically into compromised immune systems, setting the stage for a variety of adverse physical and mental health outcomes. In other words, feelings of unfairness magnify the effects of perceived stress on health. On the other hand, a sense of fairness is related to trust, which is key to employer–worker relations, high morale and productivity.

In today's fast-paced society, businesses cannot succeed without making demands on employees, and often expect a lot of sustained effort. I am not suggesting, however, that we should create workplaces that are sterile (stress-free); this would not only be unrealistic, but could lead to a decrease in productivity, motivation or innovation. It's the fairness that counts – the balance between the stressors (demands and effort) and the satisfiers (control and rewards), and the sharing of values. Most employees can cope with high demands if given appropriate control over the way they work and feel rewarded and appreciated. What I recommend is the conscientious development of both a healthy workforce and workplace, which means learning to manage the inevitable stressors and cultivating the right type of leaders.

Getting to the end of this book is like completing an important journey of discovery about often recognized but misunderstood elements of people and work. This has been a journey into the complexities of stress, self-esteem, health and work. I hope this process has helped to clarify, or perhaps even to help pave the way for, your own path toward actualizing the type of leadership and workplace that will be a part of your legacy. I wish to leave you the reader with a short motto that can sum up the messages portrayed by me: "Creating a healthy workplace is more than a good idea, is more than an altruistic objective – it also makes absolute business sense."

Exercise: assessment of your corporate self-esteem

Corporation Name: _____   Date: _____

Instructions

Read every statement carefully and indicate the degree to which it applies to your organization, or the degree to which you believe most people in your organization will endorse it. Please answer all questions.

Use the following scale for all questions by assigning a number between 0–4

0	1	2	3	4
Almost never	Rarely	Sometimes	Quite often	Most of the time

1 In social situations and public appearances, the leaders of our
   company have something inspiring to say about our firm.   ☐

2 Most people in our company seem to have more technical skills
   than other people working in our industry.   ☐

3　Our company really likes its image and therefore does not make an effort to change it. ☐

4　Whatever new business we touch, we end up messing it up. ☐

5　When the company sees a good opportunity, it recognizes it and acts upon it. ☐

6　Leaders in our company respect and like only those who are smart, witty and talented. ☐

7　To our firm, success is not imperative. The important thing is to try to do our best. ☐

8　The company's actions in general deserve to be applauded and respected. ☐

9　We really have to go out of our way to maintain a positive image within the industry. ☐

10　In our firm's culture, the prevailing belief is that being honest and transparent is a recipe for failure. ☐

11　When things go wrong, the company finds someone to blame right away. ☐

12　When things go well, the company attributes success to its leaders and they become instant heroes. ☐

13　The company cannot tolerate or deal with failures. ☐

14　If we don't do as well as other companies, it means that we are inferior. ☐

15　Many people in the firm feel that if we (the company) disappeared from the face of the earth today, nobody would notice. ☐

16　A common belief in the company is that a partial failure is as bad as a complete failure. ☐

17　A common belief in the company is that if someone makes a mistake, they will lose the affection and respect of others in the firm. ☐

18　We will never amount to anything significant in our industry. ☐

19　We have what it takes to succeed and we do not need external help. ☐

20　We think that as a company we are a total success. ☐

21　We will never be as capable a company as we should be. ☐

22　People comment that arrogance is a prevailing attitude of the leaders in our company. ☐

23　A common belief is that we are doing so well that we should continue doing the same. ☐

24　Humility is a cherished value in our company. ☐

25　The general feeling in the company is that we are really "the best". ☐

Interpretation of the scores

Important note: before calculating the total score, you need to reverse the scores for the following 10 items: # 4, 7, 9, 14, 15, 16, 17, 18, 21, 24 (this means: if you marked

0 it becomes 4; 1 becomes 3; 3 becomes 1; and 4 becomes 0). Only after reversing the scores, should you total it.

0–20 Your organization suffers from low self-esteem which can at times generate stress for employees as members of the organizations do not identify with the company and do not take pride in their organization.

21–60 Your organization has a normal level of self-esteem. These levels of self-esteem rarely provoke high levels of stress.

61–80 Your organization has a high level of self-esteem that may be a source of contentment for most employees.

81 or higher Your organization is bordering on arrogance, which produces high levels of stress.

REFERENCES

1 Dolan, S.L., Garcia, S. and Auerbach, A. (2003). "Understanding and Managing Chaos In Organizations", *International Journal of Management*, 20(1): 23–36.

2 Senge, P. (n.d.). "Meeting in Safe Spaces" in *Experiments in Silence, Journal of the Call-of-the Time Dialogues.* info@callofthetime.com.

3 Collins, J. (2001). *Good to Great: Why some companies make the leap ... and others don't* (New York: HarperCollins).

4 McClelland, D.C., Atkinson, J.W., Clark, R.A. and Lowell, E.L. (1953). *The Achievement Motive* (Princeton: Van Nostrand).

5 Empretec is an acronym derived from the Spanish words *empresas technologicas*, which means technology-based enterprise. However, the program is also very relevant to service oriented and other kinds of enterprises including the manufacturing sector.

6 García-Sanchez, G.J. and Bayés de Luna, A. (1990). "Psychological Stress and Sudden Death", in Bayés de Luna *et al.* (eds), *Sudden Cardiac Death* (Dordrecht: Kluwer Academic).

7 McGregor, D. (1960). *The Human Side of the Enterprise* (New York: McGraw-Hill).

8 This is the core concept of managing by values explained in our book: Dolan, S.L., Garcia, S. and Richley, B. (2006). *Managing by Values: A corporate guide to living, being alive and making a living in the 21st century* (Basingstoke: Palgrave Macmillan).

9 Tomará, N. and García S. (2000). "El conocimiento helénico a través de las palabras: apuntes para directivos humanistas". *Perspectivas de Gestión* V-2 pp. 46–59.

10 Kets de Vries, M. and Miller, D. (1993). *La organización neurótica* (Barcelona: Clásicos Management Apóstrofe).

11 Kohlberg, L. (1992). *Psicología del desarrollo moral* (Bilbao: Desclée de Brouwer).

12 Hamel, G. (2000). *Leading the Revolution* (Boston: Harvard Business School Press).

13 Handy, Ch. (2002). *El Elefante y la pulga. Mirando hacia atrás hacia el futuro* (Madrid: Ediciones Apóstrof); Handy, C. (1999). *The new alchemists* (London: Hutchinson).

14 Boyatzis, R. and Mckee A. (2005). *Resonant Leadership: Renewing Yourself and Connecting with Others Through Mindfulness, Hope, and Compassion* (Boston: Harvard University Press).

15 Greenleaf, R., (1977). *Servant Leadership: A Journey into the Nature of Legitimate Power and Greatness* (New York: Paulist Press).

16 Section was inspired by García. S., Dolan S.L. (1997) *La dirección por valores* (Madrid: McGraw-Hill); and Dolan S.L., García S. (2002) "Managing by Values: Cultural redesign for strategic organizational change at the dawn of the 21st century", *Journal of Management Development*, Vol. 21(2): 101–117.

17 Rockeach, M. (1973). *The Nature of Human Values* (New York: Macmillan).

18 Kluckhohn, F. and Strodtbeck, F.L. (1961). *Variations in Value Orientations* (Evanston, Il: Row Peterson).

19 Schwartz S.H. and Bilsky, A. (1987). "Toward a Universal Psychological Structure of Human Values". *Journal of Personality and Social Psychology*. 53 (3): 550–562.

20 Savater, F. (1993). *Etica para Amador* (Madrid: Ariel).

21 Begley, P.T. and Stefkovich (2004). "Education, ethics and the 'cult of efficincy': implications for values and leadership". *Journal of Educational Administration*. Vol 42. No 2, pp. 132–136.

22 George, S. (1999). *A Short History of Neoliberalism*. Conference on Economic Sovereignty in a Globalizing World. March 24–26.

23 Allport, G., Vernon, P. and Lindzey, G. *A* (1961). *Study of Values* (Boston: Houghton).

24 Ibid.

25 Goleman, D.P. (1995). *Emotional Intelligence: Why It Can Matter More Than IQ for Character, Health and Lifelong Achievement* (New York: Bantam Books).

26 Dolan, S.L., García, S. and Richley, B., (2006) *Managing by Values* (London: Palgrave Macmillan).

27 Ibid.

28 Bertalanffy, L. von (1968). *General System Theory. Foundations, Development, Applications* (New York: George Braziller).

29 Bennis, W. (1962). *Toward a Truly Scientific Management: The Concept of Organisational Health*. General Systems Yearbook, 7, pp. 269–82.

30 Argyris, C. and Schön, D.A. (1978). *Organisational Learning: a theory of action perspective* (Reading, Mass: Addison-Wesley).

31 Cummings, T.G. and House, E.F. (1989). *Organisational Development and Change* (New York: West Publishing Company).

32 Peters had tremendous success with his book *In Search of Excellence* (1982), with Robert H. Waterman, Jr. In some circles such as NPR, his books were ranked as the three best management books of the 20th century. He also

published other books such as *A Passion for Excellence* (1985, with Nancy Austin), *Thriving on Chaos* (1987), *Liberation Management* (1992), *The Circle of Innovation: You Can't Shrink Your Way to Greatness* (1997); *The Tom Peters Seminar: Crazy Times Call for Crazy Organizations* (1993) and *The Pursuit of WOW! Every Person's Guide to Topsy-Turvy Times* (1994).

33 Schein, Edgar H. (1992) *Organisational Behavior,* 2nd edition (San Francisco: Jossey-Bass).

34 Blanchard K. O'Connor (1997). *Managing by Values* (San Francisco: Berret-Koehler).

35 Hall, B. P. (2001). "Values development and learning organizations". *Journal of Knowledge Management.* vol 5, no. 1, pp. 19–32.

36 Fernandez, A. (2001) "You Lead Consistent: the Direction by Habits", *Direction and Progress,* 2001 Sep–Oct.

37 García, S. and Dolan, S. (2003). *La Dirección por Valores: el cambio más allá de la dirección por objetivos* (Madrid: McGraw-Hill). (2 ed.)

38 García, S. (2002). "La dirección por valores". in: *Management español: los mejores textos.* Chapter 8, pp. 225–65 (Madrid: Ariel).

39 Dolan, S., García, S. and Richley, B. (2006). *Managing by Values* (Basingstoke: Palgrave Macmillan), pp. 212–13.

40 García, S y Borrell, F. (2002). "Empowerment: El Poder de una palabra". *Dimensión Humana,* 6(2) 74–7.

41 Thomas, K. and Velthouse, W. (1990) "Cognitive Elements of Empowerment: An 'Interpretive' model of intrinsic task motivation", *Academy of Management Review,* October: 666–81.

42 Sheth, J. and Sisodia, R. (2005) "Why good companies fail?" *European Business Review,* Issue 22, Autómn: 24–31.

43 Handy, C. (1994) *The Age of Paradox* (Boston: Harvard Business School Press).

A Contract with Myself

I, ..., who reside in ...., following
the completion of reading this book on "Stress, self-Esteem, Health and
Work" by Professor Simon Dolan, have decided that for my own sake (and
health) I will introduce the following changes in my life:

IN MY PERSONAL LIFE:
*

*

IN MY FAMILY LIFE:
*

*

IN MY PROFESSIONAL LIFE:
*

*

                                        Signature:
                                        Date:
                                        In witness of:
                                        ....

Index